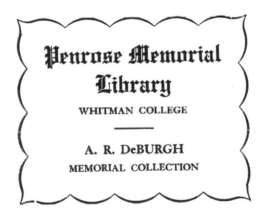

# THE TRUMAN
## SCANDALS

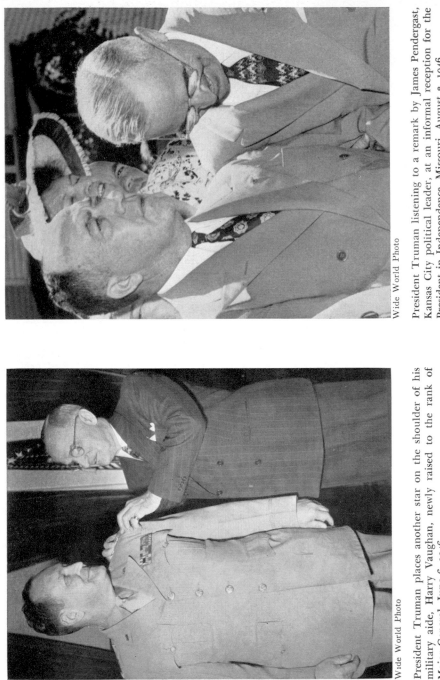

President Truman places another star on the shoulder of his military aide, Harry Vaughan, newly raised to the rank of Major General. June 6, 1946.

President Truman listening to a remark by James Pendergast, Kansas City political leader, at an informal reception for the President in Independence, Missouri. August 3, 1946.

# THE TRUMAN
# SCANDALS

## JULES ABELS

**HENRY REGNERY COMPANY**

CHICAGO · 1956

# FOREWORD

*Quis custodiet custodes?*

"Who will guard the guards?" asked Juvenal. In one form or another this question has been repeated through the centuries with varying answers.

The answer to that question is especially urgent today. Government has become too big, the power wielded by public officials too important, and the impact of their decisions on private individuals too frequent, to tolerate immorality or laxness in public office. The problem of obtaining competent and honest public servants, whose decisions will be based on public rather than private interest, is all the more acute because salaries of government officials are so small in relation to the billions of dollars affected by their decisions.

This is an ethical and political problem which, to be understood, requires a knowledge of its nature and causes, just as a study of symptoms and causes is necessary for the curing of a disease. The need to find a cure for the disease becomes the more imperative when one finds how virulent the disease can be. This book, which deals with the most corrupt era of government in our history, is an attempt to lay bare the facts for public examination.

During the Truman era, the vast powers of government were dedicated to the strengthening of a political organization. This example corroded the moral values of the office-holder and so brought about corruption not only for the benefit of the party but for individual benefit.

The great mass of public servants were not corrupted. They carried on in the face of the chicanery around them. "We should not let this incident weaken our morale but carry on as we have," an official of the Bureau of Internal Revenue pleaded with his colleagues after a questionable action by Commissioner Joseph Nunan.

In this book there will be innumerable instances in which the conflict between the great mass of honest officeholders and the political clique over them was sharply defined. A powerful governmental agency, the Reconstruction Finance Corporation, was reduced to rubble despite the competence of its many honest and loyal employees. Employees wrote memoranda which granted tax rulings only under orders, or refused to sign them. Angry protests were made. Memoranda were put into the files calling attention to extraordinary occurrences. And, in the end, the honest civil servants won out because these protests and memoranda came to light.

*This book is not an inside or confidential or gossip account.* The preponderant part is taken directly from actual Congressional investigations conducted during the Truman and the Eisenhower administrations. The remainder is from reputable, verified and published sources. Insofar as possible, the author has stated the facts as they appear in the record without color and characterization.

J. A.

# CONTENTS

SOME OF THE FRIENDS OF
HARRY S. TRUMAN MENTIONED IN THIS BOOK

TOM PENDERGAST — *Kansas City political boss.*

JIM PENDERGAST — *Tom's nephew and heir to the machine, whom Truman called his "friend, comrade and adviser."*

ROBERT HANNEGAN — *Who, as Chairman of the Democratic National Committee, put Truman on the Presidential ticket. The worst elements entered the Bureau of Internal Revenue during his regime and that of his successor, Joe Nunan, who was sentenced to jail.*

GEORGE SCHOENEMAN — *Truman's White House administrative assistant and Nunan's successor as Revenue Commissioner. A good friend of the fixer, Henry Grunewald. It was revealed that wholesale frauds occurred during his administration.*

WILLIAM M. BOYLE, JR. — *National Chairman, who resigned after disclosures of his activities in behalf of the American Lithofold Corporation.*

JOHN SNYDER — *Secretary of the Treasury, implicated in the case of the campaign contribution raised by Judge Mayock in 1948. Also implicated in special tax rulings which were granted.*

MATTHEW J. CONNELLY — *Truman's appointments secretary, indicted December 1955 for conspiracy to fix the tax case of Irving Sachs.*

Tom Evans

*Secretary of Harry S. Truman Library, Inc. Business associate of Harry I. Schwimmer, who was indicted for conspiracy to fix tax case of Irving Sachs. Evans is involved in the case.*

Donald S. Dawson

*Truman's administrative assistant; close friend of Merl Young and a source of power for the influence ring.*

Merl Young

*Convicted perjurer who was accused of influence peddling in the RFC.*

Gen. Harry L. Vaughan

*Whose friendship made possible the activities of the fixer and convicted perjurer, John Maragon, and of the five percenter, Col. J. V. Hunt.*

Brig. Gen. Wallace Graham

*Truman's White House physician. He was involved in commodity speculations and gave what he admitted was "not an accurate statement" as to his activities.*

Clark Clifford

*Truman's legal counsel, involved in the questionable Michigan School of Trades case.*

James P. Finnegan

*Revenue Collector in St. Louis; jailed on various charges of official misconduct.*

Edwin W. Pauley

*Whose nomination as Under Secretary of the Navy was withdrawn in connection with disclosures about contributions from oil interests.*

Paul L. Dillon

*Manager of Truman's 1934 senatorial campaign. Convicted of tax fraud; implicated in parole of Capone gangsters.*

CECIL GREEN | *Involved, with William M. Boyle, Jr., in American Lithofold case. Received fees in return for advocacy of other RFC loan applications.*

HARRY EASLEY | *Involved in Camp Crowder storage space scandals.*

DAN M. NEE | *Involved in Camp Crowder storage space scandals.*

## The Roll Call in the Tax Scandals

Joseph D. Nunan, Commissioner of Internal Revenue — *Convicted of tax fraud.*

Daniel A. Bolich, Assistant Commissioner of Internal Revenue — *Convicted of tax fraud.*

Carroll A. Mealey, Deputy Commissioner of Internal Revenue in charge of the Alcohol Tax Unit — *Indicted for tax fraud.*

Matthew Connelly, Appointments Secretary to President — *Indicted for conspiracy to fix a tax case.*

Charles Oliphant, Counsel for the Bureau of Internal Revenue — *Resigned under fire.*

Theron Lamar Caudle, Assistant Attorney General in charge of the Tax Division — *Fired, and indicted for conspiracy to fix a tax case.*

James W. Johnson, Collector for the 3rd District, New York (Manhattan) — *Removed.*

Monroe Dowling, Collector for the 3rd District, New York (Johnson's successor)

*Removed.*

J. B. E. Olson, Supervisor of the Alcohol Tax Unit, New York

*Indicted for tax fraud.*

Joseph Marcelle, Collector for Brooklyn and Queens Districts

*Removed.*

Denis W. Delaney, Collector for Boston area

*Pleaded guilty to tax fraud.*

James P. Finnegan, Collector for St. Louis area

*Indicted on several counts, including RFC and tax frauds. Convicted on two charges of misconduct.*

James G. Smyth, Collector for San Francisco area

*Indicted for tax fraud.*

Frank Scofield, Collector for southern Texas

*Removed.*

Ernest E. Killen, Collector for Delaware

*Removed.*

# THE TRUMAN
# SCANDALS

# · I ·

# PROLOGUE

It had been expected that after the hectic war period Washington would subside and contract. Instead the city burst at the seams. Hotels were jammed. New, gleaming-white office buildings mushroomed all over the downtown area. The swollen bureaucracy was only slightly dented.

In control of the vast complex of government, highly developed and expanded during the war, stood the Democratic party and its chieftain in the White House—machine-trained and machine-minded. Never did a political party have such riches at its disposal. There were the huge governmental expenditures in a budget many times what it had been before the war. There were billions in war surplus to be disgorged. There was cheap, long-term government credit to be had. There were opportunities in new programs, such as that for housing. Most important of all, there was the tax system, the most significant element in business life of the postwar period, wonderfully intricate with countless opportunities for special rulings, immunities, and loopholes.

The city was thronged with those who had made a career of "dealing with" the government or, speaking less euphemistically, of "milking" it. These included politicians, lawyers, lobbyists and manufacturers' representatives. But there was also another breed of men who offered a key to government—fixers, five-percenters, influence-peddlers of various descriptions whose price was high because they brought about results through special influence and collusion. The sun shone bright on Merl Young, Henry Grunewald, Col. J. V. Hunt and their like.

1

Government officials were wined and dined, given free trips, gratuities and bribes. The bills were charged to tax-deductible expense accounts, so that the cost of subverting the governmental process was defrayed mostly by the government itself. Deals were arranged in hotel rooms, taxicabs, and by furtive phone calls. And then there was the endless cocktail circuit of private get-togethers and parties in hotels like the Mayflower, Statler, and Carlton—a city-wide meeting ground for arranging marriages of interest between those who sought and those who could deliver.

These were the happy times of Harry S. Truman, thirty-third President of the United States, and the setting for our story.

# · II ·

# PRESIDENT TRUMAN AND
# CORRUPTION—I

*My people are all honorable—all of them are. My
house is always clean, what are you talking about?*

—PRESIDENT HARRY S. TRUMAN
March, 1951

*Scandals in Government are not a new phenomena.
What seems to be new about these scandals is the
moral blindness or callousness which allows those in
responsible positions to accept the practices which
the facts reveal. It is bad enough for us to have corruption in our midst, but it is worse if it is to be con-
doned and accepted as inevitable.*

—SENATOR J. WILLIAM FULBRIGHT,
Democrat from Arkansas, March, 1951

THERE is no evidence that Harry S. Truman could get mad
about corruption in his administration or at those guilty of
corruption. He could get boiling mad at a war hero like General MacArthur, or at a Washington music critic who failed
to appreciate his daughter's vocal technique, or at Senator
Fulbright, his fellow Democrat, who exposed the RFC frauds
and whom the President called "an overeducated s.o.b." But
it is questionable that he could get even moderately mad at
those who traduced the good name of the government and be-
trayed its trust.

He seemed always to be fighting a rear-guard action against
the forces which were demanding a clean-up in his administra-

3

tion. He termed Senator Fulbright's report exposing the scandals in the RFC "asinine" and only later proposed a reorganization of the RFC in response to the findings of the report. He proposed a reorganization of the Internal Revenue Bureau in January, 1952, when even those who were his friends said that the plan would have been more impressive if it had not been so long delayed.[1]

He did remove office holders, but he often did so under duress when they had become unbearable political liabilities. For example, he fired Theron Lamar Caudle, assistant Attorney General in charge of the tax division, and Joseph Marcelle, Brooklyn tax collector, on the eve of their public testimony, after word had been transmitted to him from closed sessions as to the nature of the disclosures. He let go his friend, Collector James P. Finnegan of St. Louis, after federal judge Moore had threatened to blast open the collector's office with a grand jury investigation unless Finnegan resigned. He gave a clean bill of health to his pal, Bill Boyle, Democratic national chairman, who was caught in the toils of the RFC scandals by his association with the ill-famed American Lithofold Company, and consented to Boyle's resignation only under pressure from within the party. He fired his Attorney General, J. Howard McGrath, whose continuance in office had become an unbearable political liability, but all the circumstances suggest that the axe was timed to fall so that McGrath could be made the scapegoat for Truman's decision to terminate the abortive clean-up drive headed by Newbold Morris.

The President sheltered within his own official family men who were intimately associated with the scandals. He defended his military aide, General Vaughan, whose friendship was the source of influence for the fixer, John Maragon, and the five-percenter, Col. J. V. Hunt. He shielded his aide, Donald S. Dawson, whose friendship was the main factor in making possible the activities of the RFC influence peddler, Merl Young.

1. See *Washington Post* editorial, January 4, 1952.

4

There was no indication that Truman ever censured or rebuked them for their conduct; there is no indication that Truman was emotionally affected by the frauds as was President Harding. He took no sweeping action against fraud, nor, except for one statement in his message proposing the Internal Revenue reorganization, did he make any ringing declaration against fraud.

### The President and the RFC Scandals

The Congressional investigation of the Reconstruction Finance Corporation started out not as an investigation of scandal but as an investigation of bad business judgment. In the days of Jesse Jones it would have been unthinkable to have levelled that accusation against RFC, but Jones had been gone since the beginning of 1945, and the prestige of the great lending agency had dimmed. Operations which had been profitable like its synthetic rubber plants and its Texas tin smelter plant now ran heavily in the red. Some of the losses RFC had incurred were not its fault, but they did not help publicity-wise. The RFC subsidiary, Defense Plants Corporation, had, on orders from the White House, lent $50,000,000 to Howard Hughes for his flying boat, Mars, but the boat refused to fly. That, certainly, was not the fault of RFC.

In late 1949, a series of events began which set Congress wondering what in the world the RFC was doing with the taxpayers' money. In September it voted to lend $10,100,000 to Texmass Petroleum, an obvious relief measure to two New England insurance companies which had gone wildcatting for oil and got clipped. In October, it voted $34,000,000 to Kaiser-Frazer although it was obvious that, with the auto shortage over, Kaiser could not compete with the Big Three. In February, 1950, Waltham Watch Company, to which the RFC had lent $4,000,000 a year earlier, suspended operations.

Later in that month, the wretched $37,500,000 loan to the prefabricated home-builder, Lustron, came to an end when the RFC in a welter of confusion filed suit to foreclose. A subcommittee of the Senate Banking and Currency Committee launched an investigation.

The chairman, Senator J. William Fulbright of Arkansas, had no desire to kill or cripple the RFC. On the contrary, he wished to contribute his great talents to enlightening it and putting it on the right track. The hearings in the spring of 1950 in which Fulbright discussed loan policy with the board were like a classroom seminar with Fulbright as a guide, albeit a severe one. There was no hint of the explosion that was to come. Although it was obvious from the start that there was something rotten in Denmark, and that that something was White House influence which had twisted the loan policy out of shape, Fulbright skirted the issue. Even though Fulbright argued against the wisdom of the Texmass loan, he did not attempt to stop disbursal under the loan, which started in June.

In August the President made his first blunder, and it was a costly one. He announced that Walter Dunham and William Edward Willett would be retained on the board, and that Chairman Harley Hise, and the other two directors, Harvey Gunderson and Henry A. Mulligan, would be replaced. The Fulbright Committee cited testimony that the President's aide in charge of patronage, Donald S. Dawson, tried to dominate the RFC, and that Willett and Dunham were his two puppets.[2] The other three were apparently too independent to suit Dawson's taste. Dawson handpicked the new chairman, W. Elmer Harber, and another new member was a buddy of Willett, Judge C. Edward Rowe.

The appointments were an affront to Fulbright whose recommendations had been overlooked. He and Senator Douglas had summoned Charles Murphy, the President's legal counsel

2. "Favoritism and Influence"—Report by Fulbright subcommittee on RFC (82nd Congress), p. 8.

to Capitol Hill in July and had told him that Dunham and Willett were objectionable to them. Chairman Hise, who had taken a fearful moral battering, was now released from the bonds. Harvey Gunderson was on personally friendly terms with Fulbright.

The Senate committee now went into closed sessions taking 1,250 pages of testimony. The administration became nervous and Truman ordered the RFC to tighten up.[3] The new board responded with a series of orders, raising the interest rate from four percent to five percent, requiring three votes for a loan (Texmass had been approved with only two votes) and requiring that no RFC borrower was to hire RFC personnel for two years from the time of the loan.

By the end of the year Fulbright believed that he had the full sordid story of what was going on in the RFC. He had no desire for a public scandal. With Senators Douglas and Tobey he obtained an interview with the President. Mr. Truman listened to their tale, told them not to worry and showed them to the door.

The Senators preferred not to be treated as schoolboys. There was now no choice but to publicize the story. On February 5, 1951, the committee issued its report, "Favoritism and Influence," which disclosed the activities of an influence ring in which power stemmed from the White House itself through Donald S. Dawson, administrative assistant to the President of the United States. It gave facts and names, including sundry characters such as Merl Young, Joseph Rosenbaum and Rex Jacobs. It accused two RFC directors, Ed Willett and Walter Dunham, of being peculiarly susceptible to influence.

The President's reaction was instantaneous. He labeled the report "asinine." He again submitted to the Senate his slate of five directors, including Dunham and Willett, with a request for confirmation. The issue was promptly joined. "I

3. See testimony of RFC Director Rowe, Hearings before the Fulbright subcommittee on the RFC (82nd Congress), p. 1642.

would not vote to confirm them," Senator Fulbright announced. "I do not believe these men are fit to serve in the RFC," said Senator Douglas. When the impact of the report had sunk in, the President felt differently. On February 19, he proposed to Congress a reorganization of the RFC, replacing the board of five members with a single administrator, as Fulbright had proposed.

The President moved from the defensive to the offensive, undoubtedly under the coaching of his administrative assistant, Donald S. Dawson. A publicity man was hired by the RFC expressly to wage newspaper warfare against the committee. Dawson's wife, Alva Dawson, was in charge of the RFC files and the committee got wind of the fact that she was pulling out of the files any and every letter that had been sent by congressmen or senators in behalf of constituents or friends requesting RFC loans. Some 900 letters were being photostated. This was obviously a pressure tactic designed to intimidate the Fulbright subcommittee, counteract the unfavorable publicity which had been heaped on the executive branch and persuade Congress that it might be dangerous to pursue the attack on the administration too far.

The subcommittee summoned various members of the RFC to explain why the letters were being pulled out of the file. The directors for awhile played "Button, button, who's got the button" with the committee, but finally the truth came out that the White House had instructed Chairman Harber that photostats be made and sent over to Dawson. Senator Tobey said he had recordings of phone conversations with the President. In the first conversation the President announced that he had "good information" that a "great many" congressmen had accepted fees in return for getting RFC loans. In a subsequent conversation, the President admitted he had no such evidence. The President said that it was "outrageous" that these recordings had been made.

It was a shabby maneuver in the committee's eyes. Temporarily the President might have won an inning with his unruly Congress, but members of the committee announced that they would pursue the investigation more stubbornly.

The President's strategy fizzled out. The real pressure had come from the Administration. There were cases in which Congressional pressure had wangled RFC loans, but it was difficult to prove that any remuncration or emoluments had been paid to the congressmen as a consideration beyond the latter's expectation that he would get votes. This is routine. The President was forced to take another tack. Dawson testified that the President had requested letters from the files merely in order to inform himself as to the method of operations of the RFC in regard to the reorganization plan. No more was heard about the letters.

Fulbright was stung by the President's characterization of his report as "asinine" and infuriated by the attempted intimidation. Although the President had agreed to reorganize the RFC, Fulbright announced public hearings. "These hearings have a very limited objective," he stated, "that is to demonstrate, I hope, to the Congress and the people that the report that we issued in the early part of February was not an asinine report."

Fulbright was the Grand Inquisitor incarnate. He dragged forth into the public spotlight all the personalities who were involved in his report "Favoritism and Influence." Eschewing the normal practice of using outside legal counsel, he conducted all the questioning himself. He was hard, cold and implacable in his examination, obviously contemptuous of the various RFC officials and the retinue of the influence ring who appeared before him. "I have never heard so much lying in my life," he stated. He would recite a passage from his report as if he were reading the litany. Then in response would come the substantiation from the witness. As if addressing the world, Fulbright observed sardonically that his report was not so asinine after all.

The committee wanted to summon one of the important personalities in the report, Donald Dawson, to the witness stand, but the President refused. Finally, however, public opinion forced another retreat by Truman. On May 10, Dawson appeared before the subcommittee. It was revealed that David K. Niles, another administrative assistant to the President, had gotten in touch with former Senator Burton K. Wheeler, and had asked him in turn to get in touch with Senator Tobey, so that Tobey would "go easy" on Dawson. It appeared quite clear from Dawson's testimony that the President's assistant did not have as high a set of moral standards as one might expect from a person with his responsibilities. The man who dominated the RFC sought to give the impression that he labored in a miasmic fog unconscious of his connection with the agency.

The testimony before the Fulbright committee was far more damaging than the report. The report had been merely barebones. The detail supplied flesh, blood and color. This was the story of the prostitution of a great and powerful government agency to mean personal and political ends. The fortunes of the once mighty RFC had sunk to their nadir as directors pleaded for understanding with the committee or beat their breasts with *mea culpas*. Said Ed Willett, "It was a bad board," and that "I was just as bad as the rest of them." An employee of the Dallas office put it more tersely, "RFC stinks." Fulbright continued to assert that his only desire was to reform RFC, not to kill it, but it was hard to see how the agency could recover its prestige after the pulverizing blows it had received.

When the house lights had dimmed and the curtain had gone down on the hearings before the Fulbright subcommittee in May, it appeared that the RFC would now have a reprieve in order to work out its salvation. Only a few months later, however, in October, the house lights suddenly went on again, the curtain went up, and the country witnessed another act in the RFC drama. This time, it was before the Hoey Investigations Subcommittee of the Committee on Expenditures. Many of the *dramatis personae* were the same as before the Fulbright subcommittee, but the leading man was different. It was none other than the distinguished chairman of the Democratic National Committee, William M. Boyle, Jr., who stood accused of having been paid to intervene in behalf of the American Lithofold Corporation while he was vice-chairman of the Democratic committee.

There was a difference between the amount of the retainer that Boyle had undoubtedly accepted and the fee he was alleged to have received. But no matter how you sliced it, the result was the same—that he had profited from his party position and was thus guilty on the test that the President applied. The President exonerated Boyle on the basis of the well-known Truman Exception for Special Friends. Boyle, nonetheless, resigned. The questioning of Boyle and the other parties to the matter was protracted and bitter. It was by now a familiar pattern. American Lithofold had been turned down at all levels of the RFC and then a call, a single call to RFC Chairman Hise by Bill Boyle, had thrown all the machinery in reverse and Lithofold had received three loans for over $600,000. Disgust with RFC now welled up on both sides of the aisle.

There would be no salvation now for the RFC. Loan activity contracted. Personnel deserted the agency in droves. The RFC was a sinking ship destroyed by scandal.

### The President and the Tax Scandals

The tax scandals grew out of an acorn of a dispute. Credit for prying the lid off must go to Senator John J. Williams, Republican of Delaware. A cashier in the office of the Wilmington collector in 1946 was indiscreet enough to include

11

the senator's tax payment in a swindle that involved five hundred taxpayers and some $30,000. What shocked Senator Williams was that even after Williams called the attention of the Wilmington collector to the embezzlement, for months no action resulted. The cashier, it seemed, stood high in Democratic circles in Delaware.

With this sample of how the tax office was being operated in his own state, Williams next cast a piercing eye on the corrupt New York and St. Louis collectors' offices. Williams became a Savonarola on the need for tax reform, with his desk in the Senate as his pulpit. The administration showed no interest in a clean-up. The Commissioner of Internal Revenue, George Schoeneman, a former White House administrative assistant, was a Truman crony. The Senator presented his findings on the Senate floor. Finally, in 1951, the public clamor was loud enough to induce Congress to set up the King subcommittee of the House Ways and Means Committee to investigate the operation of the internal revenue laws.

As 1951 progressed, the tax scandals were warming up. In July the collector for Boston, Denis W. Delaney, was fired, and in September he was indicted on charges of tax fixing and bribery. New York Collector James Johnson was fired in July. In August James B. Olson, supervisor of the alcohol tax unit in New York, resigned under fire. In September, James G. Smyth, collector for San Francisco, and eight others in his office were suspended. Smyth was soon afterward indicted.

The Administration was conducting a dogged retreat, but was still unwilling to admit that the burgeoning scandals called for a clean-up and reform. The King subcommittee in executive sessions was reportedly uncovering some sensational cases of official misconduct, but a Republican member of the subcommittee, James Byrnes, charged that the Justice Department was stymying the tax investigation by withholding files from the committee. Senator Williams revealed that he was no longer getting co-operation from the new Commissioner Dunlap, in checking tips that he had given. Commissioner Schoeneman had resigned in June 1951 for reasons of ill health. Senator Nixon told newsmen that the Justice Department had "not been enthusiastic in its support of Congressional investigations of scandals in the government."

By November 1951, the scandals had flared into the headline stage. The President fired Theron Lamar Caudle, assistant Attorney General in charge of the tax division, for improper activities, which included the acceptance of a $5,000 commission for the sale of an airplane to a person intimately connected with a tax case in which Caudle had exhibited suspicious interest on the part of the defendant. As we shall see later, a Chicago lawyer, Abraham Teitelbaum, alleged that he had been the victim of a shakedown attempt for $500,000 by an extortion ring which he was told included Caudle, Charles Oliphant, the general counsel of the Internal Revenue Bureau, and Jess Larson, the head of the War Assets Administration. Oliphant resigned.

The President returned from Key West, where he had been vacationing, amid speculation as to the steps that he would take in launching a clean-up offensive. On December 13, he held a press conference in which he appeared jaunty and undisturbed. He maintained that there was nothing new or unusual about the present scandals and that not drastic action but only continued drastic action would be taken. He was asked: "Mr. President, would you care to indicate some of the instances where you have taken drastic action in the past?" The President said there had been plenty of them. He said he had dispensed with several cabinet officers in times past. The collector in Boston was fired before anybody began to look into his situation except the Treasury Department. The collector of Internal Revenue in St. Louis was dispensed with long before anything was looked into by the committee. The collector in San Francisco was fired before anybody looked into it, and the grand jury in California had just indicted him.

It is difficult to find any facts to support Truman's statements. Not one cabinet officer had been dispensed with because of an intimation of fraud. Delaney had been fired after three and a half years, during which charges had been leveled against him. The administration had been notified time and time again that the collector's office in San Francisco was a rotten one. Corruption in the San Francisco office had been exposed in 1950 by the Kefauver crime committee, but nothing had been done.

In September 1952, former Assistant Attorney General Caudle revealed to the Chelf committee the background of Collector Finnegan's resignation. Ellis Slack, who was the emissary of the Justice Department to the grand jury in St. Louis, returned on March 13, 1951, and told Caudle that Judge Moore had threatened an investigation of the collector's office unless Finnegan resigned immediately. Caudle called Bill Boyle, the chairman of the Democratic National Committee. "Now, Bill, you better move fast because this judge is determined about this matter. We do not have any facts about Finnegan, but I do know that the judge is determined to have a grand jury inquisition about his affairs." Boyle undoubtedly contacted the President. Caudle assumes Boyle called Secretary Snyder. Caudle called Charles Oliphant, Internal Revenue counsel, who, he presumed, also called Snyder. Caudle called Revenue Commissioner Schoeneman and said, "This judge means business." Caudle also called Under-Secretary Foley. "I covered the waterfront," said Caudle. Finnegan's resignation followed and he was indicted several months later. When Senator Williams wrote to Secretary Snyder congratulating him on Finnegan's removal, Snyder replied that "the collector at St. Louis voluntarily resigned."

To return to the press conference of December 13. Doris Fleeson, the columnist, had written a column which had appeared in the Washington *Evening Star* the evening before, and the President had undoubtedly seen it. It was a highly imaginative piece depicting the effect of the scandals on the President. It quoted Hobbes' statement that hell was "the truth seen too late." It described him as "despondent." It said that the frauds were a "blow to the President" and referred to his "deeper pain." The President's demeanor certainly did not reflect any of these characterizations. In the middle of the press conference, he turned to Miss Fleeson and asked her why she was looking at him that way. Was she thinking of writing a sob sister piece about him? He didn't need any sob sister pieces.

Nonetheless, according to Democratic National Chairman Frank McKinney, Truman felt "let down" by his friends and so, day by day, there were predictions that the President would take this means or that for retrieving the reputation of his administration, since the tax scandals had been piled on the RFC scandals in the same year.

The general expectation was that he would appoint a special prosecutor in the way that Coolidge after Teapot Dome had appointed Owen J. Roberts and Atlee Pomerene, and Wilson had appointed Charles Evans Hughes as a special prosecutor when the airplane industry didn't turn out planes in World War I. The President sounded out Federal Judge Thomas F. Murphy to join a clean-up commission. Murphy, who had been the prosecutor of Alger Hiss, first accepted and then declined.

Then came the news which floored just about everybody. The clean-up drive would be conducted by none other than the Attorney General, J. Howard McGrath himself. It had been expected that McGrath would be forced to resign since the Justice Department was the most suspect agency in the mess. McGrath seemed the least qualified person to conduct a clean-up. Before the King subcommittee, he admitted that he had approved Caudle's acceptance of a $5,000 commission for the sale of an airplane and had also approved a trip abroad by Caudle with a wine merchant, for which Caudle's expenses had been paid. He had defended Caudle, saying that the President had fired him by going over his head.

McGrath had shown a total apathy for the anti-corruption campaign. In July 1951, he had written to Senator Douglas that he had a "lack of enthusiasm for attempts to legislate generally in the field of simple morality." On December 6, 1951, he told the Federal Bar Association, "I believe that when all the storms and the winds have passed, not one lawyer working for the United States will be found to be derelict in his duty or to his oath of office." In October, Judge George H. Moore of St. Louis had told a Washington newspaper that in the previous March he had telephoned McGrath, asking in vain for Justice Department aid in the grand jury investigation of tax scandals which culminated in the indictment of Collector Finnegan. He had obstructed the work of the King committee by hindering its access to the files of the Department of Justice. This was the man whom Truman selected to head his clean-up campaign. In effect, he had asked McGrath to investigate McGrath.

On February 1, 1952, Newbold Morris was appointed by McGrath as a special assistant to the Attorney General to investigate corruption in the federal government. Mr. Morris had been the last Republican candidate for Mayor of New York and had been president of the City Council. There was one thing seriously wrong with the appointment—Mr. Morris was himself involved in a matter which had been under investigation for months by the criminal division of the Justice Department. This was a deal for tankers acquired as war surplus and sold at a juicy profit. He was president and lawyer for China International Foundation Inc., a report about which had been sent by Secretary Sawyer in June 1951 to the Justice Department. James McInerney, head of the criminal division, had told McGrath that Morris was "on the edge of the tankers transactions" and McGrath instructed him to check into it and let him know.[4]

Morris asked, "If he knew it [the investigation by the Justice Department], he knew more than I did. Therefore why would he have brought me down to carry on this work if he knew that I was under suspicion by his criminal division?" The Chelf committee reported that McGrath's haste to appoint Morris "might justifiably be interpreted as an attempt to appoint to office a man who might be susceptible to pressure."

Morris, in spite of long softening-up lunches and other acts of kindness, looked like a man who wanted to do a job. Morris said there was an apparent lack of interest in his work from the outset; no one seemed to want to discuss it or help him work out his methods of investigation; there was a pall or chill whenever he discussed it with anyone, although no one was openly opposed to him.

The President had given an effusive welcome to Morris and had assured him that he would be granted whatever powers he needed for his investigation. Morris wanted the power to subpoena witnesses; he made it clear that he did not require the right to grant immunity from prosecution for witnesses in exchange for testimony. Nonetheless, when a joint resolution was introduced in Congress, it contained a provision joining the subpoena right together with the right to grant immunity. Congress rejected the resolution altogether.

Morris had another club that would be effective in exposure of corruption. He proposed to send out questionnaires to higher officials, at the $10,000 level and over, of departments which he wished to investigate. This type of questionnaire had proved very effective in discovering wrongdoers in police departments in New York and Washington and in the Internal Revenue Bureau. If answered truthfully, it might

4. Report of Chelf subcommittee to investigate the Department of Justice (82nd Congress), p. 11.

reveal a great increase in wealth for an official not commensurate with his salary. If not answered truthfully, the official is subject to prosecution for perjury. In an interview with Morris, the President expressed his willingness to have these questionnaires distributed, insisting that he would fill one out himself, including Margaret's income.[5]

On March 18, the questionnaires were delivered in McGrath's absence to the Solicitor General's office for distribution. On March 19, the Justice Department notified Morris that no further personnel could be hired unless a loyalty check had first been made on the prospective employee. Mr. Morris' relationships with the Attorney General had evidently taken a turn for the worse.

A week later, Col. Becker, Mr. Morris' aide, called on McGrath and requested certain of McGrath's personal records —his engagement book, diary and telephone call records—together with some other material which included the files of undisposed-of prosecutions. The material was refused. The situation had become monstrously absurd, as might have been expected. A man hires an assistant and the assistant tells his boss that his first action is going to be to investigate him.

On March 31, in testimony before the Chelf subcommittee, Mr. McGrath stated that if he had it to do over again, he would not have hired Morris. He also said that he didn't know whether or not he would fill out the questionnaire and that he would not distribute them until he was satisfied as to whether they were proper.

It was obvious that a showdown was in the offing. On April 2, a Presidential party went to Washington airport to greet Queen Juliana of the Netherlands and Prince Bernhard. Reporters were astonished to see McGrath and the President detach themselves from the waiting group and engage in a discussion which was described as either highly spirited or a

5. Newbold Morris, *Let the Chips Fall*, p. 26.

violent argument. Press Secretary Joseph Short joined the two and the voices rang higher on the field. Then Queen Juliana's plane appeared and all was smiles.

The next day, April 3, was the day on which Morris and McGrath were scheduled to arrange for a grand jury to be impaneled which would give Morris a substitute for the subpoena power. That morning Mr. Morris received a curt note, addressed "Sir," from the Attorney General, saying that he was dismissed effective immediately. No reason was given. A few hours later, the President had fired McGrath. Morris was unable to reach the President. As Morris commented, the drama ended in true Shakespearean style with two corpses lying on the stage. Said Morris, "If I got rid of nothing else, I got rid of Howard McGrath."

As the successor to McGrath, the President appointed James P. McGranery, who was a federal district judge in Philadelphia. The Democratic district attorney there, Richardson Dilworth, immediately said that the "appointment is so bad as to be unbelievable." McGranery had been special assistant to the Attorney General prior to becoming a federal judge. He said that he would not use the questionnaire method but would use the FBI to root out corruption. The FBI by law could not investigate Treasury personnel. He stated there was no point in investigating Justice Department employees since they had already undergone an investigation (this investigation, of course, is conducted prior to hiring). The only dismissal he sponsored was of a federal attorney in Topeka, Kansas, for fee splitting. On the basis of this record, on August 8, McGranery triumphantly announced that the progress in the government clean-up had made it abundantly clear that exposure and punishment would fall on wrongdoers. On September 5, he abolished the federal rackets grand juries convened the previous January, saying that they smacked of showmanship. Simultaneously, he abolished the racket squad in the Department of Justice which had been set up to assist U. S. attorneys. That rang down the curtain in the Truman clean-up.

Who fired Newbold Morris? According to Arthur Krock of the *New York Times* whose sources in Washington were of the best, Truman had agreed that Morris was to be fired.[6] In a cabinet meeting on March 28, McGrath had complained bitterly about the questionnaires and the President told him to do nothing about them for a week. On April 1, the President ostentatiously asked for a copy of McGrath's testimony before the Chelf committee in which McGrath had said that he had doubts about the questionnaire. The President could not have been surprised by McGrath's attitude. Was he at that time preparing the sacrificial lamb? The next day, the President praised McGrath for his testimony, told him not to distribute the questionnaires, and agreed with him to do the firing. Later that day Charles Murphy, Truman's legal counsel, told McGrath that he should do it, since he had hired Morris. McGrath wanted a statement of accord from the White House, which was the subject for dispute at the airport. McGrath decided to go ahead with the firing anyway. His dismissal was unexpected. As for Morris, if the President had wanted him, he could, of course, have retained him merely by lifting the phone.

At a Gridiron Club dinner soon afterwards there was a song parody which portrayed McGrath as "taking a fall for Clark" (presumably McGrath's predecessor, Supreme Court Justice Clark) and for the administration he had served so well. McGrath in excitement grabbed a microphone and shouted, "That's the truth, damn it, that's the truth."

6. *New York Times*, April 6, 1952.

# · III ·

# PRESIDENT TRUMAN AND
# CORRUPTION—II

*He was my friend and I was his.*

—Vice President Harry S. Truman,
leaving Washington for the funeral
of Tom Pendergast, January, 1945.

Harry Truman owed his phenomenal rise in life to one of the most corrupt political machines in America—the Pendergast machine of Kansas City.[1] Everything under Pendergast was for sale to the highest bidder, including the police. Nothing that happened during his administration could have shocked Harry Truman since it was strictly *comme il faut* in Kansas City. At the time of Truman's election to the Senate in 1934, one of Pendergast's chief lieutenants was the notorious Johnny Lazia, ex-highway robber, who made appointments to the police department and gave a yes or no answer as to whether you could run a racket in Kansas City. Lazia's own take from slot machines ran to seven figures. Kansas City was known as a center of activities of the Mafia and the locus of a narcotics ring which was not broken up until 1942.

Harry Truman got his first political job as judge of the county court of Jackson County (that is, county commissioner) because he was recommended by an Army friend, Jim Pendergast, to his uncle, Boss Tom Pendergast. In his *Memoirs* Truman says that Pendergast asked nothing of him. He

1. For background of Truman see Maurice Milligan, *Missouri Waltz* and W. Reddig, *Tom's Town.*

21

did not have to ask anything of Judge Truman—there was only one concrete company, the Ready-Mixed Concrete Company, supplying the building projects voted by the county commission. It was owned by Pendergast and no one else could muscle in.

In 1934 Pendergast was on the defensive because of bloody and shocking outrages in the March elections. Needing a candidate not too prominently identified with him, he chose Harry Truman for the Senate and in a three-way fight Truman won the nomination. His plurality was 41,000 votes statewide. Jackson County and Kansas City gave him 138,423 votes to the combined votes of his two opponents of 10,437. That measures the extent of his debt to Pendergast who, it was estimated, could dispose of up to 60,000 "ghost" votes.

In the same year Roosevelt appointed Maurice Milligan U. S. attorney for western Missouri. He broke the Pendergast machine for a time, securing 259 convictions for frauds in the 1936 elections, and Tom Pendergast himself went to jail for income tax evasion in 1939. In February, 1938, Senator Truman moved to prevent the confirmation of Milligan for another term. He attacked him violently on the floor of the Senate saying that "a Jackson County, Missouri, Democrat has as much chance of a fair trial in the Federal District Court of Western Missouri as a Jew would have in a Hitler court." A Republican senator arose to ask Senator Truman if he wished to go on record as condoning vote frauds. Truman's version is that he opposed Milligan's re-appointment because abler men could be found. That argument must have been made privately.

After a conference with Pendergast, the senator withdrew his opposition. The *New York Times* (February 17, 1938) commented editorially:

> An official has sinned against Mr. Truman's benefactor. It was for the protege to show the depth of his devotion. His colleague, Mr. Clark, the governor of Missouri, the Mayor of St.

Louis, many Democratic organizations are on the other side. As it turned out, Mr. Truman stood alone in the Senate against confirmation. What of it? Wasn't it affecting to see Cato cling to a beaten cause? Mr. Truman sailed into the Republican judges. All they wanted was to convict Democrats. . . .

He poured his soul into several pages of the Congressional Record. Say not the struggle nought availeth. Tom Pendergast may have lost the cemetery vote but he can't lose Harry Truman.

Milligan never accused Truman in connection with any fraud. Truman's role has been well described by William W. Reddig, formerly of the *Kansas City Star:* "Truman was a dues-paying member who ran with the pack; never struck a blow against bossism and consistently threw his weight against reform although he seldom had to make an embarrassing public display of the boss tag."

With the Pendergast machine apparently broken, President Roosevelt said to Milligan: "I told Harry Truman the other day that he had better get away from that crowd out there." But Truman did not. Of Pendergast's conviction, Truman said, "I am sorry that happened, but I am not going to desert a ship in distress." He won renomination to the Senate in 1940 by the narrow margin of 7,000 votes with the remnants of the Pendergast strength and the help of a St. Louis politician who switched from Governor Stark, a young man by the name of Robert Hannegan.

In 1945, when Pendergast died, the Vice President flew out to his funeral. A few weeks after Truman became President, he fired Maurice Milligan. In his place he appointed Sam Wear as U. S. attorney; Wear had been chairman of the Democratic State Committee of Missouri. He pardoned fifteen of the Pendergast people who had been in prison for the vote frauds. On December 7, 1945, the President wrote to Jim Pendergast, Tom Pendergast's nephew who was the heir to the Pendergast machine: "Dear Jim: I am enclosing you a check for $6 in payment of my Jackson Democratic Club dues. I hope the outfit is still going good. Sincerely yours, Harry." On the wall of Jim Pendergast's office hung a White House portrait of Harry Truman with the autograph "To James M. Pendergast—friend, comrade, and adviser."

## Kansas City—1946

On July 18, 1946, President Truman announced that he was opposed to the renomination of Congressman Roger C. Slaughter from the Fifth District of Missouri, which included Kansas City. Slaughter had offended him by his vote in the House Committee on Rules to bottle up the FEPC Bill which the President considered politically important for the 1946 Congressional elections. "If Slaughter is right, then I am wrong," he said, and the President was not wrong. He had summoned Jim Pendergast to the White House and Pendergast, who had previously supported Slaughter, now voiced his opposition. The President favored Enos Axtell, an unknown with whose name Mr. Truman was obviously unfamiliar.

In the August 6 primary, Slaughter was the overwhelming favorite to win. The President himself went to Kansas City on primary day to lend his great prestige to his fight against Slaughter. To the amazement of everybody, Axtell was the winner by 2300 votes. He went down to defeat in the November elections, but the President had achieved his purpose, to purge Mr. Slaughter.

The election, according to descriptions, was as crooked as any ever held in Kansas City. Johnny Lazia had gone to his death years before in a rain of machine-gun bullets, but Charles Binaggio, the gangster, was a new power in Kansas City politics. Flying squadrons of ghost voters were sent out from his clubhouse to cast ballots again and again. Binaggio

24

voted them not only from the grave but "from England and France." Election inspectors marked ballots for voters. The count consisted of putting the ballots in three piles, the first marked "straight machine," the second "Republican" and the third "mixed." All in the first pile were counted for Axtell. In many precincts Slaughter received no votes. In four wards the vote was 6 to 1 in favor of Axtell. Slaughter said that the Kansas City election board in issuing credentials to official watchers and challengers "gave practically all such posts to followers of the Pendergast machine."

The *Kansas City Star* cried fraud. It sent around investigators to collect affidavits and 1400 were collected. Here is part of a typical statement, cited by Milligan, from Estalla R. Carter.[2]

> On August 6, 1946, at about 6:45 p.m., I went to the polling place located in a radio shop in the 700 block on East Eighth Street. I went there to cast my vote at the primary election. I was met at the door by a man whom I would describe as about 5 feet 11 inches tall or 6 feet, having a large frame, and wearing glasses, white, about 180 pounds. I told him my name and that I wanted to vote. This man I judged to be a precinct worker. He was holding the poll book. He said, "I voted you." I said, "How could you? Nobody could vote for me as no one knew how I wanted to vote." I said, "I haven't been here before today," and he said, "Nellie Rentie told me you weren't coming to vote." Nellie Rentie is my apartment manager and she worked at the precinct on the primary election day. I told him I hadn't discussed this with Nellie. He said, "Wait a minute," and he went out and talked to some people in a car. Then he came back and asked me if I knew "Lovey." I told him I didn't. Later as we walked up the street this man pushed at me some folded bills. He handed these folded bills to me. I didn't take the money. As he handed me, or attempted to hand me, the money he said, "Here take this and buy yourself some beer."

In October the general clamor forced Attorney General Clark to permit an investigation of the vote by the FBI. The

2. For affidavit, see Milligan, *op. cit.*, p. 252.

assistant Attorney General in charge of the criminal division, Theron Lamar Caudle, gave instructions to the FBI. It was not until June 1947[3] that it was disclosed that Caudle had authorized the FBI to make only a "preliminary investigation" and had instructed the FBI to interview only two reporters from the *Kansas City Star* and four election inspectors. As former Attorney General Biddle testified before the Chelf committee this was unprecedented and "improper" since even a "preliminary investigation" of civil rights cases was by practice unrestricted. Caudle's office drafted the instructions three times before submitting the memo to Attorney General Clark who approved it and transmitted it to J. Edgar Hoover.

The FBI in submitting a 245-page report stated that "Its contents do not constitute the results of an investigation but pursuant to the specific instructions of the Attorney General are merely a summary of the data developed by the *Kansas City Star* and the Election Board." The memorandum stressed this point "to prevent the possibility of our reports being cited as a result of investigation proving that further investigation or prosecution is not justified."

U. S. Attorney Sam Wear prepared a twenty-three page synopsis of the report. He submitted it to three federal judges in Missouri, who rightly concluded that there was no basis for a grand jury investigation. These judges testified that they assumed the investigation would continue; they were not informed of the limitations in the FBI report; they were not asked as to an opinion of an additional investigation and they said that on the basis of the full FBI report, their opinion would have been different. Wear informed the Justice Department in Washington of the opinion of the judges based upon his synopsis. On January 6, 1947, assistant Attorney General Caudle stated that the investigation was closed. The department said, "The investigation in the case was thorough." In 1952, testifying before the Chelf committee,[4] Caudle

3. Reports of the judiciary subcommittee on Senate Resolution 116, July 1947 (80th Congress).

admitted frankly that the investigation by the FBI had been a highly restricted one.

Senator Kem of Missouri started asking questions. Attorney General Clark told Kem, "The FBI at my instance conducted a full investigation as to the charges of fraud in the primary— no evidence of a Federal violation was established." A Senate subcommittee under Senator Ferguson of the Judiciary Committee started a preliminary scrutiny of the Justice Department in the Kansas City vote frauds. There was great consternation in the Justice Department. Caudle worked arduously with Attorney General Clark in preparation for the hearings. On the night before the start of the hearings, May 28, they were together in Clark's home until the wee hours wrapped in blankets when the heating went off. At four in the morning, Clark dismissed Caudle and stayed up for the remainder of the night himself. At the hearings, he was calm and confident.

The previous day a county grand jury of Jackson County, which had been investigating the vote frauds, made its report in the courtroom at Independence, Missouri. It declared that the evidence showed that "there had been a deliberate and calculated plan to miscount votes and otherwise steal the election." It said that Slaughter had been deprived of the nomination by fraud. All ballots and records used by the jury in investigation were returned to the vaults of the Kansas City Board of Election Commissioner for safekeeping.

While Clark was testifying in the public hearing on May 28, Senator Ferguson announced that he had just received a wire from Kansas City: "Last night primary ballots stolen from election commissioner vault."

The vault in Kansas City had been blown open with nitroglycerin and the ballots and other records needed for prosecution had been stolen. No doors in the building had been

4. Testimony of Caudle before Chelf subcommittee to investigate the Department of Justice (82nd Congress), p. 1169, discussing the Kansas City case.

forced except the vault door. A wastepaper sack had been left conveniently in the vault so that it might serve to carry the loot away.

The President had been sleeping in the Muehlebach hotel in Kansas City three blocks away when the theft was carried out.[5]

Now Attorney General Clark authorized a "full and complete" investigation. The President concurred. Seventy-one persons had been indicted but without the evidence prosecution was fruitless.

Senator Kem proposed a full-dress investigation of Clark's conduct in the frauds by the Senate. The Judiciary Subcommittee voted it down 7 to 6 with Senator Langer switching to the Democrats. The resolution went to the floor of the Senate in mid-July, two weeks from adjournment. A filibuster went on for days in the Senate until Senator Taft was forced to let the resolution die.

Chairman Ferguson of the Senate Judiciary Subcommittee condemned Clark for not having conducted a full investigation. The minority report said in reference to his replies to Senator Kem: "It is the opinion of the subcommittee that the replies of the Attorney General indicate an intentional misrepresentation of facts to a member of the United States Senate in answer to an official inquiry." Caudle testified that Clark, who had been caught in embarrassing misstatements, reproached those who had prepared the letter for his signature. Ferguson pointed out that in Clark's own file there were 28 memos with a summary of evidence showing that 159 persons were shown to vote who did not vote; 10 persons voted who were not on the election records and 14 persons could not vote because they had already been voted.

Caudle testified in 1952 before the Chelf committee that no case in his seven years' experience at the Department of

5. Report of the Chelf subcommittee to investigate the Department of Justice (82nd Congress) p. 93.

Justice had received such "top level attention." It was a "rat race." He guessed it was because the "case was from the state the President was from and since the President indicated he would like to see Mr. Axtell elected." The Democratic Chelf committee pointed out that all in the Department of Justice who took part in the Kansas City vote fraud case were rewarded.[6] Mr. Clark was promoted to the Supreme Court. Peyton Ford built an administrative empire and went on to become deputy Attorney General. Herbert Bergson moved ahead to become head of the antitrust division. William Holloran who did the "leg work" in the case got a choice spot overseas where he would be safe from questioning. Nor was Theron Lamar Caudle overlooked. In the fall of 1947, he was given the choice plum of assistant Attorney General in charge of the tax division. By 1951 it can be said that Mr. Caudle had managed to make a name for himself.

## Federal Plunder and the Democratic Machine

Truman's personal association with Pendergast is only part of the story. There were powerful compulsives which arose simply out of the character of the Democratic party after the war. Those who remember the Democratic convention of 1944 know that Truman was nominated for Vice President, in spite of the great sentimental wave for Henry Wallace, by the city bosses who delivered their delegations— Ed Flynn of the Bronx, Ed Kelly of Chicago, Frank Hague of Jersey City, and, of course, the Pendergast machine. The vitality of the Democratic party depended upon the health of these machines. Without Boston, it could not carry Massachusetts; without New York City, it could not carry New York State; without Jersey City, it could not carry New Jersey; without the Cook County machine, it could not carry

6. Report of Chelf subcommittee, *op. cit.*, p. 95.

Illinois; and without the Kansas City machine, it could not carry Missouri. The same situation applies in other States too in which rural areas are heavily Republican.

Prior to the war, the bounty from the federal machine was limited since the budget was small even though it was considerably higher than in the days of Herbert Hoover. In 1940, for example, the federal budget was less than $10 billion. Jobs were the staff of life of the city machines. WPA jobs, post office jobs and others were the crumbs that could be distributed in those depression days when having a job was the most important thing in life.

The war changed the complexion of things and offered new sources for plunder. Plunder lay in the huge federal expenditures and in special relief from the federal controls which enveloped the country. During the war, there was no systematic attempt to exploit these new sources or, to put it more bluntly, to get onto the new gravy train. Bonanzas were plentiful and Democratic control was secure. It was not until after the war that the machines sensed the new opportunities.

There had been a huge increase in tax revenues from under $10 billion to over $60 billion. Thousands of businesses could save untold amounts of money by a nod from the right Treasury official, which would mean the difference between a favorable or unfavorable tax ruling. One man's say-so could mean the difference of a million dollars and who was to find out if a little pressure had been applied or if a little inducement had been given. If an individual were in a ninety-percent income bracket, he would have to earn $10 million in income to get the equivalent of that $1 million nod. There was gravy in government loans, particularly in the huge loans being made by the RFC in which decisions were made on purely arbitrary grounds. There was gravy in government contracts which were still being ladled out even though the war was over. There was a huge government surplus for sale. There were permits to be given out for radio stations by the

Federal Communications System and new routes for the embryonic airline industry. These privileges could lay the foundations of fortunes for decades to come. All of these were within the reach of the politicians.

Truman had thrust these politicians in control. Never were the city machines so closely knit with the administration in Washington, bound together by what Lincoln Steffens called "the cohesive power of public plunder." Truman could not act with freedom or forthrightness to clean up the government. There was a basic contradiction in fighting the forces on which his party relied.

Undoubtedly, the brazenness of these politicians stemmed from their confidence that they would be in power forever. Harry Truman set the keynote. In his *Memoirs* he records that on May 8, 1951, he wrote the following memorandum: ". . . If we can find a man who will . . . continue the Fair Deal, Point IV, fair employment, parity for farmers and a consumers' protective policy, the Democratic party can win from now on." He explained the Republican victory in 1952 this way: "The popularity of a war hero like that of General Eisenhower seemed to provide a rare political opportunity to a rebellious Republican clique."

## *Executive Clemency*

The Constitution gives the President of the United States power to grant pardons. In exercising this right of pardon, Truman exhibited a certain moral obtuseness considering the nature of the crimes and the interests of the public.

Mayor James M. Curley of Boston, a prince of demagogues, had been convicted of mail fraud with Donald Wakefield Smith, who had served on the National Labor Relations Board. Curley went through a lot of theatrics to escape sentence, such as appearing in the court for sentence on a stretcher, but he served time, while collecting a salary as mayor of Boston. Truman commuted his sentence to the period served and the pardon covered an earlier conviction of Curley for fraud in impersonating another man in a federal Civil Service examination. His executive clemency was later extended to Donald Wakefield Smith.

The Falstaffian Edward F. Prichard, Jr., surnamed "Prich", a protege of Felix Frankfurter and formerly counsel to the Democratic National Committee, was convicted of stuffing ballot boxes in Kentucky in the 1948 election. The fact that Prichard was a brilliant Harvard law graduate is not extenuation for such a crime but rather is reason to censure one who had the benefit of the best in law education. Truman commuted his sentence in 1948, after Prichard had served five months.

In an article, "The Scandalous Years," in *Look* magazine, two other strange parole cases are summarized:[7]

James J. Gavin, partner in the Greyhound gambling joint in Jeffersonville, Indiana, was serving a five-year term for dodging income taxes on horse-race winnings. James Gavin's brother Willie tossed $1000 into the Democratic national campaign fund. Then he visited William M. Boyle, Jr., Mr. Truman's former secretary who was assistant to National Democratic Chairman Robert Hannegan. Boyle said he'd do what he could. Senate Democratic Leader (now Vice-President) Alben W. Barkley and Congressman Emmet O'Neal of Louisville, later Ambassador to the Philippines, also developed an interest in Gavin. O'Neal asked the Justice Department to give the case "careful consideration."

Harry E. (Cueball) Whitney, a Pendergast wheel horse and World War I Battery D mate of the President, talked to White House Secretary Matthew Connelly about Gavin. On September 13, President Truman quietly commuted Gavin's prison sentence. A week later, four months before he was eligible for parole, Gavin was free. Attorney General Tom C. Clark said

7. *Look* magazine, May 1951.

he had been a "good prisoner" and that a large number of respected persons had requested that he be released.

The following month, the President pardoned Joseph M. Schenck, another heavy contributor to the party chests. The movie magnate had served one year of a three-year term for income-tax evasion.

Robert Gould, who had been sentenced to six years for selling liquor on the black market, had a lawyer, William H. Neblett, who was a close friend of General Harry Vaughan. Gould got a parole, and Vaughan collected a campaign contribution. In 1949, Truman issued a pardon to Frank W. Kraemer, who had been convicted of unlawfully soliciting and receiving political contributions from federal employees.

Four members of the Al Capone gang, Louis "Little New York" Campagna, Paul "the Waiter" DeLucia, Philip D'Andrea and Charles "Cherry Nose" Gioe, had been sentenced to prison for ten years for conspiracy to extort a million dollars from the movie industry. (Willie Bioff, who testified against them was executed in November, 1955—when he stepped on the starter of his car, he was blown up.) Their lawyers had pleaded for light sentences, arguing, "There is not one chance in a thousand that they will be paroled." In August 1947, they were paroled after having served only three-and-one-half years of their ten-year terms.[8]

A House subcommittee investigating the granting of paroles was hampered by Attorney General Clark and the Justice Department in getting information. It learned, however, that two or three members of the parole board were Clark's appointees and that the parole had been granted in direct opposition of the recommendations of the trial judge and the prosecuting attorney. There was testimony of an agreement to "deliver" a block of votes as partial payment for the paroles. The gangsters were still under indictment for a sec-

8. Report of Kefauver committee, *Third Interim Report of Senate Committee to Investigate Organized Crime* (82nd Congress), p. 51.

ond racket involving use of the mails to defraud members of a union of more than $1 million. This indictment was quashed with the knowledge and consent of Attorney General Clark despite a plea by the special prosecutor that the case be kept open. Income tax liens which were outstanding were reduced from $670,000 to $128,000 and the Treasury accepted the smaller sum in settlement. Paul Dillon, who was a personal friend of Truman and had been manager of Truman's senatorial campaign in 1934, made one appearance before the parole board for which he was paid $10,000. A few days later, the paroles were granted. For services rendered in the quashing of a mail fraud indictment, a fee of $15,000 was paid to Maury Hughes, a Texas lawyer who was an intimate and lifelong friend of Tom Clark.[9]

Senator James M. Kem, a Republican of Missouri, stated, "The password of the White House seems to be 'Pardon me, Mr. President.' "

The President exercised another type of executive clemency in behalf of William O'Dwyer, mayor of New York City.[10] Curious facts about O'Dwyer's career in the public service emerged from various investigations. While O'Dwyer was district attorney of Kings County (Brooklyn), he prosecuted various members of a group of killers known as Murder, Inc. There were six bosses of this combination, Joe Adonis, Bugsie Siegel, Meyer Lansky, Lucky Luciano, Longie Zwillman, and Willie Moretti. All of them were friends and associates of Frank Costello. Although various killers were convicted, including Louis Lepke, none of the Big Six was touched.

A key witness was Abe Reles, who was induced to turn state's evidence. He was kept under guard for twenty months by O'Dwyer. O'Dwyer refused to let him testify as a witness against Bugsie Siegel in California. Reles was the key witness

9. Speech by Senator Ferguson before Senate, August 18, 1949. See *Congressional Record*, 81st Congress, p. 11704.

10. Matters discussed are from report of Kefauver committee, *op. cit.*, pp. 124-40.

in what O'Dwyer called a "perfect case" against Adonis' man, Albert Anastasia, who was known as the executioner for Murder, Inc. O'Dwyer obtained no indictment against Anastasia. Reles in November 1941 was found dead, fully clothed on a balcony of a hotel five stories beneath his room, and with him the case against Anastasia fell out of the window. O'Dwyer said Reles had been trying to escape; Frank Bals, head of the six-man police guard, said that Reles had tried to climb out of the window to the floor below in order to tease the cops. O'Dwyer appeared as a witness in behalf of the six men at a departmental trial and also, as mayor, appointed Bals seventh deputy police commissioner.

John Harlan Amen had been appointed as special prosecutor in Kings County and had started a waterfront investigation into the affairs of six racketeering unions that Anastasia controlled. When Amen obtained court action for production of books and records of the unions, O'Dwyer started his own investigation. Amen suspended his investigation and turned all his records over to O'Dwyer's office since O'Dwyer was showing unusual activity. Two weeks later, the O'Dwyer investigation was suspended and never reopened. O'Dwyer said he was too busy with murder cases.

O'Dwyer had a crony of many years standing, James J. Moran, who was once a court attendant. When O'Dwyer became district attorney he made Moran chief clerk, which gave Moran power to open and close investigations. After Reles' death, the wanted cards on Anastasia who was then missing were removed from the files by Moran, and Anastasia returned to Brooklyn. When O'Dwyer was in the Army, Moran handled his personal financial affairs. Moran did not claim experience or training, but as he testified before the Senate Crime Committee, he had a "certain amount of gutter wisdom." This in O'Dwyer's eyes rated high enough for an appointment as deputy fire commissioner and then a life job as commissioner of the board of water supply. Moran was convicted in 1952 on charges of being the "guiding genius" of the $500,000-a-year fuel oil shakedown racket while he was in the fire department. Pressure was put on Moran to squeal in return for a reduction in his sentence, the squeal, of course, being the cut with O'Dwyer. John P. Crane, president of the International Association of Fire Fighters, testified that he turned $55,000 over to Moran, $35,000 as a gift and $20,000 as a campaign contribution for O'Dwyer's 1949 race for mayor. He said that $35,000 was in the hope that "he would come across and be kind to the men" in the fire department. He said "Moran allegedly was strong enough in his position in the O'Dwyer administration that if he said no, nobody could move O'Dwyer to say yes." Crane said he gave O'Dwyer $10,000 in an envelope on the porch of his Gracie Mansion and O'Dwyer took the envelope without looking into it.

By the summer of 1950, when Miles McDonald was starting an investigation of the bookmaking racket in Brooklyn, the finger was pointing at O'Dwyer. Tammany remembered that the scandals concerning Jimmy Walker had thrust La-Guardia into power while Tammany starved for years. Russell Sherwood's position vis-à-vis Jimmy Walker was analogous to the position that James J. Moran had with O'Dwyer. In the earlier scandal, it was Sherwood, the pay-off man, who fled to Mexico; this time it was the mayor himself, under happy auspices. Harry Truman lifted O'Dwyer out of the crucible and rescued Tammany by honoring him with the position of ambassador to Mexico. This was one month before Harry Gross, kingpin of the Brooklyn bookmaking racket, was arrested, who also had a tale of pay-offs to Moran and others close to O'Dwyer.

It is doubtful if our southern neighbors felt honored by the diplomatic representation of William O'Dwyer. No one had ever conceived of the diplomatic service as a sanctuary for corrupt politicians until Harry Truman entered the White House.

## · IV ·

## THE PRESIDENT'S PALS

*The choice of a prince's ministers is a matter of no little importance; they are either good or not according to the prudence of the prince. The first impression that one gets of a ruler and of his brains is from seeing the men that he has about him. When they are competent and faithful one can always consider him wise, as he has been able to recognise their ability and keep them faithful. But when they are the reverse, one can always form an unfavorable opinion of him, because the first mistake that he makes is in making this choice.*

—MACHIAVELLI,
The Prince

THE attitudes of any large organization are modeled after the attitudes of its leader. The low moral tone of the Truman administration flowed in part from the President's condonation of the low moral standards of his friends and associates or his continued acceptance of them as his friends.

### Edwin W. Pauley

Pauley was an oil millionaire who was a successful fund raiser. As treasurer of the Democratic National Committee between 1942 and 1944, he converted a deficit of several hundred thousands of dollars into a surplus. He was a pal of

Truman and might be said to have been "for Truman before Chicago." The President rewarded him by making him a fund raiser of a different type by appointing him reparations commissioner with the status of ambassador. Then he submitted his name to the Senate as Under Secretary of the Navy. There was trouble.

Secretary of the Interior Harold Ickes testified against Pauley. The Under Secretary represents the government in oil dealings and Honest Harold could see the ghosts of Albert Fall and Edwin Denby walk again. Ickes said that on the train coming back from the Roosevelt funeral at Hyde Park, Pauley told him that if the government did not prosecute the suit for the ownership of the oil-rich tidelands, Pauley could raise several hundred thousand dollars from oilmen for the Democratic party. Thus, from the moment of F.D.R.'s interment, Pauley was setting the note for the new order. Ickes recorded in his diary, "This is the rawest proposition that has ever been made to me. I don't intend to smear my record in oil at this stage of the game."

Norman Littell, a former assistant Attorney General, testified that Pauley had sought his influence saying, "These men have contributed to the campaign and they expect something for their money."

Truman at a press conference on February 15, 1946, declared that the Justice Department should not look into Pauley's testimony for a "political argument." Ickes retorted, "Every wardheeler in the land, if the Nation accepts such counsel, can now claim immunity for all his sins, whatever they may be, on the grounds that those who challenge his acts, their honesty or their worth, are just engaging in political argument." Openly at odds with Truman, Ickes resigned on February 13, 1946, saying, "I don't care to stay in an Administration where I am expected to commit perjury for the sake of the party."

The Pauley nomination was withdrawn.

## Brigadier General Wallace H. Graham

When Pauley denied the statements attributed to him by Ickes, the latter said, "I will have to say that was not an accurate statement." General Graham, the President's physician, admitted to the Senate Committee on Appropriations on January 13, 1948, that a press release he made was "not an accurate statement."[1] There is a short ugly word for persons who do not make accurate statements.

The President often denounced gambling on the commodity exchanges as a cause of high food prices after the war. "Grain prices should not be subject to the greed of speculators who gamble on what may lie ahead in our commodity markets." However, members of the President's entourage were deep in speculation. Pauley admitted he made close to a million. General Graham had 30,000 bushels of wheat bought on margin.

Commodity prices are influenced by crop reports of the Department of Agriculture which are highly secret until released, and there is other government information useful to a commodity trader. It is beyond belief that a person who was a member of the President's official family residing in the White House could consider himself morally justified in speculating in commodities.

In a press release General Graham announced that he had closed his account soon after the President denounced grain speculators in early October. He admitted later it was not true. He remained in wheat until November 29, when he had switched to cotton futures. He got out on December 18, the day the Senate passed a resolution authorizing the release of names of government officials trading in commodities. He was so ignorant, he said, that he didn't know that cotton was classed as a "commodity."

1. *New York Times*, Jan. 14, 1948.

Graham was not fired by the President, and there is no evidence that he lost face. Incidentally, a House committee found that more than 800 government employees had $213,-000,000 in investments in the commodities markets in 1946 and 1947.

## Donald S. Dawson

The power and prestige of Donald Dawson was the mainspring for the operation of an influence ring which dominated the affairs of the RFC. Dawson's association with the perjurer, Merl Young, should have been enough to have disqualified him from sitting in the White House. There is no evidence that it had any effect on Truman. We shall consider Dawson in the RFC scandals.

## Matthew J. Connelly

Matt Connelly had been a clerk and WPA investigator before he got a job in 1941 with the Truman committee which was set up to investigate war contracts. He hit it off with the senator and was appointments secretary for the President. When Harry Truman left the White House Connelly accompanied him to Kansas City and worked with him for awhile.

During the Truman administration, Connelly had been mentioned only peripherally with the scandals. He was reputed to have exercised a baleful effect on the President in quenching what little ardor Truman might have had for cleaning house. He accepted a deep-freeze from Albert Verley & Co., a story which primarily concerns General Vaughan. He accepted an expensive camera from the American Lithofold Co., which had made seduction of public officials a way of life.

In December 1951, one month after he was fired from his job as assistant Attorney General, Theron Lamar Caudle let it be known that Connelly had intervened with him in the tax evasion case of Irving Sachs of St. Louis and Shu-Stiles Inc. Although Caudle had recommended against prosecution because of the health of Sachs, a runaway grand jury in St. Louis had nonetheless indicted Sachs in March 1951. Sachs had pleaded guilty and was heavily fined. In September 1952 Caudle discussed the case at some length before the Chelf committee investigating the Department of Justice. In an executive session he had mentioned an oil royalty transferred to Connelly, but for some reason the matter did not emerge at public sessions.

On November 18, 1955, the attorney for Sachs, Harry I. Schwimmer, was indicted in St. Louis on a charge of perjury. He had testified that he had received $10,000 from Sachs as a legal fee; the government contended that it "was a fund for the purpose of bribing and corrupting public officials." There was allegedly documentary evidence in Schwimmer's records which he had overlooked in a midnight inspection after a flight from Puerto Rico shortly before the records were subpoenaed. On December 1, 1955, Connelly, Caudle and Schwimmer were indicted on a charge of conspiracy to fix the Sachs case. Ellis Slack, who had been sent as an emissary from the Justice Department, allegedly to hold the grand jury in check, was named as a co-conspirator. Connelly was charged with having contacted Internal Revenue Commissioner Schoeneman, Chief Counsel Charles Oliphant and Caudle about the case and to have received an oil royalty interest in January 1950, and $1,650 around January 14, 1952.

On November 25, 1955, the St. Louis *Globe-Democrat* reported that Connelly had asked to change his testimony before the grand jury after Tom L. Evans had changed his testimony. Evans, who was associated in business with Schwimmer, is a good friend of Harry Truman—having raised money for him in two campaigns—and is secretary of Harry S. Truman Library, Inc. At first Evans testified that he had lent $750 to Connelly to buy the royalty and that Connelly had repaid him. Later he testified that Schwimmer had repaid the loan. After Evans' attorney had visited Connelly and had told him of the change in Evans' testimony, Connelly asked for an opportunity to testify again before the grand jury. Connelly at this writing is scheduled to be tried in May, 1956.

## Major General Harry Vaughan

The influence stemming from General Vaughan was one of the most sinister in the Truman era. Vaughan was an old National Guard friend of the President. After rattling around in private industry, mostly as a tea salesman, he was picked up by Senator Truman and made his secretary. After the war, he became his military aide. The President was reputedly charmed by his ebullience, his raucous personality, and his barnyard humor. Vaughan was a throwback to Jess Smith of Harding's day. Since his capacity and judgment were obviously limited, the President was responsible for Vaughan, who acted in his job as he might have been expected to act.

Vaughan came first into public view in early 1949, when the President called a columnist an "s.o.b." for criticizing Vaughan for the acceptance of a decoration from dictator Peron of Argentina. That summer Vaughan got into more serious trouble when it was revealed that the five percenter, Col. James V. Hunt, had capitalized on his friendship with Vaughan and had used it to build up a lucrative business in influence peddling. When Vaughan returned from a vacation in Guatemala with his family, the reporters gave him a rough time, inquiring, for example, where he got the money for the trip. (His base pay was $8,800). He told them to lay off. "After all," he said, "I am the President's military aide, and you guys will want favors at the White House someday." Of his five percenter connections, he said, "That is nobody's goddamn business and you can quote me." The President pinned a medal on Vaughan for "Operation Union Station."

One phase of Vaughan's activities concerns Col. Hunt, which we shall discuss in chapter sixteen. Here we shall confine ourselves to his friendship and sponsorship of the Kansas City bootblack and, later, convicted perjurer, John Maragon. A report in 1950 by the Senate Investigations Subcommittee headed by Democratic Senator Hoey said, "There is no doubt that Maragon's friendship with General Harry H. Vaughan made his activities in his dealings with the Federal Government possible."[2]

The story opens in May 1945 before VE Day.[3] It was unheard of to see an American tourist or businessman in Europe at this time since all transport facilities were pre-empted for military use. But on May 1, 1945, General Vaughan wrote a letter on White House stationery: "To Whom It May Concern: This will serve to introduce Mr. David A. Bennett, owner of Albert Verley & Co. of Chicago, Illinois, who is contemplating travel in Europe. Mr. Bennett is a prominent businessman of Chicago and is entitled to the courtesies of American officials abroad."

Mr. Bennett, a perfume manufacturer, left on May 11 with a Mr. Otto Baptiste. The purpose of his trip was personal business. They used Air Transport Command facilities. They returned on June 6, at which time they declared through customs forty-one kilos of perfume essence, valued at $53,405. This trip came to the attention of the investigating committee

2. Report of Hoey investigations subcommittee, "The 5-Percenter Investigation" (81st Congress), p. 14.

3. Except as otherwise noted, the matters in this chapter concerning General Vaughan's activities are taken from testimony before the Hoey investigations subcommittee, "The 5-Percenter Investigation" (81st Congress), August 8 to September 1, 1949.

He was employed from November 1945 to March 1946 and returned, spending several days in Rome and Paris en route. Maragon had been a terrible nuisance on the mission. Said Henry F. Grady, head of the mission: "I learned that he was showing a picture of himself with the President and stating or at least implying that he was sent by the President to report to him directly on the activities of the mission." He got into difficulties with the Air Transport Command because he began investigating them saying that "he was doing this on authority from Washington." While Maragon was employed by the Greek mission on a salary plus $15 a day expenses, he was also on the payroll of Albert Verley & Co. at $1,000 a month. He charged to Verley the expense of his return trip, even though it was paid for by the government. His expense account totaled $9,500, including items such as $378.30 for a dinner party and "3 tickets for Jackson Day dinner, Mayflower Hotel, $300." Like many other items in his income, Maragon never reported this in his income tax.

In October 1946, Milton R. Polland met General Vaughan with John Maragon at a brewery party in Milwaukee. General Vaughan had introduced Polland, on a previous Washington trip, to the President, and when Polland saw Maragon in Vaughan's company, he immediately discerned a man of influence. Polland's nephew, Harold M. Ross, president of Allied Molasses Co., had exceeded his authorization for molasses under War Food Order No. 51 by 771,000 gallons by a shipment to Pepsi-Cola. He therefore had been cut off from further allocations of molasses. Polland gave Maragon two payments of $500 each in return for Maragon's promise to do something about getting molasses for Ross. Maragon's agreement with Ross was that he would get $2,000 if successful in getting Ross a molasses allocation.

Herbert C. Hathorn, an attorney in the Agriculture Department, in November 1946 found on his desk a note to call General Vaughan at the White House. Vaughan said he had been referred by the Secretary. He opened the conversation with "We Democrats have to stick together." Then he went on to confide an indiscretion—he was at a football game and "in the course of my conversation, I discussed the fact that everything was being decontrolled, especially sugar, rice and rents, and this Mr. Ross asked me if that meant molasses, and I told him 'Yes, there was nothing to say that molasses was not to be decontrolled,' and he said that on that basis, he, I think, has contracted for a very large quantity of molasses, and it could prove very embarrassing to me here at the White House, and you will have to do something about this."

Hathorn suggested that Vaughan take up the matter with the assistant Secretary. Then Vaughan became rough. He indicated that he had taken up the matter with the Secretary, who said it was perfectly all right. "He ended up with a statement that he was very close to the President and that a friend in the White House could mean an awful lot to a man in one of the governmental agencies and also that he could get my job or get a job." The amount of molasses that Ross had presumably bought on Vaughan's inside tip might run up to half a million dollars.

Vaughan then went to work on Joseph T. Elvove, assistant director of the sugar branch, with whom Polland and Ross had been talking before about the hardship they suffered. Vaughan made a call to Elvove on November 19, in which he reiterated the hardship to Allied Molasses. He did not refer to a huge quantity of molasses but only a tank car, which had been purchased and was now incurring demurrage charges and asked for its release. The next day, John Maragon appeared. The company was given permission to convert inedible blackstrap into edible products, but then it appeared that the molasses in the tank car was actually higher grade refiner's syrup. The authorization was withdrawn but the company thumbed its nose at the Department and used the molasses anyway. The company asked for further modifica-

there had been a change of ownership which had negated the former ban but that contention was doubtful. Then he switched and said that Congress had not banned race track construction after all. That stunned the senators who had been under the impression that they had voted for a law which did precisely that.

The affidavit of change of ownership certified that William G. Helis was the new owner of the track. Helis, according to testimony, was a partner of Frank Costello and "Dandy Phil" Kastel, the gambling czars. Helis gave money to Vaughan in 1946 to be used for the Kansas City campaign. Maragon collected campaign funds, including a check for $1,000 from George Skouras.

Drew Pearson testified that while he was talking to James McGranery, who was then assistant to the Attorney General in 1946, General Vaughan telephoned McGranery asking him to intervene in the case of the income tax fraud prosecution of W. T. Burton, a very good friend of Helis. McGranery made the statement that he was darned if he was going to stand for any political influence in this very important case. McGranery at the time of Pearson's testimony was a U. S. district judge and later became Attorney General, succeeding J. Howard McGrath. Pearson reported that there were rumors in November 1946 in Louisiana of large contributions that had been made to the Kansas City primary to prevent the conviction of Mr. Burton.

General Vaughan also collected a campaign contribution from William H. Neblett, who intervened with him in behalf of Robert Gould of Cincinnati, who had been convicted for six years for selling liquor on the black market. Mr. Gould got a pardon and General Vaughan got a campaign contribution.

In the years since 1946, Vaughan was repeatedly active in helping Maragon in his career in making a living off the government. On May 20, 1949, General Vaughan's office requested assistance from ordnance for the Austin Metal Products Inc.

The problem was to meet the Army specifications with regard to windshields. Major Prosser of the ordnance division was summoned to the office of the Secretary of Defense, where he met John Maragon, who advised him of General Vaughan's interest. In January 1949, officials of the Atlantic Marine Salvage Co. in Milwaukee, Wisconsin, went to the Maritime Commission with John Maragon, who gave the impression to government officials he was doing this for General Vaughan. The government attorney in the Maritime Commission received a telephone call from a person identifying himself as General Vaughan, inquiring as to the status of the contract.

In 1948, Maragon hooked up with a British adventurer named Dawson in a company called Trans-America Traders, Inc., the purpose of which was to deal in surplus property. Dawson, who is said to have made $100,000,000 dealing in surplus, had a criminal record, according to counsel for the Hoey committee. In January, 1948, on White House stationery, Vaughan wrote to General Hyssong, who was the Foreign Liquidation commissioner in Europe: "My Dear General Hyssong: This will introduce my good friend, John Maragon, who is representing George Dawson & Co. and who is interested in purchasing materials from the Foreign Liquidation Service."

The ubiquitous General Vaughan appears as the sponsor of one Franklin Lamb, who was hired without an FBI check as an assistant to Charles Wilson, head of the War Mobilization Board. In a letter of February 28, 1952, Wilson wrote to Senator Williams, "Lamb was recommended for the position by General Vaughan."[4] Lamb was vice chairman of Tele-King headed by Louis I. Pokrass, and in which his friends, Frank Costello and Meyer Lansky were stockholders. We shall meet Pokrass again.

The discrepancies in the statements of Maragon as to his financial dealings and the records would fill many pages. He

4. Speech of Senator John Williams before the Senate, July 20, 1954.

was convicted of perjury in 1949 and served a jail sentence. At the conclusion of the Senate hearings Vaughan was asked for his opinion of Maragon. He replied, "Maragon is a lovable sort of chap. You can't get mad at him."

The President found Vaughan also a lovable chap. During the hearings the President stated that he did not know if the statements attributed to Vaughan were true. Vaughan said that the freezers he received were experimental models and were rejects. Truman said that the committee was publishing only material unfavorable to Vaughan, not the favorable facts. This nettled the committee, so it published its executive sessions on the freezers. The subject under discussion was whether the freezers were rejects. This was indignantly denied by Gross and the manufacturers of the cabinets.

SENATOR MUNDT: These were not classified as factory rejects?

MR. GROSS: We had no such animal.

In October 1949, Vaughan announced, "The only two people I have to please are Harry Truman and Mrs. Vaughan. I am considered in many circles to be unethical and I am sure that I will continue to be. But I am going to continue to be the way I have been." Taken at its face value, this means that the President approved of Harry Vaughan's well-publicized activities.

In August 1951, ninety cadets at West Point had their careers blighted when they were dismissed for violations of the honor code in examinations. The military aide to the President in collecting campaign contributions was guilty of violating Army Regulations (Para. 17, AR 600-10) which state that members of the Army "will not be permitted to participate in any way in political management or political campaigns." All officers come under the Hatch Act and violation means instant dismissal from the service. But General Vaughan was a law unto himself.

# ·V·

# THE NATIONAL CHAIRMEN

## Robert E. Hannegan

In 1941 the Democratic machine in St. Louis was discredited and demoralized by an unsuccessful attempt to "steal" the governorship from Forrest Donnell who had been elected in November 1940. The Speaker of the state legislature had the duty to open the returns and publish them, but the Democratic legislature by resolution restrained the Speaker from doing so. The scheme was to have the legislature declare the Democratic candidate elected, but the plan went awry and a writ of mandamus was unanimously granted by the Supreme Court directing the Speaker to do his duty.

Robert E. Hannegan, of the Twenty-first Ward of St. Louis, who was a power in the St. Louis machine and a leader in the plot, was considered through in politics. In the 1940 primary elections, Hannegan's switch from Governor Stark had made the difference of the 7,000 votes which had renominated Truman. As a move to revive the prestige of the shattered machine, and the personal prestige of Robert Hannegan, Senator Truman in 1942 proposed him for the vacant post of collector of internal revenue for the western district of Missouri. The local newspapers conducted a campaign against the appointment. Senator Truman, according to the *New York Times*, painfully explained to President Roosevelt Hannegan's fitness for the job. He had carried St. Louis for Roosevelt and for Truman. "If Hannegan is not nominated, there will be no collector in St. Louis," he said. The St. Louis *Post-Dispatch* called the appointment "an affront to thousands."

In 1943, when the job of commissioner of internal revenue

fell vacant, the Senators from Missouri, Truman and Bennett Champ Clark, prevailed on the chairman of the Democratic National Committee, Frank Walker, to give the job to Hannegan. In the spring of 1944, Hannegan had risen to the post of national chairman. He now moved in behalf of his friend and benefactor, Harry Truman. He insisted to the weakening Roosevelt that Henry Wallace must get off the ticket. He organized sentiment among the city bosses for Senator Truman. In 1945, Senator Truman was President and Robert E. Hannegan was a member of the cabinet as Postmaster General. Such is the road to glory.

Robert E. Hannegan was a wardheeler by background, by temperament and by philosophy. He knew nothing of public service, he knew only the party. A hard party worker himself, he was convinced that the road to political power was to reward hard party workers down to the grassroots and precinct level with patronage and all that the party had to give. He modeled the Internal Revenue Bureau on this principle. The worst elements entered the bureau under his regime and that of his handpicked successor, Joe Nunan. Both Nunan and James P. Finnegan of St. Louis in the investigation of their official conduct gave almost identical testimony, that they were not tax experts but that Hannegan told them that it was immaterial because the jobs were political.

Hannegan resigned as party chairman in 1947 when he bought the majority interest in the St. Louis Cardinals with Fred Saigh, Jr., later convicted of tax fraud. He died in 1949. He was not known to have had any money when he came to Washington in 1943, but he left a fortune of well over $1,500,000.

## J. Howard McGrath

Truman's choice to succeed Hannegan as chairman was J. Howard McGrath, who guided the party to victory in the uphill campaign in 1948. In early 1949, he was moved to the post of Attorney General to succeed Tom Clark, who had gone up to the Supreme Court. The vacancy that Clark filled had been expected to go to a Catholic, so McGrath's appointment was interpreted as a step in grooming him for the Court. Instead of becoming a judge of the highest court of the land, however, he was ignominiously bounced in the tax scandals.

McGrath was only 46 when he became Attorney General but he had had a sensational career. He had been U. S. attorney for Rhode Island, governor, and United States senator, besides having been the U.S. Solicitor General. He had also accumulated a few millions by a judicious mixture of politics and business. Rhode Island had been known as a wide-open gambling state, its cities like Providence and Woonsocket reeking of graft and gangsterism, and McGrath was a close crony of the racing crowd. Published analyses of his career state that as U. S. attorney, he dropped an investigation under the Hatch Act of alleged contributions to politicians by the Narragansett Racing Association and was one of the group that built Lincoln Downs Race Track. As governor, he never cracked down on the gambling syndicate. He was hardly the man who could be expected to take action against gamblers or gangsterism as Attorney General. He lived up to expectations.

The Chelf committee in the Democratic 82nd Congress investigated the Department of Justice. It had this to say about Mr. McGrath: "He exhibited a deplorable lack of knowledge of the Department he was supposed to administer. He lacked information as to its organization and personnel and specific events of importance were unknown to him. . . . Mr. McGrath showed no enthusiasm for purging his department of wrongdoers or incompetence. . . . his testimony and his record as Attorney General indicate that he was content to let the status quo remain without knowing what the status quo was."

The caliber of his department is illustrated by the case of the deputy Attorney General, A. Devitt Vanech.[1] His biog-

1. Report of Chelf subcommittee to investigate the Department of Justice (82nd Congress), p. 16.

55

raphy in *Who's Who* stated that he received a B.S. degree from Peekskill Military Academy. This school could not grant degrees. The number two lawyer of the country, while he was in law school, took the Virginia bar examination and flunked. He took the bar examination of the District of Columbia three times and flunked each time. Four years had elapsed and Vanech still could not become a lawyer. So in 1940, he took the Tennessee bar examinations and barely got a passing grade.

Vanech took the bar examination under a provision of the Tennessee law that nonresidents might take the examination by declaring under oath their intention to reside and practice law in Tennessee. Vanech took this oath and never resided in Tennessee. The President of the Tennessee Bar Association stated, "If Vanech was never a resident of this State, he is not entitled to a license." When the committee made its revelations public, Vanech resigned, declaring that the purpose of his resignation was to run for the Senate in Connecticut. He has not been heard from since.

The administration of the Justice Department was lax and its record was poor. Let us consider its record concerning prosecution of government claims on accounts between private contractors and the contracting agencies of the government. Of the $21 million in claims that were certified by the Comptroller General to the Department of Justice up to June 6, 1952, only $300,000 was recovered by the Justice Department. This is a startlingly low figure, approximately 1.5 percent, when compared with over 11 percent—$493,000 out of $4.3 million —which the General Accounting Office collected from known overpayments. The GAO, unlike the Justice Department, could use no legal pressure whatever and simply afforded the contractors the opportunity to make voluntary refunds. We can understand why the figure was so low when we consider the facts in a case that was investigated.

The General Accounting Office claimed that payments to

the Michigan School of Trades, Inc., under the G.I. Bill of Rights, were induced by fraud to the extent of $1,313,035.[2] As an example of the fraud, at least twenty-five students out of forty interviewed were never in school at the times when the school records showed they had been attending. George S. Petzer was the U. S. attorney in Detroit. There was testimony that Petzer's travel reservations and hotel reservations in Washington to confer on the case had been made by Peters, the owner of the school, and that his hotel bill on an earlier trip had been paid for by Peters and Mr. Poole, the school's attorney. George S. Fitzgerald, national Democratic committeeman from Michigan, who endorsed Petzer for his job, was hired to represent Peters and was paid a fee of $5,000. Peters was not sure if Fitzgerald had attended any conferences. Petzer admitted that in looking for his job as U. S. attorney, he had conferred with Fitzgerald. Peters also retained the firm of Clifford and Miller as Washington counsel. Clark Clifford was about to resign as legal counsel to the President and Peters called on him at the White House. After hearing a resumé of the case, Clifford said that it would be "expensive," and his firm collected a fee of $25,000. Clifford, according to Petzer, had never appeared at any of the conferences leading to settlement; his partner, Miller, had sat in on a settlement conference.

A few months later in July 1951, the Justice Department recommended that the entire claim of over $1,313,000 be settled for $125,000 as recommended by the U. S. attorney in Detroit. The GAO protested, saying that acceptance of the reported offer is "substantially less than the amount withheld by the Veterans Administration." The Veterans Administration was withholding $190,000 which was $65,000 more than the proposed settlement. But the Justice Department insisted and so $65,000 was refunded to the school. The total legal fees

2. Report of Chelf subcommittee, *op cit.*, pp. 27-30.

paid by Peters were exactly equal to the amount that he got back from the Veterans Administration.

Holmes Baldridge, assistant Attorney General in charge of the claims division, admitted that Clark Clifford had recommended him to head the antitrust division but said that he had no knowledge of how active Clifford had been in making him head of the claims division.

The Department of Justice started an antitrust investigation of the four largest liquor distillers in 1948 but dropped it in 1949. The Chelf committee reported, "While the evidence is not conclusive, the subcommittee is inclined to believe that there may have been a connection between the political contributions of the liquor companies and the tapering off of the antitrust investigation of 1949."

Ernest L. Branham, an attorney in the Department of Justice, told the Chelf committee[3] a story of being "mentally horsewhipped" by his superiors in the antitrust division for wishing to press the investigation of the distillers. In late November 1948, it was brought to his attention that the Big Four had made huge contributions to the 1948 campaign. "A high official in the Department of Justice had told the president of one of the companies that he had nothing to fear regarding the litigation against the liquor industry." Branham wrote a memorandum to Herbert Bergson, the head of the antitrust division. Bergson called him in and suggested that he destroy the memorandum. In April 1949 Bergson called him into his office and discussed the alleged threats which had been made by Branham against the liquor people. According to Branham, he said, "I understand you are going to fill up the District jail. . . . I do not want you threatening them." Branham testified, "About the last thing he said was that I had to go easy on the liquor people."

In 1946, before McGrath's time, James A. Mullaly, an attor-

3. Hearings before the Chelf subcommittee to investigate the Department of Justice (82nd Congress), p. 370.

ney in the criminal division, recommended to a friend representing Carnation Milk that they hire the law firm of Hayes, Eakle and Goldstein to represent Carnation in a pending criminal prosecution in Buffalo. The members of the firm had been in the criminal division and directions were given from Washington over Theron Lamar Caudle's signature that the U. S. attorney in Buffalo should not prosecute. The fee was $3,000; $750 was paid to Mullaly and the partners divided the rest.[4] In McGrath's time, a U. S. attorney in Illinois, Howard Doyle, in his private capacity represented a distilling company which was trying to get its half million dollar tax liability reduced, while in his public capacity he was opposing it. In the midst of the case, the judge asked Doyle, "whom do you represent?" Another U. S. attorney, Tobias Diamond of Iowa, in his private capacity was trying to collect $12,000 for his clients and threatening to use his official powers. He carried out his threat by having them indicted on a criminal charge and arrested them in Miami to answer the charges in Sioux City.[5]

The most striking "conflicts" case was that of Herbert Bergson, who was assistant Attorney General in charge of the antitrust division from 1948 to 1950. In 1949, the division had filed an antitrust suit against Minnesota Mining and Manufacturing and Carborundum; two months after his resignation he was retained by these companies to get them clearance for a merger and did so. He had refused to give a clearance to U. S. Pipe Line Co., and after his resignation, he was retained to obtain the same type of letter, which he succeeded in doing. His fees were $115,000. He was indicted under the "conflict of interest" statutes that prohibit an ex-government official from prosecuting claims within two years after his government employment if he was formerly involved. The

4. Report of Chelf subcommittee, *op. cit.*, p. 78, for Carnation case.
5. Both Doyle and Diamond discussed in report of Chelf subcommittee, *op. cit.*, p. 121.

trial judge acquitted Bergson on the technicality that "claims" refer to money or property.

Letters written by Turner Smith, who was head of the criminal section of the tax division in 1949, were recovered in December 1951 from a beach on the mouth of the Patuxent River on Chesapeake Bay.[6] Smith, who had a boat there, had thrown them into the river. The letters reflected the tone of the Department. In one to a lawyer friend, Smith said, "What to my surprise yesterday I saw a new case come in involving a Pittsburg individual. His name is Melvin Opie, 415 West Washington Street, Pittsburg, Kansas. I do not recall from the file whether he already had an attorney. In any event, for old time Army's sake, I am passing this information on to you. You will, of course, treat it in the strictest of confidence. . . ." In a letter to another friend, he wrote, "I am now in my old place in Justice in charge of all criminal tax prosecutions—in the event any of your clients have the misfortune of getting involved."

On March 1, 1951, Judge George H. Moore summoned a grand jury in St. Louis and charged it to look into violations of the internal revenue laws.[7] The U. S. attorneys and their assistants were summoned by Moore, but little co-operation was given. According to the report of the Chelf committee, the deputy foreman said of the early presentation: "They went over it very quickly. They were all busy; they told us how busy they were and they told us this and that and that is all we heard."[8] There was no stenographer to make available for "such foolishness." U. S. Attorney Watson told Moore that he had called Caudle, then in charge of the tax division, and Meyer Rothwacks, head of the criminal section

6. Report of Keating subcommittee to investigate the Department of Justice (83rd Congress), p. 79.

7. Report of Chelf subcommittee, *op. cit.*, pp. 54-69, for account of grand jury.

8. Report of Chelf subcommittee, *op. cit.*, p. 58.

of the tax division, but had received no authority for the grand jury investigation.[9]

Moore himself had telephoned McGrath on February 15 and complained that channels were clogged and blocked and pleaded for co-operation. McGrath, according to Moore, replied simply that such matters should "go through channels." "But what do you do when the channels are damned up and blocked up?" Moore asked. When Moore recounted this interview on October 15, McGrath told the newsmen that the Judge's statements "if he actually said them" are "damnable and contemptible lies." He said he didn't know the Judge and "to the best of my recollection, he never talked with me over the telephone." He said that Moore's exposures were "a campaign to discredit the Department of Justice." Two days later, McGrath said that he had seen a record of the conversation and apologized to Judge Moore.

Apparently U. S. Attorney Watson was being coached from Washington and got a reluctant green light from Washington on the investigation. Then Theron Lamar Caudle dispatched an emissary to the scene, Ellis Slack. Slack appeared before a grand jury around March 12 and reviewed the cases they had been discussing. He said that some of the cases had been presented and others were not ready. Slack then returned to Washington.

Watson told Judge Moore that Slack had suggested the grand jury make a partial report. A draft was prepared and read to the jurors who were not entirely satisfied with it but were guided by the suggestions and recommendation of the government attorneys. It was read to Slack in Washington over the phone. Watson said, "Mr. Slack thinks this report splendid. It is exactly what he wants." The report was a complete whitewash. Watson said that Slack told him on the phone, "I congratulate you on the preparation of it." Many of the jury were uneasy about the tenor of the report but felt

9. Report of Chelf subcommittee, *op. cit.*, p. 58.

they had no choice on the basis of the facts of which they were cognizant. One juror said that Watson had told them that a "partial report would take the heat off"; the only "heat" was being applied by the newspapers.

When Judge Moore read the report, he hit the ceiling. He told them that only one paragraph met with his approval and that that was the concluding paragraph which said the investigation would continue. On April 30, Judge Moore again summoned the grand jury. He told them the partial report was "quite astonishing" and based on no evidence. After this recharge, the grand jurors requested lists of cases, the case dockets and the complaint files. A large number of tax evasion indictments were returned.

The Chelf committee was severely critical of Ellis Slack. It felt that he had imposed his ideas on the grand jury contrary to his responsibility not to influence in any way its deliberations. When he declared its report was "splendid" he certainly was not referring to its literary style. The committee found the clue to his conduct in his statement, "I am a soldier." After Caudle was fired McGrath appointed Slack to fill in as head of the tax division.

The St. Louis grand jury episode was most critical for the reputation of the Truman administration. It was the general area from which Senator Truman had gotten his political start. It was the home of former Democratic Chairman Hannegan, who had made Truman President, and of Secretary Snyder.

Analyzing the testimony,[10] it is evident that the administration put forth effort to stifle the investigation. Assistant Attorney General Caudle, as well as his assistants Rothwacks and Smith, tried without avail to get a list of the cases that Judge Moore was interested in. Although Watson want-

10. See testimony before the Chelf subcommittee to investigate the Department of Justice (82nd Congress), pp. 753-894.

ed help from Washington, on February 23 Smith declared to him, "As the matter now stands, we see no necessity for it." If Washington was interested in hushing up the investigation sending a man out would have the opposite effect of putting the spotlight on it.

After Watson got the green light, his first action, on March 1, was to indict Irving Sachs in whose behalf Matthew Connelly had intervened. The case was a particularly questionable one. Watson's action might have come as a shock to his home office. Despite the fact that it had previously seen "no necessity for it," the department now sent out Ellis Slack.

Watson's attitude provoked considerable uneasiness. He had previously expressed his puzzlement as to whether he was responsible to Washington or to Judge Moore. Moore was not only interested in getting indictments but he wished to know why there had been no indictments and whether there had been fixes. Would Watson now play along with Judge Moore?

Watson's appointment expired in only two months, and he wanted a reappointment. A transcribed conversation between Peyton Ford and Watson on March 2,[11] the day after the Sachs indictment, showed the deputy Attorney General using tough language in regard to a Treasury agent, Sharp, who was talking before the grand jury. Watson might very well have concluded that the language could apply to him too. "If he makes any unfounded charges against any public official, I want him to prove them. . . the more rope you give those guys that think they know so god-damned much—we had a similar thing in Los Angeles with nothing. But if there is anything wrong, I want that brought out."

Watson did not string along with Judge Moore in looking deeply into the roots of the St. Louis tax cases.

11. Testimony before the Chelf subcommittee to investigate the Department of Justice (82nd Congress), p. 764.

## *William M. Boyle, Jr.*

The successor to McGrath as national chairman was an old friend of Truman from Kansas City, Bill Boyle. When he was installed in August 1949, Truman said, "I am as happy as I can be that my lifetime friend is the National Chairman of the Democratic party." And Truman meant it. Probably no incident in the scandals gave him greater pain than the circumstances which compelled the resignation of Boyle two years later.

Bill Boyle was born with the blood of Pendergast politics in his veins. His mother, Clara Boyle, a friend of Truman, had been an ardent Pendergast precinct worker. Bill was active in politics from his teens and attended Jackson County Democratic picnics with Truman, who was almost twenty years his senior, and was starting his political career as Jackson County Judge. Bill moved up the Pendergast ranks to police commissioner, commissioner of street cleaning, and prosecuting attorney. Truman made him his secretary when Harry Vaughan went off to war. He joined the National Committee in 1944 to help promote Truman for Vice President. Then he opened up law practice.

Boyle's law practice, while Truman was President, as one might expect, was very thriving. In June 1952, Senator Williams told the Senate that a $38,000,000 income tax claim against William Rhodes Davis of New York was settled for $850,000, or three cents on the dollar, after Boyle was hired as the attorney. The bargain-rate settlement was recommended by Joseph D. Nunan, the internal revenue commissioner, and chief counsel Charles Oliphant.

Boyle had worked on a voluntary basis for the National Committee on and off. He worked there steadily in the campaign of 1948 with Merl Young by his side. In 1949 he attached himself more firmly to the Democratic Committee as McGrath started to move out in the beginning of the year. On February 8, 1949 (the chronology is important in the Lithofold matter) he was appointed vice chairman of the Democratic National Committee; on April 20, he was granted a salary of $30,000 a year and presumably withdrew from law practice; and on August 24, he was elected chairman.

Charles Binaggio, the gangster, a main cog in the Kansas City Democratic machine, was on the arrangements committee for a dinner to the new chairman in Kansas City on September 29, 1949. He and his wife, the niece of racketeer Tano Lacoco, sat close to the President. On April 6, 1950, Binaggio and Charles Gargotta were found murdered in the Democratic clubhouse, 716 Truman Road. They were lying under a picture of the President.

In the *Readers Digest* for June 1952 Stanley High in "The Missouri Gang" told of other distinguished guests at the banquet. Here is the list along with the credentials that High gives them. Jim Finnegan, the revenue collector who landed in jail. J. A. Purdome, the Jackson County Sheriff criticized in the Kefauver crime report. Morris "Snag" Klein, a professional gambler recently under sentence for vote fraud. Anthony Gizzo, described by the Kefauver committee as a racketeer who dominated Kansas City gambling. Five persons connected with the Camp Crowder storage scandals (discussed in Chapter XVII). Sidney Smith, Jr., head of the warehouse charges unit of the CCC in Kansas City, later suspended in connection with his official duties. James A. Waechter, who, according to Senator Kem in a Senate speech, was once fired "for the betterment of the public service" from his job as St. Louis Board of Election Commissioner. Earl W. Beck, an old friend of Truman, who resigned under fire as head of a Jackson County home for children, and after nomination by Truman was unanimously rejected by a Senate committee for a $9360 job in the District of Columbia Government as "utterly unfit." There was also Morris Shenker.

Chairman Boyle proposed as a member of the finance committee Morris A. Shenker. Shenker was linked to the administration not only through Boyle, but he is also the son-in-law of Sam Kopler, a business associate of John Snyder. Shenker declined the appointment after sundry facts came to light. Before the Kefauver committee he had represented James J. Carroll, St. Louis betting commissioner, John Mooney, a bookie, and William P. Brown, part owner of a wire service. John H. Hendren, former Missouri Democratic chairman, gave this sworn testimony—that he and Shenker had together met William Molasky, who had a monopoly in the wire service to bookies in St. Louis. Molasky had given $2,000 to the Democratic party and in return asked that the Democratic candidate for governor, if elected, would put his choice on the police board. His first choice Hendren believed to be Shenker.[12]

Boyle's departure as national chairman came in connection with the American Lithofold loan from the RFC. We shall discuss that in Chapter Eight. The President exonerated Boyle, saying that it was proper for an official of the National Committee to introduce someone to a government agency, but not to accept a fee. Boyle claimed that he called Chairman Hise in his capacity as an official of the committee. But he was on a retainer on which he had collected $1250 from Lithofold and the St. Louis *Post-Dispatch* alleged that the payment had been $8000. The case had more serious overtones than the fee from Lithofold.[13]

Truman had said that an official of the Democratic Committee must not accept a fee or profit out of his position. From

12. Testimony of John Hendren before Kefauver committee, Senate Committee to Investigate Organized Crime (82nd Congress), part IV, pp. 153, 154.

13. See testimony before the Hoey subcommittee, "American Lithofold Corporation," (82nd Congress) p. 7. Also see testimony of William M. Boyle, Jr. (p. 890) and of Max Siskind (p. 777) before the Hoey investigations subcommittee, "American Lithofold Corporation" (82nd Congress).

February, when he joined on an unpaid basis, until April 20, when he went on salary, Boyle had obtained cases the appraised value of which was $158,500. From the time Boyle moved in, he was accepted as chairman, sitting in McGrath's office. Can one doubt that his position was the prime reason for his getting these lush cases?

Another matter was also brought out before the Hocy subcommittee. When Boyle decided to withdraw from his practice, according to him on April 20, he turned over to his associate Max Siskind, twenty-five pending cases in which they agreed that the potential fees amounted to $410,000. According to Boyle, Siskind orally agreed to pay $150,000, including $56,000 in accounts receivable. By October 1951, Siskind had paid Boyle $99,268, leaving a balance of over $50,000.

The transaction is most suspicious. There was no formal written agreement as one might expect of two lawyers to protect the heirs of Boyle and Siskind. The payments to Boyle were to have no relation to the fees Siskind would eventually collect. To the accountant for the investigation subcommittee, Siskind waved a yellow sheet of paper with figures written on it but unsigned. The sums paid to Boyle were treated by Siskind and listed as forwarding fees on his tax return. The case was stated succinctly by Senator Nixon: "Rather than being a sale [of a law practice] this appears to me very frankly in the light of what you have testified to as to the way it was treated for income-tax purposes, as to the legal memoranda, as to the memoranda that was prepared at the time—it appears to me to be simply a subterfuge by which Boyle continued to share in the law business."

The members of the Hoey subcommittee were unaware that the suspicion they were probing had been confirmed. Before the Fulbright subcommittee earlier in the year a memo had been submitted by Chad F. Calhoun of Kaiser-Frazer which stated that Rex Jacobs had called on Edgar Kaiser the previous day. "Jacobs indicated (I am told) that employment of Mr. Boyle or Mr. Boyle's legal firm could help to straighten things out at RFC for K-F." The date of the memo was December 13, 1949.[14] If Boyle had withdrawn from law practice, why was his friend trying to get a case for "Boyle or Mr. Boyle's legal firm"?

### Frank E. McKinney

Truman picked Frank E. McKinney, a political power in Indiana, as Boyle's successor and his last chairman. Frank McHale, who had recommended him, said that he was "like Caesar's wife—beyond reproach." McKinney, like McGrath, had many financial interests. He said that he would sell the stock in a pipeline company, of which he was vice president, which was trying to get 100,000 tons of scarce steel, but would retain his liquor holdings and his radio stations that would be trying to get television licenses when the freeze was lifted.

Two months after his selection some curious facts came to light in a bankruptcy hearing involving the Empire Tractor Co.[15] In October 1946 McKinney had bought stock for $1,000 in Empire which Empire bought back in August 1947 for $68,000, netting McKinney $67,000. McHale had received $17,000 for a $250 purchase. McHale was suing Empire for $93,500 for legal fees or 10 percent of the $935,000 won in a government contract settlement case. The head of Empire, Frank Cohen, according to the *New York Times*' account, had a notorious reputation for buying influence. In 1941, Charles West, a former Under Secretary of the Interior, who had a claim against Cohen for $70,000, or 1 percent of the contracts obtained by the Empire Ordnance Corporation, denied that he had sold influence but said that Cohen had offered to con-

14. Hearings before the Fulbright subcommittee on the RFC (82nd Congress), p. 686.
15. For facts stated, see *New York Times*, December 11, 1951.

tribute $50,000 to the Democratic National Committee if it would help him. Cohen had sought to hire Tommy Corcoran of Brain Trust fame, and Corcoran, while claiming that he got the retainer for another lawyer, did give Cohen legal advice. Senator Truman as head of the War Investigating Committee said to Cohen, "You were after anyone with influence." Years later Truman's national chairman turns up in this extraordinary deal with Cohen.

# · VI ·

# THE RFC SCANDALS—I:
# ITS STRANGE LOANS

*Get rid of it [the RFC]. It has been an abortion and
miscarriage of the RFC Act all along the line. These
are pretty sordid pictures. If the average taxpayer
sees it as some of us do up here, he is going to cry out
"Unclean, unclean," turn thumbs down and give
them the* coup de grâce.

> —SENATOR CHARLES W. TOBEY,
> during hearings of the Ful-
> bright Subcommittee investi-
> gating the RFC.

THE Reconstruction Finance Corporation was born on January 22, 1932, during the period of the deepening depression.
As the title of the agency announced to the world, it was
born to "reconstruct." It did that job. It restored the shattered
banking system, making loans to 7,343 banks. It lent money
to millions of farmers and raised the prices of commodities. It
pulled out railroads, surety and casualty companies and saved
even some insurance companies. It gave aid to hard-pressed
cities and states. In 1934, it started lending money directly
to businesses.

The RFC was a main pivot of the New Deal, so closely associated with it that it was generally forgotten that the RFC had
been established by Herbert Hoover. The chief of the RFC
was a hard, cautious banker from Houston, Texas, by the name
of Jesse Jones. He ran the RFC on sound banking principles
and enjoyed such great respect that he was subjected to a minimum of interference.

It was quite legitimate for the RFC to continue to reconstruct through the decade of the thirties, since the economy continued to languish. Roosevelt ordered business loans to be discontinued, but with the recession of 1937 loans were resumed in greater volume.

Then came the war and the riptide of boom. The RFC financed the nation's industrial mobilization. It spawned new subsidiary agencies—the Defense Supplies Corporation, the Defense Plants Corporation, the Rubber Reserve Company and the Metals Reserve Company. It bought the materials for war, it stockpiled them, it built the plants, it built our synthetic rubber industry.

The prestige and power of the RFC were now at their peak. It was a mastodon of an agency with 15,000 employees. It had been combined with the Commerce Department, and since the RFC was the more important member, Jones was now the Secretary of Commerce.

At the beginning of Roosevelt's fourth term, Jones was ousted. On January 20, 1945, the President wrote to Jones that Henry Wallace wanted the job in return for his services in the 1944 campaign, and he felt obliged to give it to him. The President was genuinely regretful, but he was enfeebled and did not have the will to resist Wallace's demand. Jones says that the President had never forgiven him for refusing, in 1942, to buy the Empire State building (then known as the Empty State building) for federal offices. The President told Jones that he wanted to help out Al Smith who was connected with the losing proposition and who had a large family to support. Despite a good deal of pressure, Jones remained adamant, insisting that it was a bad buy for the federal government.

Wallace had wanted to be Secretary of Commerce on account of the loan agency, but he was to be denied the prize. Congress confirmed him but, in anger at Jones' dismissal and suspicious of Wallace, divorced RFC from the Commerce

Department and later put it under a board of five members. From that point on, the fortunes of the RFC began a steady decline.

The years had rolled by and the RFC was now in a new era. It was postwar inflation. Price and materials controls had to be retained for a long time after V-J Day; materials had to be conserved for housing; the President campaigned in 1948 on a platform which demanded stand-by price controls to fight inflation. It would be expected that in this climate RFC loans would diminish. Instead they soared. In 1940, the RFC had made 1,125 business loans totaling $68,803,000. In 1947, it made 10,551 loans for a total of $393,000,000. In 1948, the 80th Congress, in renewing the charter of the agency, gave it a set of directions, the Buck Report, of which Senator Fulbright heartily approved. It instructed the RFC that "it should not engage in lending of a purely private character where the benefit of the general public is remote, whether the loans be large or small." It also instructed the RFC to put emphasis on small business loans. The plain intent of the instructions was to restrict loans, not to expand them. Instead, the RFC quickened its loan activity. For the year ending June 30, 1950, the loan figure was well over $500,000,000.

The agency which had been born to "reconstruct" was now making loans to concerns vital to our economy, such as a gambling casino, a rainbow trout fishery, night clubs, snake farms, swank resort hotels in Miami Beach, movie houses, and a grower of cactus plants for sale in dime stores.

At this point an explanation is necessary. The disaster which overtook the agency was not of its own making. Its personnel on the whole were the best trained and the most competent in Washington. It was wrecked by the administration, which wanted to continue it on a loan binge. The administration was obsessed with the fear of a depression and considered inflation the best means of prolonging the boom even though it gave lip-service to the need to stop inflation. This depression complex gave it a spending complex. In the second place, it did not intend to give up its power to make loans, which was a valuable political asset.

The RFC had to take orders. On the one hand there was the sound business judgment of the personnel trained for years under Jesse Jones, and on the other hand there was the administration, which didn't give a hang about business judgment when it wanted to accomplish its objectives. The result was a schizophrenia in which the RFC lost its balance.

Such a situation was made to order for abuse, waste of the public money, intrigue, favoritism and influence. Despite Truman, the scandals could not be suppressed. After the American Lithofold affair, it was evident that the agency was in a state of liquidation. On July 31, 1953, the new Republican Congress gave it the coup de grâce. Thus, after twenty-one years of life, the agency that was born to "reconstruct" was consigned to its grave, unhonored and unsung.

## Loan Policy

The loan policy of the RFC had to be fashioned to conform to the administration's orders that it lend more, lend faster, and lend to the right ones. So its loan policy was not a policy but a blank check.

An RFC loan, it must be emphasized, was a valuable privilege for many businesses. The loan was a long-term one, up to ten years at a low rate of interest (four percent, until the end of 1950, when it was raised to five percent). The RFC would lend on fixed assets. Commercial banks go in for short-term credit, up to a year—where they lend for a long-term on fixed assets, they restrict the amount to a fraction of capital and surplus.

Not until the time when Stuart Symington was administrator in mid-1951 did the RFC establish a loan policy which declared certain classes of business ineligible. Until that time, the sole test was the "public interest." And what was that? Before Fulbright, the RFC defended loans as in the "public interest" if the loan prevented people from losing their jobs or creditors from losing their money. On that test, a loan to a house of prostitution would be in the "public interest" and, in fact, some of the loans were little more in the public interest than that.

The RFC would defend some bad loans, for example the one to a snake farm, because it was a loan to a small business. This misread Congress' instructions which were that *all* loans should be in the "public interest" but that more loans should be made to small business. The RFC set up a small-loan division, which really had little connection with Congress' intent. It used the same personnel in RFC but simply processed loans under $100,000. A small business may need more or less than $100,000. The sum is not the test as far as a small business is concerned. The division was just a dodge to impress Congress. There was another line of defense the RFC could fall back on to justify a loan—it could point out that someone was a veteran or that the business was in a distress area.

Many of the loans the RFC made were for what are called "bail-outs." The RFC objected to the use of the term, but that is what they were. In a sample that the Fulbright committee made, of 103 loans, 49 percent of the money went to "bail-out" existing creditors. That is, the money didn't go to the borrowing businessman at all, who already had credit; the funds went to banks, insurance companies or private creditors who wanted to get their money out. The obligation switched from them over to the RFC.

Now, it is true that it was important in many cases for this to take place because the RFC was a long-term creditor and part of its operation did consist of financing short-term into long-term credit. In many cases, it was necessary to replace a tough Scrooge of a creditor with a more complacent one. How-

74

ever, it also opened the way to let Uncle Sam hold the bag. Where a bank or insurance company was threatening fore-closure, it was evident that the loan was shaky. Under such circumstances, the government was being saddled with a bad risk. That was certainly the case in the Texmass loan. It is true that the RFC was originally set up to bail out banks, but after the war, Congress certainly did not intend that the business loans made by the RFC should go to banks. In a letter to Senator Fulbright on April 10, 1950, Jesse Jones wrote: "I did note in one of the corporation's reports, probably at the end of the year, an item carried as 'loans for consolidation of debt.' That sounds very much like loans to pay creditors of the bor-rower, which should not be a function of the corporation and I am sure was never intended by the Congress."

The RFC construed its authority that it had the power to make what are called equity loans. How in the world it ever came to the conclusion that it had this power, it is hard to determine. There are two types of capital, the lender's risk and the owner's risk. The lender's risk is called borrowed cap-ital, the owner's risk is called equity capital and in a new company, equity capital may be called venture capital. The RFC had a policy of making venture capital loans to new busi-ness, if, as a rule of thumb, the owner put up half the money.

The RFC was speculating with public money and on the most absurd terms. To put it bluntly, the RFC was the big-gest sucker of all times. Let us suppose two persons go into a new business, and each puts up $100. If there should be a profit of $1,000, it would be split, each one getting $500. But when RFC went into an equity capital deal, it would collect only $100 with interest, and the other party would collect the $900. This, of course, played right into the hands of entrepre-neurs, who always want as much fixed capital as possible in order not to dilute their equity. This is what is called "lever-age." The entrepreneur doesn't have to spread the profits but could keep the gravy for himself. The RFC loan gave him that chance. As far as the public was concerned, it was a "heads you win, tails I lose" proposition. It is interesting that the RFC made more loans in Texas than anywhere else, even though Texas had the biggest crop of new millionaires. As Senator Fulbright put it: "When rich people find out that they can do this and therefore they do not have to take anybody in on a good thing, I can see an unlimited demand for capital of this kind."

There were other aspects of RFC practice which made for loose lending:

RFC accepted appraisals of collateral made by persons employed by the borrower. In 1947 the appraisal of collateral in the Novelty Plant and Pottery loan was $97,000—in a bankruptcy sale in 1949, it was sold for $2,000.

RFC made loans even though the company had been badly milked by its owners. In September 1949, RFC approved a loan of $175,000 to Wheeler Reflector Company even though the president in the previous three and a half years had drawn out $250,000 from the business.[1]

There was no docket of loan applications, they were taken up in any order, loan examiners were assigned at will, there was no registration of attorneys, there was no publicity given to approvals. RFC functioned as if it were behind a silken curtain. Behind the curtain, the warning of Jesse Jones was amply borne out. "Where the sugar is, you will always find the flies."

### Some RFC Loans

Let us see how the RFC loan policy worked out in application of various loans.

*The Mapes Loan.* The Mapes hotel was competing with the Riverside hotel in Reno and decided to build two extra

1. Hearings before the Fulbright subcommittee on the RFC (82nd Congress) p. 312.

stories, one of which would be a gambling casino equipped with the most up-to-date gambling paraphernalia, including roulette, blackjack, fan-tan, bingo, vingt-et-un and other attractions. The creditors of the hotel, including an insurance company and a bank, at that point decided to step out. The RFC stepped in with a loan of $975,000. Most of it was a bail-out. The loan was approved, even though the RFC review committee pointed out that the loan would be paid for out of gambling. Thirty percent of the net profit of the hotel came from the gambling casino, which guaranteed the hotel a minimum of $5,000 a month. Pictures of the swank casino were splashed all over *Life* magazine. It would be operated by the notorious gambler Lou Wertheimer, and it was believed that he was associated with Mickey Cohen of Los Angeles and Bernard (Mooney) Einstoss.

Senator Fulbright could not understand the public interest involved in this loan.

MR. FULBRIGHT: Mr. Hise [RFC chairman], I would like to know what it was that led you to believe that there was sufficient public interest in this loan.

MR. HISE: I might point out that you overlooked one very important public interest in Nevada when you overlooked divorces and marriages and concentrated on gambling.

SENATOR FULBRIGHT: Then you were trying to help promote divorces?

MR. HISE: I would say if those people go there to get divorces, they should have the facilities of a fine hotel.

Senator Fulbright was very obtuse. He could not see a scintilla of public interest involved in helping people get divorces. He pointed out that since the RFC was in the gambling business, if the Riverside improved its casino, the RFC would have to lend more money to Mapes to keep up.

*The Ribbonwriter Loan.* Ribbonwriter Corporation of America had a new gadget, the most revolutionary since the invention of the typewriter. It was an attachment to a typewriter which would turn out five copies without using carbon paper. The Jacksonville office originally recommended that some part of the $400,000 requested be granted but later recommended decline after receipt of a technical report which stated that the gadget was impracticable. The loan request went to Washington. The Washington examiner was an honest man. He had known one of the directors for forty years, and the director had assured him that the gadget was sound. The examiner cannot be censured. This was a venture capital loan, and in making venture capital investments, people's tastes differ. Some people like ravioli and others don't. The examiner liked the gadget. The RFC approved a loan of $400,-000. Two months after the loan had been disbursed to the tune of over $300,000 the company went bankrupt, and there was only $100 cash in the till. No one was sure where the money had gone.

The interesting aspect of this loan is that one of the largest stockholders in Ribbonwriter was Sheriff Clark of Broward County, close to Miami.[2] Miami for years after the war was a wide open gambling spot. Clark reportedly made a fortune by participating in the profits of gambling ventures. The agency manager of the Jacksonville office, in his letter of August 26, 1949, to the general counsel of RFC, stated, "You perhaps know that Sheriff Clark of Broward County (Fort Lauderdale), Florida, is the president of this company. It is generally understood that Sheriff Clark is 'in the money.' It has been said also that he is a very close personal friend of the President."

*Saxony Loan.* The RFC lent a good deal of money for hotel building. It lent $563,000 to hotels operated by the American Hotels, Inc. It accepted the appraisals of the Hockenberry

---

2. See report of Kefauver committee, Third Report of Senate committee to investigate Organized Crime (82nd Congress), p. 36. For details of Ribbonwriter Loan see Hearings Before Fulbright subcommittee, *(op. cit.)* p. 30 ff.

system; E. J. Hockenberry was vice president of American Hotels. In May 1949, the RFC approved a loan of $1,500,000 to the swanky Saxony hotel in Miami Beach. The loan requested by Saxony of $2,500,000 was at the rate of $10,000 a room. The Kefauver report stated, "There are 30 to 40 punchboard manufacturers in the United States. The Sax interests in Chicago are probably the largest manufacturers of punchboards." Mr. H. W. Robertson, the RFC examiner on invitation from the hotel, spent ten days from January 29 to February 9 as a guest of the hotel with his wife and daughter. His room rent was paid for by the hotel. After being a guest at the Saxony, Mr. Robertson on an amended application recommended that Mr. Sax be permitted to withdraw $200,000 from the account to pay his personal income taxes. When asked by Fulbright what the public interest was in the loan, Robertson replied, "You asked for the public interest. If you take 15 or 20 subcontractors waiting and hollering for their money and other accounts and notes paid all on a temporary basis, I think you are absolutely justified in approving the loan." Presidential aide Donald Dawson was a nonpaying guest of the Saxony.

*Harrington and Richardson Arms Company Loan.* In April 1950, the RFC approved a $300,000 loan to this company of which C. Edward Rowe had the principal ownership and control. Shortly afterwards, Rowe was appointed a director of the RFC. His appointment began to be rumored a full year before it occurred.

Rowe was a long-time friend of Director Ed Willett of the RFC. Examiner Bergen in the Boston office recommended decline and the office and advisory committee concurred. The inventory of shotguns and rifles was inadequate, he felt—an opinion confirmed by the Boston engineer-examiner. Rowe visited Willett on March 23 and spoke to Examiner Hoover. On the day the Bergen report was received in Washington, Rowe spoke to Willett by phone and again three days later.

Examiner Hoover then recommended the loan, saying that the appraisal should be made not on the basis of what it would fetch in a distress situation but the fair value of it. The regular basis of the RFC was the distress test. The board granted the loan and Willett congratulated Rowe by phone.[3]

Willett admitted that he had hand-picked an examiner and let Rowe confer with him. "I did it as a personal favor to Judge Rowe. . . . I would do it for any friend."

*Reliance Homes of Lester, Pennsylvania.* The RFC voted a loan of $3,838,000 on June 27, 1949. It disbursed $501,468 on July 15. According to Senator Williams, RFC was warned that the company was insolvent and that the financial statements were false. New statements that were submitted on July 31 showed that the company was insolvent to the extent of three-quarters of a million dollars and that it had lost $1,000,000 in the previous four months. Nonetheless, RFC disbursed another $832,946 on August 26. It had disbursed the entire loan by August 31, 1950. On September 7, 1950, the loan was declared in default and three months later the firm was bankrupt. No one knows what sponsorship induced the RFC to throw away millions of the taxpayers' money.

*The Texmass Loan.* The loan to Texmass[4] ranks as one of the most atrocious made by the RFC, attributable to gullibility, political pressure, or both. Homer Snowden of Dallas promoted a plan for development of oil properties in Texas and raised $8,600,000 in Boston during 1945. Contributors included Boston Brahmins, Wellesley College and Harvard College. He reorganized the company several times under different names until in October 1946, Texmass Petroleum Company obtained a charter in Texas. The development of the oil properties showed no profits and more money was pulled

3. See hearings before Fulbright subcommittee to investigate the RFC (82nd Congress), p. 1612.

4. See hearings before Fulbright subcommittee, "The Texmass Loan" (82nd Congress), April 13-27, 1950. Also report of the Fulbright subcommittee, "Texmass Petroleum Company Loan."

in. The Second National Bank of Boston put in $400,000, and $8,000,000 was sunk into the enterprise by two New England insurance institutions—the John Hancock Mutual Life Insurance Company of Boston and the Massachusetts Mutual Life Insurance Company of Springfield.

The investors were becoming more impatient and still the enterprise showed no results. The only consolation was that the board of directors was becoming more and more distinguished and the widows and orphans were in the company of the Cabots and the Lodges. Snowden left the company and the $436,000 he owed the company was charged off as a bad debt.[5] Texmass had exhausted all possibilities of raising more money in the private markets. There was only one source left—Uncle Sam—so, in December 1948, Texmass applied to RFC for a loan of $22 million, employing Ross Bohannon, a Dallas lawyer. It is a significant commentary on the value of the Texmass proposition that almost all the money that was sunk into it came from New England, not from Texas.

The Dallas examiner to whom the application went first, made this comment: "The loan value which could be assigned to the collateral tendered is not, in my opinion, a sufficient amount to reasonably secure the loan requested." The wells were stripper wells, which could not produce much oil and they were scattered so widely that the cost of operation would be high. A geologist hired by the RFC stated that the oil in Texmass property might pay off the loan in 20 years, but the RFC loan could be for no more than 10. A geologist of the SEC stated that the reserves would be insufficient to pay the loan. The advisory committee of the Dallas agency recommended a loan for $15,925,000. One of the members of the committee was the vice president of a bank in Dallas which was to receive $250,000 of the loan. Another member had a partner who had been connected with Snowden.

5. Report of the Fulbright subcommittee, "Texmass Petroleum Co. Loan," p. 3.

The advisory committee in Washington recommended that the loan be declined, saying that "there was little if any public interest." It pointed out, moreover, that the loan was a bail-out of the present investors. Nonetheless, the RFC on September 29, 1949, voted to lend Texmass $10,100,000. Eighty-one percent of the loan went to creditors. Massachusetts Mutual received $2,448,203 and John Hancock $1,831,265, according to the Fulbright committee.[6]

The Fulbright committee prior to the time the loan was disbursed in June 1950, investigated the loan and questioned the directors. The loan was passed, not by a majority of the RFC, but by a 2-to-1 vote. Chairman Hise declined to vote, Harvey Gunderson and Walter Dunham voted "aye." Gunderson apparently was impressed by the need for oil as a long-term reserve. Dunham, who was from Detroit, knew that oil was important for automobiles, and "we would not have Detroit without the oil business." He said to Senator Fulbright: "After you get to a certain point, you can't lose in the oil business."

> FULBRIGHT: You can't lose?
> DUNHAM: It is the most depression-proof business that I know.
> FULBRIGHT: I think the evidence shows clearly that these people did lose in the oil business and that is the reason they came to the RFC.

In December 1955 three-quarters of the loan was still unpaid.

As rotten as the RFC Board was, it was not internal weakness which caused the final collapse. It was unendurable pressure from the outside to which it was subjected by the White House and the Democratic National Committee.

6. Report "Texmass Petroleum Company Loan," *op. cit.,* p. 20.

## · VII ·

## THE RFC SCANDALS—II:
## THE INCREDIBLE MERL YOUNG*

*May I briefly summarize. I did start at the bottom in
life. I have bettered myself. This ambition was given
me as a child when I was taught that in this land of
opportunity, there was nothing wrong in hard work
and trying to progress up the ladder of success.*

—MERL YOUNG, testifying before
the Fulbright subcommittee investigating the RFC.

IN THE eyes of the men who ran the RFC, Donald S. Dawson
was next to God—because in another sense, he *was* next to
God. He was administrative assistant to the President, in
charge of personnel matters and was therefore the master of
their fate. It was Dawson who gave the word as to whether
they should remain in their jobs. This he coolly demonstrated
in August 1950, when he retained on the board his two puppets, Walter Dunham and Ed Willett, while purging the
board of the independent members, Chairman Hise, Harvey
Gunderson and Henry Mulligan. Chairman Hise testified
that Dawson tried to dominate the RFC. Hise, Dunham, and
Gunderson said that Willett did whatever Dawson told him
to. Dunham admitted that he did not resist Dawson's domination. Hise, as a matter of fact, in moral confusion, usually

* Unless otherwise noted, the matters in this chapter were brought out
at the hearings before the Fulbright subcommittee on the RFC (82nd
Congress), pp. 595-1872 (February 21 to March 11, 1951). Also report,
"Favoritism and Influence," by Fulbright subcommittee on the RFC
(82nd Congress).

voted with Willett and Dunham. Dawson did not have to put much effort into domination—a wink and a nod were enough.

Dawson was well acquainted with RFC affairs. He was an alumnus of the institution, having graduated from the post of personnel director of the RFC to his White House job. He had eyes and ears in the RFC. His wife, Alva Dawson, was in charge of the RFC files—a copy of every memorandum leaving an office in the government immediately goes to central files. Moreover, the personnel director of the RFC, Donald W. "Snuffy" Smith, was a buddy of Dawson.[1]

Walter Dunham, Dawson's obedient friend, who became a director in March 1949, was a penitent from a period which, coincidentally, dated from the time of the Fulbright investigation. He lifted the veil, to a degree, on his relationship with Dawson. "Upon my arrival in Washington, I went through Mr. Donald Dawson to meet the President. After my appointment, Mr. Dawson told me that top personnel matters should be cleared at the White House. Mr. Dawson introduced me to Mr. Willett, a fellow director, stating that the White House had great confidence in Mr. Willett." Dunham was then told that there was ill feeling between Dawson and the chairman, Mr. Hise.[2]

Mr. Dunham had previously met Mr. Rex Jacobs, president of F. L. Jacobs Company. Jacobs said he had known Dunham for twenty-five years. Jacobs introduced him to his assistant, Mr. James C. Windham, a former assistant to George Allen, RFC director. Windham had joined Jacobs as treasurer and director of F. L. Jacobs Co. after the company had gotten a loan from RFC of $3 million. A couple of days later, Windham brought in to meet Dunham a close friend of Dawson, a man in his early thirties, who was an employee of Jacobs and, like Windham, a former employee of RFC. His name was

1. Report, "Favoritism and Influence," *op. cit.*, p. 8.
2. Testimony of Walter Dunham before Fulbright subcommittee, *op. cit.*, p. 1319.

# THE RFC INFLUENCE RING

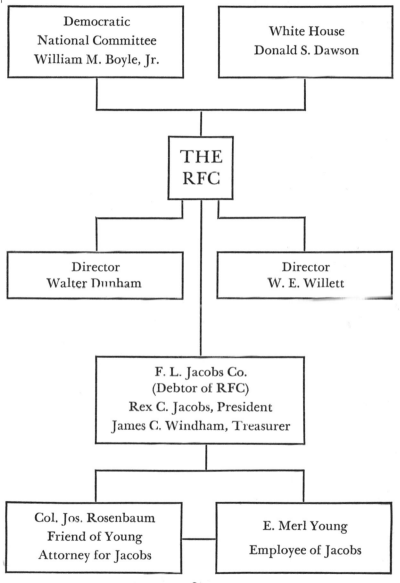

Democratic
National Committee
William M. Boyle, Jr.

White House
Donald S. Dawson

THE
RFC

Director
Walter Dunham

Director
W. E. Willett

F. L. Jacobs Co.
(Debtor of RFC)
Rex C. Jacobs, President
James C. Windham, Treasurer

Col. Jos. Rosenbaum
Friend of Young
Attorney for Jacobs

E. Merl Young

Employee of Jacobs

E. Merl Young. "My impression," says Dunham, "was that the group was solely interested in the welfare of the Truman administration and that any RFC interest they had was along the line."

## Introducing E. Merl Young

Only in the degraded moral climate of the Truman administration could the story of Merl Young have occurred. He left high school in Missouri in 1932 and had no further training. He drifted to Washington from Jericho Spring, Missouri, in the mid-1930's, became a clerk in Peoples' Drug Store and then worked for a dairy, reportedly driving a milk truck. Just before the war, on the basis of merit, Young had risen to the position of assistant messenger for the General Accounting Office at a salary of $1080 a year.

Already, however, Merl Young was on the road to dizzy success. His wife, Lauretta, was a stenographer in the office of the junior senator from Missouri, Harry S. Truman. While hanging around the office, Merl had become well acquainted with an aide of Senator Truman by the name of William M. Boyle, Jr.

After a hitch in the Marine Corps, he returned to Washington in 1945 and the breaks came thick and fast. Senator Truman was now President Truman. Lauretta Young was now in the White House as an assistant to Rose Conway, the President's secretary. Young got a job in the RFC in the surplus disposal branch. He picked up his acquaintance with William M. Boyle, Jr., who was practicing law in Washington, and who was now a big political wheel in the administration. Young had a White House pass. He worked on the same floor of the Lafayette building as the personnel director of the RFC, Donald S. Dawson. He now forged the final link that was to bring him dubious fame, fortune and a jail sentence for perjury. Young and Dawson became friends; they found that Dawson and Lauretta Young came from the same county of Missouri, Cedar County.

The common friendship of Young and Dawson with Bill Boyle was one of the ties which bound them together. Young now shot up fast. His personnel record for 1946 shows that on September 20, he was "reinstated" as an examiner at Grade 13 and a salary of $4,500. This is a grade that a person starting at the bottom usually takes 10 to 15 years to reach —that is, with luck. He was then moved to the highly responsible position of a financial examiner at a base salary of $7,193 a year. In this job, he had to pass on examinations involving millions of dollars of government money. He took an accounting course, but didn't bother to pursue his studies. He didn't have to.

Then Dawson moved up. He went on loan to the White House for some special work and then went over on permanent assignment as the President's assistant for patronage.

To those who observed him at the hearings, Young did not seem impressive. However, he had traits which made for success. He was sharp, brash, likeable and the simplicity of his mind left him free of moral and intellectual inhibitions. He was a hustler, a "What Makes Sammy Run" type rare in the government. Moreover, he knew how to take advantage of every favorable circumstance.

A fortuitous circumstance that Young capitalized on was the fact that the President's mother's maiden name was Young. There was testimony that from the time he worked in Peoples' Drug Store he claimed that he was Harry Truman's nephew. Later on, he didn't have to say very much about this. His friends propagated the myth and it was generally so widely circulated that it *was assumed that you knew* Merl was related to the President and that out of a sense of delicacy, he couldn't discuss it. At times, Merl's imagination would flower wondrously. He would say that he had campaigned with "The Boss" for the Senate in Missouri and that they had slept together in the same bed. He was always privy to "The Boss's" thinking. There is a recorded instance, shortly after he left RFC, when he stopped off at the St. Louis office between trains and gave the boys a pat on the back saying, "The Boss wishes he had an office in Kansas City like the office he has at St. Louis," and walked off with some valuable information.[3]

In August 1948, Young started to cash in the chips. According to Carl A. Strandlund, the president of Lustron, Director Gunderson suggested to him that he hire Young for $12,000 a year. Since Lustron, building prefabricated homes, was indebted to RFC to the tune of $37 million and was completely at its mercy, and it was all government money anyway, Strandlund agreed. Gunderson wanted Strandlund to hire another man by the name of McGrath, but because Young objected, McGrath's appointment was dropped.[4]

Young was indicted and convicted for perjury in denying that he had anything to do with the Lustron loan. Records showed that he had "concurred" in a second loan to Lustron in 1948 and resigned to join Lustron the day the loan was approved. Undoubtedly Strandlund saw the value of having him as his representative in Washington to "service" the loan.

That summer and fall, Young worked with Boyle in the Democratic National Committee for the re-election of Truman. A book published in 1948 by Edward Brown, publicity man for the Democratic National Committee, called *Democracy in Action,* shows Young's picture as assistant, besides that of Boyle.[5] Young, together with Dawson, organized the President's itinerary and Young was on the campaign train with the President in the last week of the campaign.

Young's salary and expenses all the while were being paid

3. Testimony of Oliver Kraft before Hoey investigations subcommittee, "American Lithofold Corporation," (82nd Congress), p. 309.

4. Testimony of Carl A. Strandlund before Fulbright subcommittee, *op. cit.,* p. 933.

5. Testimony of Merl Young before Hoey investigations subcommittee, "American Lithofold Corporation," (82nd Congress), p. 487.

by Lustron, out of government money. Strandlund left Young to his own devices in Washington. In the fall, Chairman Hise told Strandlund that he would like "to see Young get something out of it," so Strandlund promoted Young to vice president of Lustron at $18,000 a year. Young testified "my salary was increased to $18,000, which Mr. Strandlund told me that I had earned as he felt I had done a good job." That job apparently consisted of helping get Truman reelected.

Since Young held one honorarium, there was no reason why he should not accept a second. Rex C. Jacobs, president of F. L. Jacobs Company, saw in Young a man of influence with whom it was desirable to become intimate. The wartime accounts of Jacobs' companies, including sums such as $65,458 for jewelry and $35,822 for night clubs, showed that he paid heavily for cultivating people.[6] He hired Young for $10,000 a year, presumably to promote the installation of vending machines in Washington for an obscure drink called Coca-Cola. Carl Strandlund swore under oath that he had never had the slightest idea that while Young was working for him, he was also working for Jacobs. Young sent duplicate expense accounts to both firms. He collected $9,000 from Jacobs in 1948 and 1949 and $11,000 from Lustron. The job with Jacobs was never cleared by the RFC, although Jacobs was a debtor of RFC, since only jobs over $12,000 a year had to be approved.[7] Ed Willett knew of the double employment and so did Dunham. Perhaps other directors did too.

To milk the situation to its fullest, Young had to hook up with a lawyer, since RFC clients approached the agency and negotiated with it through lawyers. Through Jacobs, who had used him for tax work for years, Young, in the fall of 1949,

6. Testimony of Rex Jacobs before Fulbright subcommittee, *op. cit.*, p. 1039.

7. Testimony of Rex Jacobs before Fulbright subcommittee, *op. cit.*, p. 707, and of Merl Young, before Fulbright subcommittee, p. 1013.

became a friend of Col. Joseph Rosenbaum, head of the Washington law firm of Goodwin, Rosenbaum, Meacham and Bailen, which had eighteen lawyers. Col. Rosenbaum specialized in tax law and the human equation and never missed a trick. Even his cable address, GOVPRAC, advertised what his firm did. He developed a good practice by representing loan applicants with the RFC; a tabulation shows that, including the time Rosenbaum teamed up with Merl Young, he submitted 38 loan applications for $59,618,000 and got loans approved for $25,155,000.[8]

Merl Young with his contact in the White House with Dawson and with Bill Boyle and his power over directors Dunham and Willett, was the key man of the influence ring. He was variously referred to as the contact man or the expediter. He was cherished sufficiently so that Rosenbaum, who was not a charitable institution, lavished substantial gifts on him:

1) The most highly publicized was a mink coat for Young's wife. The royal pastel mink cost $8,540 less a 10 per cent discount. Guenther Jaeckel, the firm from which the fur was bought, filed an application for an RFC loan, which was approved in May 1950, though not disbursed.

2) For a payment of $500, Rosenbaum got for Young the down-payment on an option for either $4500 or $12,000 to purchase half of the Atlantic Basin Iron Works, a company which had real estate in Brooklyn worth $200,000 and $1,500,000 of other assets. The company could be gutted of its assets, but then it would be valuable for sale as a tax loss.

3) Atlantic Basin advanced Young $30,000. Rosenbaum got an RFC loan for Central Iron and Steel. Atlantic Basin then bought 2500 tons of steel plate from Central Iron and Steel at a time when steel was very tight and delivered it to Price Iron and Steel at a profit of $80,000. The steel, as Sen-

8. Testimony of Joseph Rosenbaum before Fulbright subcommittee, *op. cit.*, pp. 1214, 1215.

ator Capehart saw it, went into the black market. That profit more than covered the money given to Young.

4) Young went into the insurance business in 1950, after resigning from Jacobs' firm and Lustron, and Rosenbaum advanced him $11,000 without collateral.

5) Rosenbaum organized the Martin Investment Company. Young bought 60 shares from Rosenbaum in May 1950 at $1 a share, and on July 15, Rosenbaum's firm was paying $200 for the same shares, thus giving Young a paper profit of $12,000.

6) Rosenbaum's father advanced Young $8,500 and Young spent $2,500 of it to go into the brewery business with George Fitzgerald, the Democratic national committeeman from Michigan. Soon before the brewery had put in and had withdrawn two applications for RFC loans.

There were other knicknacks such as a sixteen-foot boat that Young got from Rosenbaum, which he, in turn, had bought from Jacobs for $1,000. Rosenbaum could not explain why he showered this largesse on Young.

SENATOR FULBRIGHT: You do not expect this committee to believe that just out of a clear sky you suddenly fell in love with Mr. Young and dealt him those wonderful little bits of participations in deals, do you? Do you think we are so naive that we think you do it because you like the color of his eyes?

MR. ROSENBAUM: No, he is a friend of mine, a business associate.

The cost of subsidizing Mr. Young also ran high for Mr. Jacobs, whose spending always ran on a prodigal scale. When, in 1950, Young went into the insurance business (for which he had no license), his only client was Jacobs. His tax estimate of income for 1950 was $60,000. In September 1950, he went back to Jacobs' employ at $18,000 a year plus expenses. Jacobs frankly said he hired Young again as a contact man. In early 1950, as we shall see, Jacobs lent Young $37,500 on unsecured notes for an oil venture.

The tax angle of these transactions should be noted. Young received money as loans so that he would not have to report them as income. When the loans were not repaid, they would be charged off as bad debts. So by "lending" money to Young, Rosenbaum and Jacobs were delaying the time when they could deduct the amounts from their tax bill.

Rosenbaum's connection with the influence ring was through Young and Jacobs. He didn't know Dunham and had met Willett only casually. The close teamwork between the members of the ruling clique in the RFC is evident in the diary that Dunham kept of his activities from the beginning of April 1949 to July 30, 1950. This diary covered about 280 working days and shows how many days he either conversed by phone on incoming calls or lunched with various members of the clique. It has no reference to outgoing calls or dinner engagements which were very frequent: Dawson, 45 days; Merl Young, 89 days; Herschel Young (Merl's brother), 15 days; Rex Jacobs, 39 days; James Windham, 47 days; William Boyle, 26 days.

Dunham's diary generally shows what the subject of discussion was in these calls, except for the calls from Merl Young. For some reason, a reference was rarely included. Ed Willett also kept an office record from August 9, 1948 to February 28, 1951. It shows ninety calls from Merl Young.

Besides frequent get-togethers at the usual meeting ground in Washington, the Colony Room of the Statler, the group met frequently in Jacobs' home near Homestead, Florida. Dawson visited, with his wife, and Boyle visited there too. Young and his wife were generally present. Rosenbaum was a guest.

An investigator for the subcommittee, while going through Merl Young's files, came across an interesting file, entitled "The McCutcheon Drilling Co.," which set forth the terms of an oil venture in Gaines County, Texas, involving various personalities connected with the RFC. The investigator took careful notes. The next day, when he returned, Young refused to let him see the file again. A copy of this arrangement was torn up by Rex Jacobs.

This venture, which was set up in early 1950, according to a letter from Windham to Jacobs dated June 12, 1950, listed the interests as follows:

| | |
|---|---|
| Rex Jacobs | 20 per cent |
| James Windham | 20 per cent |
| E. Merl Young | 20 per cent |
| Phil Regan (the actor) | 20 per cent |
| Donald Dawson | 10 per cent |
| William Boyle | 10 per cent |
| Total | 100 per cent |

The venture looked good at first and even Ed Pauley, who knew oil, tried to buy in but was unsuccessful. According to Jacobs, Dawson and Bill Boyle backed out, because they could not afford it. But of the $160,000 that was put up, F. L. Jacobs Co. supplied $120,000, so Dawson and Boyle might not have been called on for money. Perhaps they thought their involvement in the venture was unwise. Young, as usual, put up no money. Funds of F. L. Jacobs Company were advanced to him for a total of $120,000, but notes were given to him by other parties so that his liability was only $37,500. The notes matured but were not paid for by September 1950. The law firm which represented the joint adventurers was Goodwin, Rosenbaum, Meacham and Bailen.

A single event evidences Merl Young's strong influence. When Carl Strandlund in the fall of 1950 decided to oust Young from Lustron, he asked Dunham's advice. Dunham, in turn, asked Dawson's advice. Dawson, in turn, asked the President of the United States if it would be all right to fire Young. The President made an historic decision, *pro bono publico,* that Lustron and the $37,500,000 of the public money were more important than Merl Young.

## Texmass

It is much easier to document where influence was peddled and a deal was not made than cases where the sale is successful. In the latter cases, the purchasers cannot talk, because they are *particeps criminis*. In the former case, they have no reason for silence. Ross Bohannon, an attorney in Dallas, was hired to swing the loan for Texmass. He got a call from a friend named Rucker, inviting him over to a New Year's Eve party, where he met one John Skiles, the chief of personnel of the Dallas RFC office. Skiles admitted that they talked about the Texmass loan—he said that Bohannon talked of Washington connections in between his statements that "that ain't whiskey talking." Bohannon said that Skiles advised him that to swing the Texmass loan in Washington he had better contact Merl Young, who was close to the President, whose wife was the President's secretary, and who had all the influence in Washington.[9]

Young contacted Bohannon at the Raleigh hotel in Washington and they met for lunch at the Statler Colony Room. Young advised Bohannon to bypass the Dallas office and make application directly to Washington. He said his fee for getting a loan would be $10,000 plus $7,500 a year for 10 years. Bohannon gulped—his own fee was only $55,000. Bohannon said that he had considered hiring Bill Boyle of the Democratic National Committee. Young replied that it would make no difference, since Boyle would hand the case over to him. Bohannon had Young investigated and discovered that he wasn't the President's nephew after all.[10] Senator Connally

9. Testimony of John Skiles before Fulbright subcommittee, *op. cit.*, p. 782, and of Ross Bohannon, p. 597.
10. Testimony of Ross Bohannon before Fulbright subcommittee, *op. cit.*, p. 631, and of Edward P. Morgan, p. 730.

told him that he shouldn't bother with Young because the political backing for the loan was strong enough. So Bohannon wrote Young advising him that he would not hire him. Skiles apparently kept after Bohannon. He wrote to Young in February 1949, saying, "I haven't heard from Ross, but I assume you got together with him." He wrote also that he would protect Young's interests.

Young denied flatly that he had solicited the fee. However, there is written proof of the fact that Bohannon talked freely about the suggested fee to others. Young said that he met Boyle of the Democratic National Committee and discussed the case with him and that Boyle replied, "Forget it." According to Young, the whole conversation had struck him as "funny" because Bohannon had asked him about the serious rupture in the Dallas office with which Skiles was involved. Fulbright and the other committee members couldn't understand why Bohannon's conversation as quoted by Young should strike anyone as "funny." A practicing lawyer like Boyle would hardly regard a fee like that in the case of Texmass as "funny."

Chairman Harley Hise had apparently gotten wind from some channel or another of the attempt by Merl Young to make a killing on Texmass. He summoned Bohannon and an attorney who was an associate of Bohannon into his office and told them that he knew of the matter. He demanded of Bohannon that he sign an affidavit explaining the whole proposal and swearing that he had done no business with Young. Otherwise, said Hise, the Texmass application would be sent back to Dallas. Bohannon furnished the affidavit. Hise abstained from voting on the Texmass loan.

### Kaiser-Frazer

In the fall of 1949 the Kaiser Auto Company, the Kaiser group having secured loans from the RFC for steel and aluminum, applied for a loan to secure funds required to tool its 1951 models. The amount of the proposed loan was $34,400,-000. Kaiser's financing through private banks was available for working capital only and could not be used for capital investments. The Bank of America in San Francisco, managed by L. M. Giannini, had a stake of about $8,000,000 in the loan, since it was financing Kaiser.

The pressure to use Merl Young's services in this case was more intense than in the case of Texmass. RFC Director Gunderson on October 1 made a record of what Edgar Kaiser had told him the previous day. Col. Rosenbaum had called Giannini in San Francisco and told him that the loan would go through but that he could get easier terms for Kaiser because of his influence with two directors, Willett and Dunham.[11] Giannini called Henry Kaiser, who called Edgar Kaiser in Washington. The Kaiser people decided that they would not employ Col. Rosenbaum.

Merl Young then tried his hand directly. He tried to reach various members of the Kaiser delegation by phone—Edgar Kaiser, Bruce Wood and Chad Calhoun—but all of them refused to take the call until the morning that the Kaiser-Frazer loan was being considered. Then Bruce Wood called Young back, and Young told him that, in behalf of the Metal Products Company in Detroit connected with Jacobs, he had been using his contacts in RFC to fix things up for Kaiser. This was a gingerly type of approach in which he offered bait for Kaiser, but Kaiser wouldn't bite.[12] The loan was approved on October 6.

There was further pressure on Kaiser. On December 7, 1949, Bruce Wood got into a quarrel with Director Walter Dunham in the latter's office, in which Dunham accused Kaiser of

11. Memorandum of Harvey J. Gunderson before Fulbright subcommittee, *op. cit.,* p. 678.
12. Testimony of Edgar F. Kaiser before Fulbright subcommittee, *op. cit.,* p. 679.

violating the terms of the loan in their use of the funds. He threw Wood out of his office. The Kaiser people were stunned. They couldn't understand what it was all about. Then the answer dawned on Edgar Kaiser. On December 12, Rex Jacobs came to Willow Run to see Edgar Kaiser. He told him that he knew all about Wood's quarrel with Dunham and that he, Jacobs, knew how to get things straightened out. The answer was that Kaiser-Frazer should hire Bill Boyle. Immediately, Calhoun put a memorandum in the files relating what Jacobs had said to Kaiser. "Thus it appears that Mr. Dunham's blow-up at Bruce Wood last week was a deliberate act on his part and it was all a part of the plan to make us kick through to the so-called right parties."[13]

Kaiser, by refusing to have any truck with the forces of darkness, undoubtedly got more severe terms than they would have gotten if they had played ball with Rosenbaum and Young. Even though the independent appraised value of the collateral was two-and-a-half times the value of the loan, the RFC demanded the personal guaranties of the Kaiser interests and these guaranties had to be secured by a pledge of marketable securities as collateral. The terms were unprecedentedly severe but Kaiser had no alternative but to accept them.

## Lustron

Someone once titled Lustron as "the house that jack built," and truer words were never spoken. The idea for Lustron was that of Carl A. Strandlund as a means of coping with the severe housing shortage after the war. It was a prefabricated, enameled steel house. Senator Fulbright couldn't understand how anybody would want to live in it. It reminded him, he said, of a bathtub. RFC Director Gunderson said the early

13. Testimony of Chad F. Calhoun, before Fulbright subcommittee, *op. cit.,* p. 686.

models reminded him of a hot-dog stand. The credit for the brilliant idea of the government investment in Lustron belongs to Wilson A. Wyatt, who was Truman's housing chief. Wyatt was Adlai Stevenson's campaign manager in 1952, but his administration of the housing problem after the war smacked less of eggheadism than it did of mushheadism. John R. Steelman, Truman's assistant, forced the Lustron loan down the throat of RFC.[14] Strandlund put in $1,000 and got a job for $50,000 a year. The equity investment raised through the sale of stock to the public amounted to around $840,000. The government put up the rest. The government leased to it the surplus war plant of Curtiss Wright at Columbus, Ohio. The house which was supposed to cost from $7,000 to $8,000 cost $11,000. By mid-1949, according to RFC, Lustron was losing $1 million a month. Strandlund, however, insisted that all he needed was time and that his problem was to coax RFC along, both as to the existing loan and as to getting more credit.

On February 2, 1950, after three years of operation, the Lustron investment came to an end when the RFC filed suit to foreclose. Strandlund claimed that continuous pressure had been applied to him by RFC since July 1949 "for the single purpose of forcing me to give up my control of Lustron to a small clique, including Mr. Dunham, Merl Young and Rex Jacobs."[15]

This is the story according to Strandlund. Strandlund[16] swears that he had no idea that Merl Young had divided loyalties growing out of the fact that he was an employee of Rex Jacobs at the same time that he was an employee of Lustron. In any event, since Young stayed in Washington, and Strand-

14. For background of Lustron loan, see *Time* magazine, July 4, 1949.

15. Statement of Carl Strandlund before Fulbright subcommittee, *op. cit.*, p. 940.

16. Testimony of Carl Strandlund before Fulbright subcommittee, *op. cit.*, pp. 932, 962, 998, 1056.

lund in Columbus, the latter probably had little idea of what Young was doing with his time. In late spring of 1949, Dunham began paying visits to Lustron and told him on one visit he wanted Rex Jacobs to look over the plant. While Jacobs was at Lustron, Dunham called from Washington and told Strandlund that Jacobs was a good friend of his and urged him to "talk freely to him," repeating the phrase several times. Jacobs proposed to Strandlund that Lustron use Jacobs' washing machine in their homes and that Merl Young be paid $15 for each washing machine used, which would mean a minimum of $50,000 a year even at Lustron's meager output. Strandlund, greatly surprised, said no. Jacobs said to him, "What shall I tell Walter [Dunham]?" Strandlund replied, "Tell Walter to keep his shirt on." Strandlund said that from that time on, his troubles really began.

In August, Dunham was getting hot and bothered about the Lustron loan and a $2 million temporary credit to Lustron included a provision that a committee should be appointed to investigate Lustron and to report back to the RFC. The committee appointed on August 31 was Rex Jacobs and E. J. Hunt, a former production man with Chrysler. On September 7, Jacobs and Hunt inspected Lustron, accompanied by Merl Young. Jacobs, Hunt and Dunham had called a few days before on Donald Dawson in the White House. Dunham's diary indicates that he discussed the case freely with Dawson. Said Dunham, "The Lustron case was a matter which worried me considerably, and I am sure I discussed it with Messrs. Dawson, Jacobs, Windham and Young whenever we were together, which was usually whenever Mr. Jacobs came to Washington and invited us to dinner."

The Jacobs report, as might be expected, recommended new management. On September 26, Strandlund was advised by Dunham and Willett that he had to give up 60,000 of the 86,000 shares he had of Lustron. Strandlund now saw Merl Young in open communication with Jacobs. Young, on October 6, urged Strandlund to accept Dunham's demand for relinquishment of the majority of the stock, saying that he would be taken care of with a salary for life.

Strandlund was now convinced that he had a Trojan horse within his gates. The question, however, was how to deal with Merl Young in view of the undoubted political power which he wielded. After getting permission from Dunham to move against Young (Dunham had checked with the White House), Strandlund wrote a cautious letter to his disloyal employee, advising him that he was shifting him from Washington to Columbus, Ohio. On October 13, Young replied, stating in a very carefully worded letter, for which Rosenbaum was quoted as having taken the credit, that he reluctantly had to decline the honor of moving to Columbus, but it all served Strandlund right because Strandlund had not taken Merl Young's advice as to how to retrench. The resignation, however, was dated six weeks ahead. Young possibly thought that by that time the reorganization of Lustron would be complete. Strandlund now got cold feet and, on November 9, asked Merl Young to reconsider his resignation but Young was adamant.

A preliminary draft of the report by Jacobs, dated September 9, states what Jacobs had in mind for Merl Young. "I believe that Mr. Merl Young should be retained in his present capacity. I believe that there should be enough Class B stock issued to Messrs. Haggerty, Hunt and Young to offset the 86,000 shares that Mr. Strand [sic] and Mrs. Strand owned."[17] The stage was now all set for the grab. As the garrote was being tightened around the throat of Strandlund, Hise ordered him to obtain the resignations of all the members of the board of directors except himself. Strandlund offered a counterproposal—to balance out his members with those nominated by

17. Testimony of Rex Jacobs before Fulbright subcommittee, *op. cit.,* p. 965.

RFC. This was rejected. RFC had passed a resolution that no funds could be expended by Lustron for inventory without RFC approval and thus operations were falling off.

Apparently, the grab was called off because at the same time as the Jacobs survey, the RFC ordered a survey by Booz, Allen and Hamilton. The report made the whole matter of Lustron academic, since it stated that there was no hope for Lustron to make good in the housing business. RFC now hurried the company to slaughter. A receiver was appointed in March 1950 and Strandlund was sued personally for $15,485,000. From the time of the Lustron matter on, Dunham said he started a withdrawal from his association with the influence ring. He got a bad scare when he attended a party at Jacobs' home in Florida and got a call from a Detroit newspaperman checking on the fact that the people at Jacobs' ranch were engineering a "grab" of Lustron. "I was impressed by the fact that the caller had an accurate guest list: Mr. and Mrs. Dawson, Mr. and Mrs. Young, Ed Hunt and several others. I told the newspaperman that I couldn't conceive of Mr. Jacobs wanting to go into the Lustron Corporation. . . . I was, however, worried about the matter, and as I look back now, I feel that my changed feeling was reflected in my attitude towards Messrs. Jacobs, Young et al."

Even though the Lustron grab fell through, there were still possibilities in Lustron for Young and for Rosenbaum. There were creditors involved in Lustron. The Commercial Home Equipment Company had contracted to transport the Lustron houses from factories to building sites; there were no facilities for warehousing Lustron homes. The Fruehauf Trailer Company furnished these trailers to Commercial Home and there was a $3 million unpaid balance owing to it. Fruehauf had therefore an important interest in Lustron. After the RFC rejected the reorganization plan proposed by Lustron in November and again in January, Fruehauf was called to Washington on January 24 by Paul Buckley, a Lustron director and also a director of Commercial Home, who told them that a crisis was on hand for Lustron.

Ray Fruehauf, head of Fruehauf Trailer, gave this account:[18] Rosenbaum joined Buckley and Fruehauf in a room at the Wardman Park Hotel and told the two of them that he could save Lustron through his friends at the RFC, Dunham and Willett, who, he said, were "in his hip pocket." He was confident that there was no one else who would be able to save Lustron. He proposed that the next day he should take Buckley and Fruehauf over to the RFC to see Willett. James Gottlieb, the president of Commercial Home, showed Fruehauf a letter of retainer which Rosenbaum had drawn up. It provided for a total of $100,000 with a payment immediately of $25,000. (Rosenbaum admitted that he asked a fee of $100,000 from Gottlieb.) Fruehauf's lawyer, Alfons Landa, told Fruehauf to discourage this retainer of Rosenbaum, saying that it bore all the earmarks of the Washington "fix."

As a creditor of Commercial Home, Fruehauf, of course, had an interest in seeing that no money of its debtor was being uselessly squandered, so he told Gottlieb to call the deal off. Rex Jacobs, who was acquainted with Fruehauf, spoke to him repeatedly on the phone urging him to take Rosenbaum as his counsel and pointed out to him the number of RFC loans that Rosenbaum had successfully swung. Jacobs apparently made these calls from Rosenbaum's office, since at one time he left Rosenbaum's number for Fruehauf to call back. Jacobs kept calling Fruehauf in Detroit and other places in Rosenbaum's behalf.

The creditors were working out a new plan with Strandlund, in which Strandlund gave Fruehauf and his associates all the powers and proxies necessary for reorganization of Lustron. Thus the condition that RFC had imposed, namely

18. Testimony of Roy Fruehauf before Fulbright subcommittee, *op. cit.,* p. 1167.

that Strandlund get out, was complied with. The new organization contemplated hiring two prominent housing specialists to aid in the sale of Lustron's homes. The responsibility of the management was to be shifted to Fruehauf, who would accept no compensation but who would act only to protect the $3 million debt.

On February 14, RFC released the news which shocked the Fruehauf group, that foreclosure action would be taken. On the morning of February 16, the Fruehauf group met in a conference with the four RFC directors, Dunham, Willett, Gunderson and Mulligan; Chairman Hise was ill. The first thing that Dunham said to the Fruehauf group was "Rex Jacobs is in town."

> SENATOR TOBEY: So what, what is the inference in that?
> MR. FRUEHAUF: I do not know, Senator.

Dunham said that even though RFC had ordered foreclosure they would welcome a reorganization since their intent had been merely to smoke Strandlund out. This sounded insincere to Fruehauf, since Dunham must have known for at least the last ten days that the Fruehauf group had proxies from Strandlund which gave them control. The RFC board was exceedingly cordial and receptive, with Dunham obviously in the driver's seat dictating RFC policy.

The meeting adjourned. Fruehauf returned at noon and the situation was completely changed. (Dunham's office record shows that he had phone calls from Jacobs and Merl Young.[19]) Dunham said that as far as he was concerned there was no solution other than foreclosure. He was outspoken in his resistance to any suggestions, constructive or otherwise, to help Lustron. His statements became incoherent and irrational. He was adamant that Lustron must cease operations.

19. Diary of Walter Dunham, testimony before Fulbright subcommittee, *op. cit.*, pp. 1363, 1365.

What had happened to change Dunham's attitude and make him do an about-face within a couple of hours? Fruehauf was sure of the answer. Even though he had told Gottlieb not to hire Rosenbaum, nonetheless Gottlieb had, in fact, signed a retainer agreement. Commercial Home had signed a retainer with Rosenbaum for $10,000 down and $90,000 additional, if an acceptable plan were effected. Gottlieb had given Rosenbaum a check for $10,000 and Rosenbaum had promised that he would not deposit the check for a week.

After the early morning conference Fruehauf told Gottlieb that everything was going along fine. Gottlieb thereupon decided that he didn't need Rosenbaum and that he had better get back his $10,000. His brother, John, rushed over to Rosenbaum's office, said something like, "Please give me the check back," grabbed it and rushed out. Gottlieb later in triumph showed the check to Fruehauf. It is apparent that Gottlieb's miscalculation had resulted in a scuttling of the reorganization plan.

The strange aftermath is that Gottlieb, deciding that he had been overhasty, on February 23 went with another check for $10,000 to Rosenbaum to reinstate the retainer so that Rosenbaum could try to work out a reorganization plan. Nothing came out of it. Another plan for injecting new capital was offered to RFC, but it was too late, since the foreclosure suit was already in the courts. But Gottlieb had been taught a lesson according to the circumstances that Fruehauf had narrated. Col. Rosenbaum had told the truth. Through Merl Young he did have the RFC "in his hip pocket."

# · VIII ·

# THE RFC SCANDALS—III:
# MORE ON THE INFLUENCE RING

*Senator Capehart: Well, I cannot conceive—and
maybe you can—but I cannot conceive of any ability
that an attorney can use in getting an RFC loan. . . .
Is it a matter of filling out the forms, presenting a
balance sheet and presenting the facts, and that is
all there is to it? Is there anything else used?*

*Mr. Casey: Senator, you could never get a loan on
that basis.*

*Senator Capehart: I think you are about right.*

—Testimony of former Congressman
Joseph E. Casey, before Fulbright
Subcommittee investigating the RFC.

THE RFC was a political agency straight down the line. The
diary of Walter Dunham over a fifteen-month period shows
that he was contacted 226 times by officials of the Democratic
National Committee. The office record of Ed Willett shows
that he was contacted 70 times by phone by the Democratic
National Committee.

There were a few cases in which Democratic members of
Congress were involved. James J. Murray, Jr., son of the
senator from Montana, represented three hotels in Miami
Beach, including the Sorrento and the Saxony. The RFC reversed itself and granted a loan to the Sorrento after the Senator had written a letter to Hise and it subsequently enlarged
the credit when a bank declined participation.[1] Murray received a fee of $21,000.

1. Testimony before the Fulbright subcommittee on the RFC (82nd
Congress), p. 1280.

Mrs. Florence Bratton, secretary to Vice-President Barkley for twenty-six years, admitted contacting the RFC in behalf of a group of Detroit realtors who wanted a $1,100,000 loan to build a luxury hotel in Miami Beach. Charles E. Shaver, then counsel for the Senate Small Business Committee, accompanied her on the visit. The RFC had turned down the loan four times, but a few days after her visit, on May 8, 1950, it approved the loan. In the midst of the public furor, the promoters of the project abandoned the idea.[2] Shaver was indicted in June 1952 on charges of taking $3,100 in fees for using his influence in cases before the RFC and ICC and pleaded guilty to the RFC charges. Mrs. Bratton continued to hold her job with the Vice-President.

In December 1951 the Hoey investigations subcommittee released to the press, without public hearings, its accounts of the events in the Stutts Lumber Industries loan. Following is a summary of the accounts in the *New York Times.*

In 1949 the Stutts Lumber Industries applied for an RFC loan but the Birmingham office turned it down on the ground that the loan was an outright bail-out of creditors. On July 16, Washington examiner Hubert Steele flew down to Birmingham and drove to Thomasville. On July 18, the RFC granted a loan of $455,000 bypassing the Birmingham office. One of the conditions of the loan was that W. C. Ribenack, a Washington consultant, should be on the board of directors. After Steele left the RFC, his partner in advising on RFC loans was W. C. Ribenack. We shall meet Steele again in the Central Iron and Steel loan. Congressman Frank Boykin of Alabama had introduced Stutts to the RFC.

In December, 1950, RFC overruled the Birmingham office again and released 20,000 acres of land, in return for $7500, which the Boykin interests had leased to Stutts' company. In this way the land was exempt from foreclosure by RFC. Allegedly as part of the package deal Congressman Boykin in a

2. *New York Times,* October 22-30, 1951.

private luncheon for the RFC Board members at the Capitol on February 1, 1951, persuaded them to grant a twelve-month moratorium on payments by W. P. Stutts' company on its RFC loan even though no payments had been made and the company was $70,000 behind in its payments. In December, 1951, the FBI investigated embezzlements from the Thomasville bank in Alabama, and arrested Stutts; according to J. Edgar Hoover $300,000 of the RFC loan was used to cover up illegal loans which were made to Stutts.[3]

The main stream of influence, however, flowed from the administration, not from Congress. Political sponsorship was carried to the point where the Mississippi State Committee vetoed a loan to a concern in Yazoo City on the ground that counsel for the concern had not been loyal to Truman in 1948.

### Donald S. Dawson

When Dawson was examined before the Fulbright subcommittee, he showed a remarkable lack of the ethical values that one might expect from a Presidential assistant. He had a hard-boiled conception of what was immoral. Senator Fulbright commented that Dawson saw nothing wrong in the fact that his pal, Merl Young, held jobs with two RFC debtors at the same time.[4] He saw nothing wrong, moreover, in the fact that he, Dawson, paid three visits to the Saxony hotel in 1949 and 1950, on one occasion with his wife and daughter and that his bill was paid for by the Saxony on each occasion. The Saxony was a large-scale debtor of the RFC and at the time was negotiating for a relaxation of the loan restrictions.

For two years after the election of 1948, the important Dallas office of the RFC was in such a state of disruption that no work could be done, and the blame was evidently that of

3. *New York Times,* December 13, 16 and 21, 1951.
4. Hearings before Fulbright subcommittee, *op. cit.,* p. 1795.

Dawson.[5] L. B. Glidden, head of the office, shortly after the election, fell into disfavor with the local Democratic party. John Skiles, an official of the Dallas agency, who seems to have been on intimate terms with Dawson and Merl Young and was a friend of Ed Willett, led the campaign against Glidden on the grounds that he was a renegade. When Skiles had first talked to Bohannon about Texmass he told him, said Bohannon, that it was good for them to get acquainted since Glidden was going to get kicked out. He had backed Coke Stevenson for the Democratic nomination for senator rather than Lyndon Johnson and had played ball with Republicans. Skiles quoted Glidden as saying he didn't care if the Republicans got in because Tom Dewey would take care of him.

The chaos in the office is hard to describe. According to the chief of the RFC investigations division, "Skiles had what he called some kind of a list, and every time he had a fight with somebody he would put them on the list, and the list was supposed to be discharged when this new management came in. He was always pretending to run out in the hall and call his Washington contacts." In May 1949, Skiles, according to a friend, was getting discouraged with the strategy and called Dawson in Washington to ask for a transfer, but "upon calling he was told to sit tight, that everything was working well and Lindsley reports that Skiles was most jubilant." Skiles was in communication with Young, having written him, "Merl— L. B. Glidden, RFC head in Dallas, is N.G."

Senator Connally asked Dawson if there was anything to the rumor that Glidden would be displaced, and Dawson replied that he knew nothing about it. The situation was impossible now for Glidden. He appealed to the RFC, but Dunham and Willett supported Skiles. He wrote a letter directly to Dawson appealing to him on the ground that it was well-

5. Hearings before the Fulbright subcommittee, *op. cit.* See particularly testimony of John B. Skiles, pp. 782-860; L. B. Glidden, p. 827; and Berriam Lindsley, Jr., p. 788.

known that he was Skiles' sponsor. Dawson ignored the letter. In 1950, Glidden gave up and resigned.[6]

When the Fulbright report was published in early February 1951, Walter Dunham was sick and dispirited. He had either shelved his associates in the influence ring or they had shelved him. He claims that he was disillusioned with his former friends. On the other hand, he may have become remorseful that he had played on the wrong side. At any rate, he wrote a letter of resignation, left it signed in his desk and went to Florida. He told RFC Chairman Harber and Dawson of the letter—there is no indication that anyone else knew but his secretary, Mrs. Smoot. On February 19, the day that Truman sent Congress his plan to reorganize the RFC, Dunham got a call in Fort Lauderdale, Florida. Director Rowe from Washington opened the conversation by saying, "I am in your corner." He then proceeded to say that he understood that Dunham had left a letter of resignation and that it was vital that it go to the President that very day. Dunham wanted to know why the hurry, but Rowe wouldn't explain. The next day Rowe got the letter and rewrote it, using the last page with Dunham's signature. The earlier part Rowe made entirely different, with the key sentence, "I am being crucified on the Hill on account of my vote for the Lustron loan and the Texmass loan." Mrs. Smoot says that Rowe told her, "I think it is important that you get this letter over to Donald Dawson today."[7] Mrs. Smoot said that she would have to call Dunham because the letter was not accurate; Dunham had never voted for the Lustron loan since it was before his time. When she read it over the phone, Dunham refused to approve it. He called Fulbright and in his absence told an aide that he

6. For denial to Senator Connally, see testimony before Fulbright subcommittee, *op. cit.*, p. 853. Also see report, "Favoritism and Influence," p. 13.

7. Testimony of Mrs. Florence M. Smoot, p. 1666. For Dunham's letter of resignation and the version prepared by Rowe, see texts on page 1405 of testimony before Fulbright subcommittee, *op. cit.*

was returning to Washington because he was suspicious of what his associates were asking him to do.

The reason for the rush seemed obvious to Dunham—he was to be the "fall guy" or the "goat."

### American Lithofold[8]

American Lithofold of St. Louis, which printed and distributed business forms, had a motto which it had tried and found true: "A GOVERNMENT EMPLOYEE IS A COMPANY'S BEST FRIEND."

Lithofold adopted the principle that a dollar invested in a government employee was its best investment whether it wanted a government contract, some tax help or an RFC loan.[9]

R. J. Blauner was president of American Lithofold. He filed his income tax in Chicago. G. Elmer Brown, accounts and collections supervisor of the Chicago Internal Revenue office, was Blauner's guest for four days, with his wife, at Blauner's home in Florida. The plane tickets to Miami Beach and return were paid for by Blauner, but Brown insisted that he repaid the amount in cash.

Walter Doxon was an internal revenue group chief in the Newark office. That is where the returns of R. A. Blauner, son of R. J., were audited. There was evidence that Blauner was having trouble with tax delinquencies. Doxon was paid $7,500 for introducing R. J. Blauner to John L. Kelly, besides receiving gifts like a Polaroid camera and a turkey. He was

8. Unless otherwise noted, the matters discussed as to the American Lithofold Corporation loan from the RFC are taken from the hearings before the Hoey investigations subcommittee, "American Lithofold Corporation," (82nd Congress), September 13 through October 5, 1951, and the report of the Hoey investigations subcommittee, "American Lithofold Corporation," (82nd Congress).

9. For G. Elmer Brown, Doxon, Kelly, O'Connor, and Moling, see report of Hoey investigations subcommittee, "American Lithofold Corporation," *op. cit.*, pp. 13-17.

retired from service. He received his money as an equal split with John L. Kelly, regional investigation supervisor of the wage and hour division, who earned his money, he admitted, with one phone call to a friend, which got the business for Lithofold.

Marion O'Connor worked in the Newark tax office with Doxon. She audited at least one year's return made by R. A. Blauner. Her brother was assigned a Blauner return to audit by Doxon. She was the guest of R. A. Blauner at the 1947 World Series and she spent two weeks in Florida as Blauner's guest.

Charles B. Moling was civilian chief of the printing contract branch of the Air Force in Washington. He was in a position to get advance information about bids and could influence the general policy for the procurement of printed materials, including business forms. He received loans of $6,100 from R. A. Blauner while he was with the Air Force, not to speak of gifts like a camera, perfume, World Series tickets, and a television set. He also borrowed $6,500 from another paper company, Laurel Printing. He left his $6,400 a year job to take a $25,000 job with American Lithofold as eastern sales manager.

In 1948, Lithofold needed some financing since it was paying twelve percent interest on a loan of $250,000 from a Chicago factoring concern. It decided that the best place to get the money was the RFC. It gazed at its motto, "A GOVERNMENT EMPLOYEE IS A COMPANY'S BEST FRIEND," and drew inspiration.

In the fall of 1948, Lithofold hired James P. Finnegan who was then collector of internal revenue in St. Louis and who was later to be convicted of official misconduct for his receipt of money from Lithofold. Blauner said that he hired him as a sales promoter, but Finnegan's sales contacts at best consisted of two or three contacts which netted no sales. Finnegan was paid $45,000 in fees and expenses. Finnegan's obvious contribution was to help with the RFC loan. He visited the St. Louis office on many occasions and did contact work in Washington, notably with Ed Willett. (Finnegan arranged a deal for Lithofold with Joe Nunan and J. B. E. Olson, which will be discussed in Chapter Fourteen.)

Finnegan was riding high, wide and handsome.[10] When asked at the hearings how he managed to spend $8,000 for expenses for Lithofold, he replied, "I could take you out on a party at the Shoreham and spend $800 so fast you wouldn't know it was gone." In June 1950, according to the St. Louis *Post-Dispatch,* he had been working on a plan with Merl Young and Rex Jacobs to acquire the Nicaro nickel plant which the government owned in Cuba. He was in frequent conversation with Bill Boyle, who was in the same hotel, but the deal did not work out. Boyle said that the entire story was a fabrication although, he said, he knew that Finnegan and Jacobs were interested in the deal.[11] Finnegan was also reported by that paper to have received $50,000 from the Zenith Corporation. According to Rep. Kean, he was to persuade the Justice Department to put pressure on movie companies to give films to Zenith for phonevision experiments. But the antitrust division had already acted to do that, so that when Finnegan approached Zenith, the information had leaked to him— he was therefore sure of success.[12] In January 1955 St. Louis newspapers had front page stories that a grand jury had started to look into a payment of $82,500 which Rex Jacobs had made to Hugh Finnegan in 1951. We shall meet Finnegan again in the tax scandals.

Oliver R. Kraft, assistant manager of the St. Louis office,

10. For employment of Finnegan see testimony of James P. Finnegan, before Hoey investigations subcommittee, *op. cit.,* p. 657.

11. *New York Times,* August 7, 1951. Jacobs discussed his plans for the deal, mentioning Finnegan and Young, before the Fulbright subcommittee on the RFC, *op. cit.,* p. 1706.

12. Hearings before the King subcommittee on the administration of the internal revenue laws (82nd Congress), p. 1706.

where the Lithofold application was filed, went on a five-day fishing trip with R. A. Blauner in Minnesota for which his expenses were paid by Blauner. The loan application had been turned down by the St. Louis office by that time, but Kraft was fired immediately after the admission.

The loan application had tough going. The St. Louis office objected to the fact that the management was milking the company. R. J., his son, R. A., and his son-in-law were taking out over $200,000 a year. Besides, instead of buying carbon paper in the open market, it was buying it from its subsidiary, American Carbon Paper, at a high price. The St. Louis office refused to approve the loan. Merl Young had called the office about the loan.

Finnegan then proposed to Blauner that he hire Cecil Green, which he did at $10,000 a year. Cecil Green was from Kansas City, was connected with the Pendergast machine, and knew the President well. He had no White House pass but had no difficulty gaining admittance. His daughter, Shirley Green, worked at the White House with Lauretta Young. He had been a saloon keeper in Kansas City and had a garbage truck. This background obviously qualified Cecil Green as an expert on RFC affairs.[13]

Frank Prince, who was chief of the loan operations division of the office of loans, RFC, until he was fired, stated that Green contacted him on about twenty different loan applications.[14] Dunham's diary shows twenty-nine calls from Green, who was also a friend of Ed Willett. In connection with one loan for $45,000, in which Green was interested, Willett called Prince into his office on at least five occasions; Prince admitted it was high-pressure by Willett. Green received sums of varying amounts from different applicants. From McPike Drug Company, which got a loan of $700,000, he got a fee of $5,000.

13. Testimony before Hoey investigations subcommittee, *op. cit.,* pp. 637, 674.
14. Testimony of Frank Prince before Hoey investigations subcommittee, *op. cit.,* p. 394.

Green scattered Lithofold largesse all over town.[15] Twenty-six Polaroid cameras costing $150 each were distributed. A camera went to Matthew Connelly in the White House and another to Charles Oliphant, general counsel for the Bureau of Internal Revenue. Prince was the recipient of many gifts, a turkey, a ham, camera, perfume, oranges; Prince did not think it was objectionable to receive a small ham.

> SENATOR McCARTHY: How large a ham do you think an RFC official should take?
> MR. PRINCE: I would say, 8 pounds, 8 or 9 or 10.
> SENATOR McCARTHY: How about, let us say, if he took one that weighed 11 pounds. Would you say that was improper?
> MR. PRINCE: I would stop at 12.

There were so many objections on financial grounds to the Lithofold loan that it got nowhere. R. J. Blauner was pressing Green to "call the White House in an effort to get some 'high influence' used to accelerate the approval of our loan." In the course of the negotiations Cecil Green suggested that Bill Boyle be hired.

### Lithofold and Bill Boyle

The Lithofold loan application was declined at all levels in St. Louis. The Washington examiner and RFC review committee declined the loan, and, thus, on January 13, 1949, the loan was declared automatically declined. There was a steady objection that the company had been "bled white." On January 14, Lithofold asked for a reconsideration of a refunding loan of $548,219 or a working capital loan of $125,000. RFC Director Willett asked Dodds, chief of the small business division, to suggest a financing plan. Since the loan was above

15. Report of Hoey investigations subcommittee, "American Lithofold Corporation," p. 16, *op. cit.*

$100,000, it was not within the jurisdiction of the small business division. Two examiners in this division recommended decline. Two other examiners in the office of loans recommended decline. On February 28, the board recommended decline by a vote of 2 to 1.

On the afternoon of February 28, within a few hours after the declination by the board, R. J. Blauner, Cecil Green, and John Toole, an employee of Lithofold's who was formerly chief loan analyst for the Smaller War Plants Corporation, called upon William M. Boyle, Jr., vice-chairman of the Democratic National Committee.[16] At the request of this group, Boyle immediately telephoned Chairman Hise to make an appointment for the officials. The officials did not need a call from Boyle to see Hise. Toole had called on Hise often before. After Boyle made the appointment, Blauner and Toole went directly to the RFC where they conferred with Hise. On March 3, three days after the loan was declined, the board voted an $80,000 working capital loan by a vote of 3 to 1. No new facts were presented. The loan went through with breathtaking speed. Of the action of one top RFC official in cutting through the red tape, Toole recorded in his diary "that was the quickest, most fruitful response I ever received from a request of an old friend."

Four months later, on June 30, Lithofold submitted an application to RFC in St. Louis for a $500,000 refunding loan. The loan application was declined at all levels in the St. Louis office. A loan of $465,000 was approved by a Washington examiner who had been assigned to the loan by Frank Prince. The Washington review committee recommended decline. On September 30, the board approved a loan of $465,000. Then, in order to eliminate the factoring company, the RFC approved another $100,000.

Boyle had been recommended for hiring by Cecil Green,

16. For Boyle and RFC loan, see report of Hoey investigations subcommittee, "American Lithofold Corporation," *op. cit.*, pp. 7-11.

who had been at one time employed by Boyle as an investigator for $5,000 a year. Boyle was hired about the middle of February at a retainer of $500 a month, at a time when he was unpaid vice chairman of the Democratic National Committee. Boyle's defense was that he had cut off his retainer from Lithofold when he became a paid official of the Democratic Committee in April. He admitted that he had collected $1,250 but stated that he had done nothing for Lithofold except arrange an appointment in his official capacity. That appointment, however, seems to have been the trick which got the Lithofold Corporation $645,000.

The St. Louis *Post-Dispatch,* defying Boyle to sue it for libel, printed an article by Theodore C. Link stating that the fee was actually $8,000. This charge triggered the Lithofold probe. The significance of the difference between $1,250 and $8,000 is that the latter sum would be recognition that Boyle did something special for Lithofold.[17] When Boyle became a paid official the retainer was shifted to Boyle's law partner, Max Siskind. Boyle had endorsed his last check of $250 for half a month over to Siskind. Siskind had received a total of $14,500.[18] It was the contention of the St. Louis *Post-Dispatch* that half of the sum received by Siskind was money that was paid to Boyle. Link claimed that he could produce two people in St. Louis who would swear to the truth of the allegation.

This charge is substantiated by some external evidence cited by the Hoey committee. It said that Siskind was not called upon by any responsible official of Lithofold for legal services. Moreover, Lithofold did not even know who Siskind was. The first check to him was made out to Sam Siscon, the next was made out to Sam Sisson, and the next two to Sam

17. Report of Hoey investigations subcommittee, "American Lithofold Corporation," *op. cit.,* pp. 1, 2; testimony of Theodore C. Link before Hoey investigations subcommittee, *op. cit.,* p. 973.

18. Report of Hoey investigations subcommittee, "American Lithofold Corporation," *op. cit.,* p. 5.

Siskind.[19] The books of Lithofold also confirmed the suspicion that Boyle was still being paid when he took over the job as chairman. Boyle and Siskind were both listed on the records of the corporation as salesmen rather than as attorneys and the fees were entered as sales commissions. Blauner claimed this was done for accounting reasons, but then the regular legal fees were carried as legal fees. The Boyle and Siskind accounts were carried on the books as a single-commission account. Miss Janet Boone of Lithofold, who made up the monthly commission statements, was told sometime in 1949 to keep the statements of Boyle's commissions turned over on her desk so that the information would not become known to her fellow employees.[20]

Bill Boyle's name was a powerful one with RFC, as is evident from other cases Fulbright brought to light. In September 1950 the Fulbright committee learned that the RFC was about to consummate a sale of certain properties it owned to the Starrett Television Corporation, owned by Jacob Freidus. Freidus and his stepfather Sam Aaron were under indictment for tax evasion and the case was set for trial. After inquiry by Fulbright, the RFC reconsidered the matter and cancelled the sale a few days before Freidus and Aaron went to prison. No Dun and Bradstreet, an elementary precaution, had been called for from Starrett, even though one had been asked from another potential bidder. The attorney for Starrett, Leo B. Parker of Kansas City, had been introduced to Dunham by Boyle and that was a sufficient warranty.[21]

On October 13, 1949, Boyle called Dunham, according to his diary, re George Tribble. On October 17, Dunham called Boyle back, advising him that RFC had recommended Trib-

19. Testimony of Max Siskind before Hoey investigations subcommittee, *op. cit.*, p. 783.
20. Report of Hoey investigations subcommittee, "American Lithofold Corporation," *op. cit.*, p. 5.
21. Report, "Favoritism and Influence," by Fulbright subcommittee on the RFC (82nd Congress), p. 22.

ble for a directorate on the board of Preferred Accident Insurance Company. On July 19, 1950, Merl Young called and discussed appointing Tribble to the presidency. "Mr. Dunham said in view of the investigation being conducted at the present time, the safest course to follow is to do nothing until the report is completed."[22]

## Central Iron and Steel

In a surprising number of cases, after an applicant for an RFC loan had been successful in his loan application, an RFC employee involved in the loan joined the organization at a fancy salary. Of course, the contact might have given an applicant firm the opportunity to get a first hand impression of the competence of the RFC employee. The acumen, too, of the examiner in seeing the merit of the application might also have incited the admiration of the applicant.

John E. Toole, as we have seen, who was a top man in the loan division of the Smaller War Plants Corporation, joined Lithofold after it had been successful in wangling a big SWPC loan.[23] As we have seen, James C. Windham, who was an assistant to Director George Allen of the RFC, was employed by F. L. Jacobs shortly after that firm obtained a loan of $3 million from the RFC. There were Merl Young and Lustron. John Haggerty, head of the Boston RFC office, took a $30,000 a year job from the trustees of the Waltham Watch Company. less than a week after negotiation of the loan.[24]

Allen Freeze took a $25,000 a year job as vice president of Texmass. As an RFC employee, he had been active in the

22. Hearings before the Fulbright subcommittee on the RFC, *op. cit.*, p. 1390.

23. Hearings of Hoey investigations subcommittee, "American Lithofold Corporation," *op. cit.*, p. 204.

24. Hearings before Fulbright subcommittee on the RFC, *op. cit.*, pp. 670, 750.

preparation of material favorable to the loan. In June 1951, administrator Symington announced that Freeze, while assistant controller of RFC, had actually been vice president of Texmass since April 18, 1950, and had submitted documents in connection with the Texmass loan.[25] He left the RFC on September 28 at the time the loan was granted. Somehow, while he was working for RFC nobody knew that he was working for Texmass even though his name was on Texmass documents.

One of the most suspicious cases occurred in connection with the successful application of Central Iron and Steel Company, in which the applicant was represented by Col. Joseph H. Rosenbaum and Joseph E. Casey.[26]

The loan application of Central Iron and Steel, a subsidiary of Barium, would be concededly most difficult to get through the RFC. The reason was that Barium Steel had a practice of milking the subsidiary companies which it owned. The head of Barium was Joseph A. Sisto, a person of most unsavory reputation. In the Jimmy Walker scandals of 1932, it was revealed that he had given the mayor of New York City $26,500 in bonds at a time when the regulation of city cabs in which he was interested was being considered by the board of estimate. His brokerage firm was declared bankrupt in 1930. The New York Stock Exchange had expelled him in 1938 for violating its rules. The Philadelphia examiner, Jantzen, who recommended decline, stated, "Barium's methods of company acquisitions appears to be to pay the purchase price from the proceeds of a loan from a financial company and then to repay the financial company from money it borrows—'takes'—from the business so acquired." Of Central Iron and Steel, he said, "the men who comprise the operating management of the

25. *New York Times*, June 19, 1951.
26. The matters in this section on the loan to Central Iron and Steel are brought out in hearings before the Fulbright subcommittee on the RFC, *op. cit.*, pp. 1413-1584, and report, "Favoritism and Influence," by Fulbright subcommittee, p. 9.

business ... are now subservient to the reckless Mr. Sisto who heads the parasitical Barium Steel and who has no sustained record of success in any line. ... His practice of putting nothing in and taking everything out has worked to the immense detriment of the applicant and to other Barium subsidiaries."[27]

All along the line through the various echelons, a recommendation for decline was made. There was no possibility of participation with a bank. In the RFC, an examiner, Brodie, was preparing a report for decline. The situation was desperate for Rosenbaum's client. Then Ed Willett came to the rescue. He took the case away from the Washington examiner, Brodie, and gave it to his handpicked examiner, Hubert Steele. "I told Mr. Steele to go up and see if he could work out a loan," testified Willett.[28] Now the appraisal of Central Iron and Steel changed miraculously. Steele went to the applicant's mill and was impressed with the knowledge of the owner with current trends in the industry and production know-how. "This examiner found Barium's practices ethical and a typical example of outstanding business acumen."[29] A justification cited for the loan was that President Truman had wanted more steel produced. Barium and Central, however, Fulbright pointed out, were not manufacturers of ingot steel, which was the steel in short supply. They were fabricators. Their total production of steel amounted to less than half of one percent.

Who was Hubert Steele, known in RFC as "Hub" Steele? He was a close friend of Ed Willett. He was also a close friend of Merl Young, having trained him as an examiner, and his daughter worked in Young's office. He was one of those who had propagated the myth that Merl Young was related to the President.

27. For Joseph A. Sisto and Barium Steel, see testimony before Fulbright subcommittee on the RFC, *op. cit.,* pp. 1495-535.
28. Testimony of Willett before Fulbright subcommittee on the RFC, *op. cit.,* pp. 1560-564.
29. Testimony before Fulbright subcommittee, *op. cit.,* p. 1549.

In May, 1949, the RFC approved a loan of $3,300,000. On June 3, the RFC approved a loan of $4,700,000 in place of the loan previously approved. Earlier that day, Dunham and Willett had lunch with Dawson and Boyle. In August Central Iron asked for another loan of $1,900,000, which was reduced to $1,650,000. Wires were sent from various outside parties like the Phoenixville Chamber of Commerce and a congressman, pressuring for the loan. Copies of these wires were found in Rosenbaum's files. The Philadelphia examiner again pleaded for decline. "The reckless Mr. Sisto makes promises first and then looks to others to supply the cash." Hubert Steele recommended approval and the board voted approval of $1,650,000. One month later, Hubert Steele left the RFC and joined Rosenbaum's law firm at $15,000 a year with an immediate payment of $5,000. His daughter was given a job by Rosenbaum. One-third of Steele's salary was to be paid by former Congressman Joseph E. Casey, who was an attorney for the applicant.

In January 1950, Central asked for a third loan of $1,000,000. The Philadelphia examiner recommended decline. Central was already violating the provisions of the loan and had recovered $800,000 from the sale of excess inventory and scrap but had not remitted $300,000 to RFC as was required. The board voted down the third loan 3 to 2 with Dunham and Willett voting in favor of it. Merl Young put pressure on Dunham. His diary of July 20 states that Merl Young called regarding Central Iron and Steel. On July 27 the board approved a disbursement of $270,000 under less rigid conditions and eased its working capital requirement.

Truman did not take any action against any of the personalities involved in the RFC scandals. Donald Dawson stayed on, and Mrs. Young resigned voluntarily. Merl Young served a jail sentence for perjury. He had lived recklessly in Washington during his heyday, having bought a $52,000 home, and had told the committee that his liabilities exceeded his assets. However, he must have salvaged a good deal out of it. He and his wife bought a $100,000 motel in Florida. In this land of opportunity, Merl Young had started at the bottom and had bettered himself.

# · IX ·

# FOR TAX HELP SEE
# DEMOCRATIC NATIONAL COMMITTEE

*The Democratic party was in battle. It was an insti-
tution for which I had the highest regard and loyalty
and in a war, sir, you tend to adopt the devil's ethics
rather than normal human ethics.*

> —JUDGE WELBURN MAYOCK, testifying
> before the Kean subcommittee on the
> administration of the internal revenue
> laws.

THE investigation of the tax frauds during the Truman administration was conducted by a subcommittee of the House
Ways and Means Committee under the chairmanship of Cecil
R. King, Democrat of California. They were continued in the
Eisenhower administration by a subcommittee of the House
Ways and Means Committee under the chairmanship of Robert W. Kean, Republican of New Jersey. The revelations
produced by the Kean investigation were, in some respects,
more damaging than those under the King investigation,
though they received far less publicity since the scandal
era was past. The Kean committee had the benefit of a
prolonged study of the remarkable conversations in a
telephone log which was left behind by Charles Oliphant,
general counsel of the Bureau of Internal Revenue, who resigned in December 1951, when his friendship with the fixer,
Henry Grunewald, came to light during the testimony in the
Teitelbaum case. Originally, the King committee was able
to examine only excerpts. Later, it was able to obtain the en-

tire log, to pore over it and to follow leads. All the cases discussed in this chapter were brought out in hearings before the Kean committee.

An understanding of the administrative set-up in the tax field is necessary. The Treasury was headed by its Secretary, John Snyder, and the Under Secretary, Edward H. Foley. Thomas J. Lynch was general counsel. The Bureau of Internal Revenue is part of the Treasury so that its general counsel, Charles Oliphant, was actually assistant general counsel of the Treasury. Where Oliphant approved criminal prosecution the case was sent to the tax division of the Department of Justice headed by Theron Lamar Caudle, who exercised considerable discretion as to whether prosecution should be conducted. Caudle's division was in charge of considerable civil tax litigation, as in the federal court of claims.

## Judge Mayock Raises a Contribution[1]

The circumstances in the Mayock case raise a strong suspicion that a tax ruling was given under the exigencies of the 1948 campaign to raise $30,000 as a campaign contribution in order to put Harry Truman on the air. It cost the Treasury Department and the taxpayers of the United States $7,750,000 in revenue. The Secretary of the Treasury, John W. Snyder, is implicated by the testimony which was given.

Judge Welburn Mayock claimed the distinction of having been the only man to unite the Democratic party in California—all factions agreed that they did not want him as a candidate for governor. Mayock, who probably wasn't entitled to use the title of Judge at all, regarded himself as counsel for the Democratic Committee in 1948 and was a member of the

1. All the matters discussed are taken from the testimony before the Kean subcommittee on the internal revenue Laws (83rd Congress), pp. 1365-539.

finance committee. He was assigned a quota of $30,000. It was difficult to raise money for the Truman campaign since the chances for the President's re-election were not regarded as good. William Solomon, who lived in New York, and who, incidentally, admitted that he was a friend of the fixer, Henry Grunewald, told Judge Mayock that he had a friend in his apartment house who had a tax problem involving millions of dollars. Mayock felt that he could be of help and so Solomon brought the two of them together.

The man with the tax problem was William S. Lasdon. The Lasdon family controlled drug patents from which they received an average of $1,150,000 a year as royalties under a contract with American Cyanamid Company. The family had little left after taxes since they were in the ninety per cent income tax bracket. The Lasdons established Lasdon Foundation, Inc., a charitable foundation to which the patents were transferred. They asked for a ruling that the payments by the Foundation to them be considered as capital gains, taxable at the capital gains rates of only twenty-five per cent.

Prior interpretations of the Bureau of Internal Revenue were against the position taken by the Lasdons. A string of attorneys were unsuccessful with the Bureau. The last of the attorneys was Norman Cann, who had formerly been an assistant commissioner of internal revenue. Mr. Cann advised Lasdon that the application for a ruling be withdrawn since a refusal to rule by the Bureau would be unfavorable to the Lasdons if the case were argued in the courts. This was done and the application was withdrawn on June 24, 1948.

Mayock at this point entered into the case. He had a talk with Lasdon, and, according to Mayock, there was no pretense as to what his role would be. The agreement was that Lasdon would pay $65,000 to Mayock if Mayock was successful. Mayock said he had told Solomon he was out to raise money for the campaign and that he was sure Lasdon understood it. "I knew and I think they knew as reasonable men that they were going or at least trying to purchase my services as a political figure rather than my skill as a lawyer, and I think that anybody who had occasion to regard all the facts and circumstances would come to the same conclusion even though it were not blueprinted and specified."

Norman Cann was told that Mayock was going to intervene in the case and Cann gave him a power of attorney. Under the rules of the Treasury, an attorney must file this power of attorney. This power of attorney was never filed by Mayock. Also, any contingent compensation agreement must be filed and this was not done. Cann also gave Mayock a brief summary of the facts of the case. He said in sending it to Lasdon that it was adequate "for the presentation of the character that Mr. Mayock plans to make." Cann explained in his testimony that "it was my understanding that he was going to argue the case on the policy level as distinguished from the technical level."

As a first step in getting the ruling, Mayock brought the matter to the attention of the Under Secretary of the Treasury, Edward H. Foley. Foley's duties did not specifically include supervision of the Bureau of Internal Revenue, but in the next two weeks, he made four inquiries of the chief counsel, Charles Oliphant, and Oliphant told him that the request had been withdrawn. His log shows that Foley replied: "That is when they thought they were not going to get it." On August 17, Mayock found that Foley was away on vacation and so he went directly to John W. Snyder, the Secretary of the Treasury. He denies that he told Snyder that a $30,000 campaign contribution was at stake but admits that it was common knowledge that he was active in raising funds and that "he knew that I was a busy little bee in the campaign."[2]

The wires now started humming as if the fate of the nation were at stake. The Secretary of the Treasury telephoned the Under Secretary at Newport, Rhode Island, where he was

2. See Kean subcommittee, *op. cit.*, p. 1423.

vacationing, asking for his report on the Lasdon ruling. Foley states that that was the only call of such a nature that he remembers. The Under Secretary thereupon called an attorney in the office of the chief counsel, who was in charge of the Lasdon case, a man named Price, and instructed him to report in two days. On August 19, Foley had a talk, too, with the acting chief counsel of the Treasury, Mr. Tietjens, who, according to Price, "indicated that he would have no objection if Mr. Oliphant should approve the application." According to Price, "I then called Mr. Foley and told him the results of my conversations with Mr. Oliphant and Mr. Tietjens. This morning Mr. Tietjens informed me that both he and Mr. Foley had talked to Secretary Snyder reporting the substance of my conversations with each of them."[3] On August 20, Mayock saw Snyder again. He left a brief with Snyder, but the merits of the case as presented by him apparently could not have been under serious consideration, since on that very date Mayock called Cann and told him that a favorable ruling would be issued.

It was not until September 22 that the favorable ruling was sent out. The Bureau had trouble with its legal help, who seemed to always be getting in the way when something important had to be done. Karl Price certainly knew the disposition of the Treasury officials, but on August 31, he submitted a strong memo recommending an adverse ruling. He said there were five cases now pending before the Bureau, which were substantially alike. All five applications, said Price, should be turned down since the transfer to the foundation was really not a sale at all. Oliphant, in a conference with Price shortly thereafter, told him that he felt differently, and Price had to write a justification for the opposite viewpoint.

Mayock pressed Oliphant for the ruling. He called him on September 22 and Oliphant said the ruling would be out in the course of the week. "Judge Mayock said that would be

3. See Kean subcommittee, *op. cit.,* pp. 1368, 1474.

too late." Immediately after the conversation, Oliphant called Lynch, general counsel of the Treasury, and asked who Mayock was. Lynch said that Mayock was counsel for the Democratic Committee. Oliphant then caused a rapid approval of the letter. As he told Lynch later in the day, "I took it to the Commissioner and got it signed. I called his office and left word it would be mailed."[4] He obviously meant that he had called Mayock, because Mayock called Cann and told him the ruling was on the way. Cann got the ruling the next day.

On September 28, Lasdon paid Mayock $65,000 in cash. Proudly Mayock took $30,000 to the Democratic National Committee at the Biltmore in New York and laid it on Louis Johnson's desk. He said, "Here is the $30,000 I have been trying to raise for the campaign." Johnson replied, "Judge, this is magnificent." However, it was returned to him in a few minutes because it wasn't in the form that it could be legally received under the Hatch Act. There were no names or addresses of the donors and there was a $5,000 limit for a contribution. So Mayock had to buzz around to get friends to write checks for the committee, for which Mayock supplied the money. A lot of people got credit for contributions which cost them nothing. Solomon and Louis Markus, who was a client of Mayock's and in whose offices Mayock met with Lasdon, both made out small checks to the Democratic Committee, saying that Mayock had given them the money. Mayock limited each contribution to $3,000, because above that amount an informative return must be supplied for income tax purposes. As for the remaining $35,000, Mayock either pocketed it or split it with William Solomon and Louis Markus, the latter claiming that they got nothing and Mayock got it all. On his income tax return Mayock filed an income of $17,500.

What did Mayock mean when he told Oliphant that a delay would make the contribution too late? The answer was

4. See Kean subcommittee, *op. cit.*, p. 1455.

that the $30,000 was required to put Harry Truman on the air. Mayock's explanation was a classic in frankness. "I know that we had various deadlines to meet because the boys at the committee made a contract for radio for speeches that they would be paid in advance. I think 24 hours in advance of the speech . . . we were up against a situation where we didn't have enough money to put the President on the air. There were several occasions and other occasions came up during the campaign when we couldn't meet the payroll."

In a reference to the Lasdon case, Oliphant noted, "This approval applies only to this case," and in spite of misgivings that Oliphant had expressed, the Bureau found a way to distinguish the other cases. "We are going to go ahead on Lasdon and try to hold the line on others."

At the inaugural banquet in 1949, the newly elected President, Harry S. Truman, praised Judge Welburn Mayock for his efforts in behalf of the party.

### Contributions to the Party

Richard J. Reynolds of Winston-Salem, North Carolina, treasurer of the Democratic National Committee in 1941 and 1942, on October 14, 1944, made a contribution to the Democratic State Committee of New York of $96,000. On February 27, 1947, he made two further contributions, one of $75,000 and one of $100,000. He contributed $39,110 to the Democratic State Committee of New Jersey. These appeared as business loans. On December 28, 1948, the deputy commissioner of internal revenue, E. T. McLarney, ruled that 90 per cent of the money which was not repaid to Reynolds could be regarded as a bad business debt. Similar consideration was given to a "loan" of $50,000 by Marshall Field of Chicago.[5]

Collections of the Young Democratic Clubs of America and the Chicago Historical Committee of the National Jefferson

5. See speech of Senator John Williams before Senate April 29, 1952.

Jubilee were held to be business expenses. However, when the New Jersey Republican State Committee sponsored a dinner in Atlantic City on December 30, 1950, the Bureau ruled that the purchase of tickets would not constitute a deduction although by New Jersey law such a purchase, if made in the ordinary course of business by one whose business is thereby benefited, is considered a business expense.

## The Oliphant Log

The telephone log of Charles Oliphant contained a verbatim account of his most intimate day-by-day conversations. It was most embarrassing to the administration. Due to his high position, all high policy matters of the Bureau of Internal Revenue funneled through Charles Oliphant. Under an agreement the King subcommittee was furnished with extracts from the log as they were requested, albeit with some delays. In September 1952, the committee delving into the decisions made by the Bureau in certain tax cases asked for an extract from the log in the case of Universal Pictures.[6] These extracts included conversations between Charles Oliphant and the Secretary of the Treasury, John Snyder. On September 18, the request was addressed to the commissioner. The commissioner balked, and this refusal continued even though the committee gave assurances (Chairman King was himself a Democrat) that no use would be made of the material in the Presidential campaign then going on.

The game of hide and seek with the log now began. On October 8, the district judge in Brooklyn at the request of someone in the U. S. Attorney's office, signed a subpoena calling for the production of the log, the subpoena being returnable within five days. The log thereby went to Brooklyn, and it was not until after it was there, on October

6. For matters discussed in this section about Oliphant log, see testimony before the Kean subcommittee, *op. cit.*, pp. 1502-19.

15, that the new counsel for the Bureau, Charles Davis, advised counsel for the King subcommittee where the log was. The Brooklyn grand jury, however, then in session on the tax frauds, was uninterested in it. The foreman of the grand jury knew nothing about it; the request had not emanated from him. So the log was sent back to the Justice Department in Washington.

Shortly afterwards, the King committee served a subpoena on the acting commissioner of internal revenue, Justin F. Winkle. On November 15, a conference was held by the Secretary of the Treasury, John Snyder, in his office, attended by Mr. Foley, Mr. Winkle, Mr. Lynch, the information officer, Mr. Siler, and Charles Davis. The conference was for the purpose of discussing a press release already prepared which would announce that Winkle in his capacity as acting commissioner of internal revenue had delivered the Oliphant log to Mr. Oliphant, who was no longer with the Department. This was the one avenue by which the log could be suppressed. If Mr. Oliphant received the log, he might refuse to deliver it up on the grounds of self-incrimination and a long legal fight might occur. In a Sunday session with his staff, Winkle considered the problem and wrote a letter to the Secretary in which he coolly refused to go along on various legal grounds which he cited. There was no alternative left but for the Treasury to surrender the log, and two days later it was delivered to the subcommittee.

The Brooklyn grand jury, which had been convened to consider the tax frauds, is directly related to the efforts of the administration to obstruct the King committee. The Bureau and the King committee had entered into an agreement during the investigation that no action would be taken on matters in which they were concerned prior to consultation among the three parties concerned, the Treasury, its Bureau of Internal Revenue and the committee.

At the end of January, the committee had concluded its first phase of its Washington hearings and had gone to San Francisco for hearings in King's own home state. The committee now was on the threshold of discoveries which reached into the vitals of the Bureau of Internal Revenue. They had evidence concerning four principal parties, Joseph Nunan, Daniel Bolich, J. B. E. Olson and Carroll E. Mealey. At this point, the Treasury and the Bureau went to Attorney General McGrath, and he agreed to convene a special grand jury in Brooklyn.

On February 11, the King committee was astonished to learn that eight agents who had worked with them on the Big Four cases had been summoned to appear before the Brooklyn grand jury, which was convened on February 18. The committee feared that once its files went to the grand jury they would be buried forever in the secrecy of its proceedings.

In the early hours of February 12, on direct instructions from King, chief investigator Dowling directed the movement of the files to Washington. They were taken by private car and placed in the custody of the sergeant-at-arms of the House of Representatives. On February 14, King accused the Treasury officials of trying to stop the investigation: "The action of the Treasury was in clear violation of an agreement that there would be no such action which could interfere with the investigation of the subcommittee without prior consultation. Moreover, we have obtained indisputable evidence that the Treasury experts familiar with the facts agree that presentation to a grand jury at this time was not advisable. Above all, we have clear evidence that the decision to refer the matter to the U. S. attorney in Brooklyn was made solely for the purpose of stifling the investigation of the committee."

## Secretary Snyder Intervenes in Tax Cases

The Oliphant log revealed that the Secretary of the Treasury, John W. Snyder, intervened actively in certain cases, particularly involving large companies. In the Schenley case, he intervened for John L. Leban, a prominent contributor to the Democratic party. He intervened for companies in which there was no evidence that a political contribution had been made or was involved. The important point, however, is that these were large companies which it was advantageous to please, whether for personal or political ends. Snyder's attitude, as revealed by the log, was that where he felt a favorable tax ruling should be given, he did not inquire about legal obstacles. Charles Oliphant, the chief counsel of the Bureau, whose sworn duty it was to enforce the law impartially, seemed willing to co-operate with his boss. The members of the legal staff inconveniently threw up obstacles by pointing out Supreme Court decisions, law, regulations of the Bureau, and past rulings.

It should be noted that the Bureau was under no compulsion to give a ruling, and it would have been good administration not to have done so in many cases. Regarding the charitable foundation group of cases of which Lasdon was one, a lawyer in the interpretative division wrote: "I do not think the Commissioner can be criticized for refusing to rule. Our function is to aid in the conduct of ordinary bona fide business transactions, certainly not to aid in prospective transactions which have as their principal motive the minimization of taxes."

*The Schenley Case.*[7] Louis Rosenstiel, the president of Schenley, is a name well-known in political circles. According to the Chelf committee, his vice-president, John L. Leban, raised up to $45,000 for the Democratic party in 1948, up to $25,000 in 1949, and $18,000 in 1950. In September 1950, the Internal Revenue Bureau was asked for a ruling on an oral agreement between Rosenstiel and John L. Leban, in which Leban agreed to purchase Schenley stock at two-year intervals until 1970 at the price the stock was selling for on

7. Testimony before Kean subcommittee, *op. cit.*, pp. 1325-44.

the day of the agreement in June, which was $26.50 a share. For example, if the price in 1960 were $60, he would have a gain of $33.50 per share, which he wanted to be declared nontaxable. In October the stock was already selling seven points higher than it sold in June. The regulations clearly stated that if property were transferred from an employer to an employee for less than its market value, the difference would be compensation. On October 19, an unfavorable letter was prepared by the taxpayers ruling branch for the signature of the chief counsel. On October 26, the interpretative division initialed the letter.

Then things happened. On October 26, Snyder phoned Oliphant. "There is a case I would like to have expedited. Understand it is with Dwan—sale of Schenley stock by Louis Rosenstiel to John Leban. Rosenstiel sails on Sunday and this must be gotten out immediately." Snyder called later in the day: "Louis Johnson [formerly Secretary of Defense] is interested in this thing. If there is anything we can do, let us try to help him out." Oliphant told Treasury Counsel Lynch that everyone was adverse, but after conferences, a favorable ruling was given, proving that where there is a will, there is a way. On October 31, a revised letter, granting the taxpayer's request, was sent down for initialing to the taxpayers ruling branch. The official who originally handled the matter refused to initial it, putting her reasons in a memorandum for the files. She objected on the ground that there was really no contract in existence. Under the New York statute of frauds, the oral contract was unenforceable; besides, the contract had been made only with the president and not approved by the stockholders.

It would be interesting to know whether Mr. Leban continued to purchase the stock since at this writing Schenley stock is selling for $20 a share.

*General Foods Case.*[8] Igleheart Brothers, Inc., wanted to

8. Testimony before Kean subcommittee, *op. cit.,* pp. 1345-63.

merge with General Foods and in early 1947 wanted a ruling that the receipt of General Foods stocks by holders of Igleheart would be declared nontaxable. The request was renewed in early 1948. There was no necessity for the Bureau of Internal Revenue to give a ruling since it was agreed that no reorganization would take place unless a favorable ruling were given. All along the line, the legal members of the Bureau ruled adversely under the analogous Court Holding Company case. Attorney Tomasulo in the interpretative division of the chief counsel's office expressed an unfavorable opinion, and he was backed up by his chief, Mr. Atkins. On December 21, Secretary Snyder phoned Oliphant about the case and Oliphant said, "I will run it down right away." The next day there was a conference at which Oliphant made it clear that the transaction should be tax-free and that a favorable ruling should be issued. On December 29, Oliphant called Snyder's secretary and said, "Will you tell him favorable ruling is in the mill." Attorney Tomasulo was instructed by Oliphant to prepare a memorandum favorable to the ruling. He did so, but refused to initial it because he did not agree that what the memorandum stated the law to be was the law.

The following March, Igleheart's attorneys went to the Secretary's office and got a closing agreement. This is stronger than a ruling because it can never be subsequently upset. The original ruling was given on the firm understanding that no closing agreement was to be requested.

Snyder called again about a case involving a corporation in which Igleheart had a substantial interest. Oliphant jumped with a favorable ruling the very same day that Snyder called. On November 9, 1950, the following conversation took place:

> SNYDER: See if you can find anything on Igleheart, Igleheart Brothers, or International Steel Company.
> OLIPHANT: I will check it and I will call you.

Later in the day:

> OLIPHANT: We will mail that Igleheart today—favorable.
> SNYDER: Good work.

*Universal Pictures.*[9] This company made an application for a refund of excess profits tax paid in the war period, a so-called "section 722" case. The agent who went to California to make the study was the recipient of substantial favors from Universal Pictures at the time he was working on their case, such as the payment of hotel bills and airplane tickets for his family to visit him. He made a recommendation for payment of $21 million by the government. On August 9, 1948, the day before the agent submitted his case report in New York, Secretary Snyder called Oliphant and said that he wanted the case expedited. Oliphant called the excess profits tax council in Washington: "The Secretary asked me about a case. Universal Pictures. He was interested in it not going back to the field." It was a general requirement that the field committee certify and review the agent's report before sending it to Washington, but a phone call by Oliphant from Washington to New York citing Snyder's interest resulted in shipping the case to Washington, the only time a field check had been omitted by the New York office.

When the excess profits tax council in Washington saw that there was no field certification, they sent it back to New York. After further delays, Snyder intervened again, after he had received letters from Universal Pictures. On November 30, Snyder inquired of Oliphant about the case. Oliphant inquired of the council: "I am a messenger boy because the Secretary called personally about it." In February 1949, the chairman of the field 722 committee was called to Washington and told to forward the case from New York without certification. The recommendation for the $21 million was intact. The

9. Testimony before Kean subcommittee, *op. cit.,* pp. 1572-86.

excess profits tax council in Washington reviewed the case and cut the $21 million down to $3 million, sending it back to New York for the certification it should have had in the first place.

*Frank C. Rand of St. Louis*.[10] Mr. Rand was suing in the Court of Claims for a refund of taxes that he had paid. The case involved the taxability of income from a trust set up by Rand for his children, which income he used to pay insurance policies on his life. On October 14, 1949, he offered a compromise of $175,000 for his suit of $335,000. But in view of the taxability of the money he would receive from the government, the difference between the compromise and the money he was suing for amounted to only $30,000. Usually, the opinion of the Internal Revenue Bureau which was sent to the Department of Justice took two to three months. In this case, it took one day, October 17 to October 18. Mr. Oliphant recommended the compromise be accepted. The reason for the haste is this conversation. Oliphant called Snyder on October 18.

> OLIPHANT: On Rand, I am sending a recommendation to Justice that we settle by paying $177,000 [misprint for $175,000].
> SNYDER: Of course, and they said they would accept that.
> OLIPHANT: I think so. I have a copy of their offer, and it is a kind of merit settlement.
> SNYDER: You think this will fix it?
> OLIPHANT: I think so.

Ten minutes later, Oliphant called Theron Lamar Caudle, assistant Attorney General of the tax division.

> OLIPHANT: Frank C. Rand. That is a claim for refund. For your information, the Secretary is personally interested. I am sending you this refund of $177,000. I talked to the Secretary and told him I would ask you to be kind enough to expedite it over there.
> CAUDLE: Certainly will. Send it to me personally.

10. Testimony before Kean subcommittee, *op. cit.*, pp. 1586-96.

The memorandum recommending acceptance of the claim was written in the office of Mr. Oliphant by an attorney to whom he assigned the case, Julius M. Jacobs. The attorney, following instructions, wrote a memorandum citing reasons for accepting the compromise. He then signed out on annual leave for the rest of the day so that he would not have to initial the memorandum.

### Housatonic Dye[11]

Criminal tax cases are not the best reading for those with weak stomachs. Among malodorous tax cases, Housatonic Dye, or the case of Garry D. Iozia, is considered in a class by itself.

In 1945, Vincent F. McNally, special agent for the Newark office of the Internal Revenue Bureau, was assigned to an investigation of Housatonic Dye & Printing Co., owned by Iozia. Bolts of cloth would be sent for dyeing in the course of which they would be stretched before the dye was applied. The same yardage would be returned, but the excess or remnants would be sold and no tax reported. McNally concentrated on D. Brodie & Co., of which Max Kossov was a partner and which was purchasing the remnants. The case was built with the most meticulous and painstaking care. Records, including invoices, were compiled from 1943 on, including cash payments and identity of shipments. There were adding machine tapes and process sheets which listed the amount in yards and pounds of goods received. The tapes bore the handwriting of Mr. Iozia. The case was cleared by the Internal Revenue Bureau and sent to the tax division of the Justice Department for prosecution. The tax evasion ran into the hundreds of thousands of dollars.

11. Except where noted, all matters discussed as to Housatonic Dye were taken from testimony before Kean subcommittee, *op. cit.*, pp. 597-986.

Garry Iozia, facing ruin for his business if he were criminally prosecuted, acted in a panic. He switched lawyers, paying out money recklessly. In 1949, his lawyer was Paul Arnold, a former employee of the Treasury, who reported to Iozia the probability that he would be prosecuted. Arnold suggested that Iozia hire a Washington attorney, Wallace Cohen. Cohen was hired in late 1949 for $5,000 and a contingency of $45,000, if he were successful. Cohen recommended to Iozia that Joseph T. Sherman, a newspaperman, be hired. Sherman was cautious and he arranged his employment by Iozia so that it would appear that he was an employee at $300 a month from May 1950 on. The total payments to Sherman were $6500, plus a rug for $866. Fifteen hundred dollars, according to Iozia and Arnold, were paid to Sherman for expenses of a trip to Independence, Missouri, so that Sherman could confer with President Truman's brother.

In the same month, Cohen also brought Iozia together with a newspaperwoman by the name of Hope Ridings Miller. Iozia claims he paid her $5,000. Mrs. Miller and Mr. Cohen said that it was only $2,500. Iozia said that he hired her on the understanding that she was the secretary of House Speaker Sam Rayburn. Arnold says that he thought she was hired because she was a friend of Sam Rayburn's and could therefore get a conference for Iozia with an awesome, inaccessible tax potentate in Washington by the name of Theron Lamar Caudle.

It was the understanding of both Arnold and Iozia that Joseph T. Sherman was hired because he would be able to get a conference with Caudle. This was plain nonsense, since Mr. Caudle was the most conferrable person on earth. Rufus T. McLean, top Justice attorney, branded the understanding as "ridiculous." "I think he fell prostrate in offering conferences. We were conferred to death. . . . All you had to do was pat him on the back and say, 'Lamar, I would like to see you', and the chances are he would open his door and let you walk in."

Mrs. Miller said that she was hired to stir up sympathy for Iozia on the ground that he was being persecuted because he was an Italian and a Catholic. She says that she asked Rayburn to investigate and he reported to her that Iozia was not being persecuted. She inquired of Deputy Attorney General Ford, whom she met by chance at a dinner, whether Iozia was being persecuted and did some investigative work, the details of which she could not remember. That was worth $2,500. Incidentally, she did not report the sum on her income tax until she was questioned about it and then she filed an amended return that day.

In dealing with Mr. Cohen and Mr. Sherman, Mr. Caudle was dealing with high powered influence. In another connection, while testifying before the Chelf committee in 1952, Caudle stated that Cohen had come to him in the Housatonic Dye Case by way of an introduction from David K. Niles, administrative assistant to the President.[12] He said that he kept Niles informed of the status of the case, saying of his relations with the White House: "Yes, sir, when I am courteous, I am just really genuinely courteous." Joseph T. Sherman, who himself became embroiled in tax difficulties, had had a long connection with the Democratic National Committee. In the 1940 and 1944 campaigns, he had been in the speaker's bureau. In the 1948 campaign, he was on the finance committee. Sherman was seen constantly in the corridors of the Justice Department close to Caudle's office.

By August 17, Caudle had approved prosecution, but the case was not sent out for action as was generally done. A memorandum written by Caudle in October reveals for the first time Caudle's attitude after he had had a conference with Cohen. He was convinced that the case against Iozia was a gigantic hoax. As Rufus McLean said, this seemed to be an obsession with Caudle from that point on. In November,

12. Hearings before Chelf subcommittee to investigate the Department of Justice (82nd Congress), p. 1327.

Iozia was visited by two men, Robert Ables and Myer Meth. According to Iozia, they said that they could fix the case for $100,000 because Meth was a cousin of Meyer Rothwacks, who was the new chief of the criminal section of the tax division under Caudle. Iozia said he paid them a total of $8,500 in cash. Meth fixed up an appointment for Iozia with Rothwacks in Washington. If the fix were on, Rothwacks would give the signal by putting his arm around Iozia at the end of the meeting. Iozia understood after the conference that the fix was on, but he may have been taken for a ride; Rothwacks was said to have the characteristic of ending conferences by putting his arm around his visitor. Rothwacks, who was mentioned in the Teitelbaum case, said that he merely explained to Iozia the policies of the Department in criminal tax prosecutions.

On January 2, 1951, there was a staff conference on the case in the Justice Department. Caudle persisted in his belief that a hoax had been perpetrated. Turner Smith, Caudle's assistant, was heard by agent James Bonano saying to Caudle, "My God, Lamar, this is a document case." On January 10 to 11, a full-dress conference was held with the attorneys for Iozia. Iozia had gotten a conference—and what a conference. It included the assistant Attorney General in charge of the tax division, the first assistant, the chief of the criminal section, the attorney on the case, the assistant head of the Bureau's penal division, a special agent and a revenue agent on the case. Joseph Sherman attended over the protest of Rufus McLean, who pointed out that he was a newspaperman.

MR. TOBIN: Did you observe any marked attitude on the part of the Justice Department attorneys toward Mr. Sherman?

MR. McNALLY: Yes, sir. That is, in fact, what raised my curiosity as to who he was. When Mr. Iozia and his party entered Caudle's office, it was noted that Caudle and his attorneys acted with considerable diffidence to Mr. Sherman. I happened to be sitting on a settee in the office and Mr. McLean was sitting next to me, so I asked Mr. McLean, who is he . . . is he a lawyer or accountant. Mr. McLean said, no, he is director of public relations for the Democratic party.[13]

McNally got the definite feeling that Caudle was trying to kill the case and wrote a memorandum to that effect to his superior when he returned to New York. His superior told him to pull no punches in writing that memorandum. The revenue agent, James J. Bonano, who worked with McNally, agreed. McNally's charge was sent to Washington.

Caudle allowed the second year of the statute of limitations to expire against the individual on January 15. The third and last year would expire on April 21, and Caudle now took some remarkable steps. The tax returns of the chief government witness, Kossov, were called for to be examined to find out if he were a tax evader himself. Kossov, a 65-year old man with high blood pressure, was subjected to a gruelling examination for three and a half hours by four government attorneys led by Rothwacks, in an effort to ascertain whether his testimony could be shaken. It was unusual for a government witness to be examined in this fashion. They asked him questions such as, "Have you been a habitual gambler?" Another question was, "Didn't you think you were playing a dirty trick on Garry Iozia by selling goods and making money on it, and, at the same time, fixing a tax case against him?" Bonano testified, "I thought maybe they were trying to frighten him to death." The revenue agents were excluded on Caudle's orders, while Kossov was being examined. After the government attorneys finished with Kossov, the defense attorneys were given a whack at him, but Kossov stood firm.

Now, there was no course open but to present the case to the grand jury. Three steps, not taken in a tax case such as this, were taken: (1) The case was presented by the tax attorneys, not the U. S. attorney; (2) the jury was told the

13. Kean subcommittee, *op. cit.,* p. 888.

government was undecided as to the merits of the case; and (3) defense witnesses were allowed to appear before the grand jury.

All this was to no avail. The grand jury returned an indictment and Iozia subsequently pleaded guilty. Thus, it would appear that justice was done in the end despite the Department of Justice.

Iozia was milked to the end. He paid $8,000 to an attorney for four days' work during the grand jury hearing and $16,000 to the lawyer who represented him at the trial when he pleaded guilty. In all, Iozia paid out $105,000. The specific tax charge on which he pleaded guilty was evasion of $150,000 in taxes.

After he was indicted, Iozia berated Meth and Ables for misleading him. Rothwacks claims that he had not fed any information to his cousin, Meth, yet Ables had gotten some information from a very well informed source, because he had told Iozia about the expiration of the statute of limitations on January 15, a very unusual date. Meth and Ables also saw Rothwacks in Florida, after the indictment, and Ables on his return, in the presence of a witness, Theodore Boss, read from a memorandum which he held in his hand and stated to Iozia that the whole trouble was that he had the wrong attorney and that there was a revenue agent, Vincent McNally, who had been a stumbling block.

Joseph Sherman was involved in another case which grew out of his work in the Democratic National Committee and which was discussed in Sherman's testimony in Housatonic Dye. While Sherman was working in the 1948 campaign on the finance committee, a Mr. Vernard F. Bond was brought to him. Bond was in an income tax jam. Sherman took Mr. Bond over to the office of Mr. Caudle. Sherman said he told Caudle that Bond was going to make a contribution to the Democratic campaign, which he in fact did. Sherman later borrowed $5,000 from Bond. The policy of the Department at that time was not to prosecute if the trial might endanger the taxpayer's life. Doctors of the Public Health Service twice certified that Bond could safely stand trial. It was the policy of the government to adhere to these recommendations, but in the Bond case, Caudle's department took the opinion of Bond's own doctors that his health was too precarious to stand trial and so declined prosecution.

# · X ·

# THE FACTS IN THE CASE OF
# MR. TEITELBAUM*

*Mr. DeWind: When did that occur?*
*Mrs. Menkin: When he was taking motion pic-*
*tures that day. Mr. Nathan said something like "this*
*is my boy," and Mr. Caudle put his arm around Mr.*
*Nathan and said, "Frank, you know there is nothing*
*I wouldn't do for you." And Mr. Sale, as I said, ad-*
*vised me most definitely to be certain that Mr. Teitel-*
*baum not try to buck them because it involved*
*Oliphant, it involved Caudle, Larson and a man by*
*the name of Rothwacks or Rotwacks, who I also met*
*among others. It was about as messy a thing as any-*
*one could ever listen to.*

> MRS. SHYRL B. MENKIN, testifying
> before the King Subcommittee on
> the administration of the internal
> revenue laws.

ABRAHAM TEITELBAUM was a Chicago lawyer who had done
well in the world. He got his big break when he was hired to
represent Al Capone, and he took great pride in the fact that
he had cut a sliver off Capone's sentence. Teitelbaum's pros-
perity continued even when his benefactor departed from the
scene. He owned some office buildings in Chicago and had a
retainer from one association for $125,000 a year. Mr. Teitel-
baum also had income tax problems.

In November 1950, Mr. Teitelbaum was walking along

* All matters discussed in this chapter, unless otherwise noted, are
from testimony before King subcommittee on the Internal Revenue
Laws (82nd Congress), pp. 1297-1915.

145

Collins Avenue in Miami Beach with a friend, J. Kenneth Edlin, and ran into an acquaintance of Mr. Edlin by the name of Frank Nathan. Edlin must have told Nathan later that Teitelbaum had income tax trouble. Edlin still later reported to Teitelbaum that Nathan had given him a quick rating—he was a "good touch." Teitelbaum said that from that point on Nathan offered him his good services to help him out of his tax jam. Nathan had friends in Washington who counted, and he showed Teitelbaum an oil agreement on which his name was listed along with those of Theron Lamar Caudle, assistant Attorney General in charge of the tax division, and Mr. Jess Larson, who was head of the War Assets Administration.

A few months after Teitelbaum had met Nathan, in April 1951, the pressure became more intense. Nathan brought over to Teitelbaum's home a new friend, Burt K. Naster. According to Teitelbaum, Naster said, "there was a clique in Washington; that Mr. Charles Oliphant, Mr. Jess Larson and that there was a former Collector of Internal Revenue by the name of Mr. Joe Nunan and another man who had just resigned from the Internal Revenue Department, Mr. Schoeneman, were all together with Mr. Larson, comprised the whole —I wouldn't say a triumvirate, but a combine—who were looking around the country to see who were soft touches, or words to that effect." Nathan and Naster told Teitelbaum that unless he let them take care of his case he would be prosecuted and sent to the penitentiary. The price for their help to Teitelbaum and his partner, Paul R. Simon, was $500,000. Mr. Naster said that he himself had served a term in the pen for income tax evasion, but "if he had known at the time he was indicted what he knows at the time he was talking to me, he never would have had to serve in the penitentiary one day."

A son-in-law of Frank Nathan, Mr. Les Sale, visited Teitelbaum, he said, and out of the goodness of his heart told him that Nathan was a ruthless blackmailer and blackguard who was holding him, Sale, at his mercy. Nathan entertained a lot of political figures, and Sale, according to Teitelbaum, "was present at a conversation between his father and Mr. Theron Lamar Caudle and my name was brought up there; and that Mr. Lamar Caudle called a Mr. Charley Oliphant on the telephone to press my case in Washington." Mr. Sale's advice was that Mr. Teitelbaum would be smart to pay up and shut up.

Mr. Teitelbaum had a friend in Miami Beach, Mrs. Shyrl B. Menkin, widely known as Mrs. Teitelbaum. She had become a canasta partner of Mrs. Nathan in early 1951 and was frequently at her home. She says that she told Teitelbaum of visible proof of the friendship between Caudle and Nathan. At a time when Caudle and Nathan were in Nathan's home making pictures of Nathan's grandson, she was introduced to Mr. Caudle as Mrs. Teitelbaum, and he seemed to know who she was. She had seen Mr. Caudle put his arm around Nathan and say that he would do anything for him. Caudle in his testimony recalled the incident when motion pictures were taken in Nathan's home, but denied that he remembered meeting a woman introduced as Mrs. Teitelbaum. He suggested that Mrs. Menkin might have peeked through the window.

At this point, Teitelbaum said that he was becoming a bit nervous. This nervousness turned into anxiety when he returned to Chicago in April and found that his case had suddenly taken a turn for the worse. Instead of a settlement for a five-per cent penalty, his case had been forwarded to Washington.

Mr. Teitelbaum requested a conference in Washington with the Internal Revenue Bureau and says that he visited the Bureau with his attorney, Eugene Bernstein, on July 16. He was mistaken as to the date, since the records of the Bureau show that the conference was held on the 20th. He was given what he called a "Count of Monte Cristo" trial and got the impression the case was going unfavorably against him. Greatly agitated, he flew to Miami Beach, called Nathan and got together with him. This must have been on the morning of the 21st. Teitelbaum accused Nathan of putting the heat on him. "Frank, what did you do about my income tax matter?" And Nathan replied, "Well, what would you expect me to do? Wouldn't you, as a lawyer, put anybody in trouble if you could make half a million dollars? How can I go back to my friends and offer them less than $500,000?" Teitelbaum testified, "I told him if I had a revolver there I would have killed him."

Teitelbaum says that within a half hour after he had left Nathan, he received a phone call collect from Palm Beach, Florida. A man was speaking in a guttural voice with a thick German accent. He gave the fictitious name of Mr. Watson. He advised Teitelbaum to take Mr. Nathan and Mr. Naster's advice "because they have Mr. O., [meaning Mr. Oliphant] and Mr. Caudle, in their vest pocket."

Now Mr. Teitelbaum was in a state of intense nervous excitement. He left Miami on July 24 bound for Chicago and the plane stopped in Atlanta. From that point on, his story jibes with that of Mr. I. T. Cohen, a lawyer of Atlanta with whom he struck up a conversation in the lounge of the plane. Mr. Cohen related that "Teitelbaum was rather nervous looking and I asked him what was the matter. I thought perhaps it was his first flight or that he was nervous or upset from something." Teitelbaum told his story of the extortion ascribing it to a third person and mentioned the name of Theron Lamar Caudle. This was an astounding coincidence since Cohen was a very good friend of Caudle. In fact, his law firm had given Mrs. Caudle the mink coat which was a subject under investigation by the King committee. Cohen was casually interested. Then Teitelbaum said something which made Cohen sit bolt upright. He said that Nathan in his presence had called Caudle at the George Cinq hotel in Paris. This convinced Cohen that there was substance to Teitelbaum's story since Caudle had recently left for Europe and was, in fact, at that very time at the George Cinq hotel. Cohen asked Teitelbaum to put down his name and address on the back of a hotel bill of Cohen's and this in Teitelbaum's handwriting was submitted to the committee. Cohen understood that the third person was Teitelbaum. Alarmed by the story, Cohen called Turner Smith, Caudle's assistant in Washington, and they discussed whether to communicate with Caudle. Cohen wrote to Caudle in Rome, saying that he had something of the gravest import to discuss with him when he returned.

When Caudle returned from Europe in August (an expense-paid junket also a subject for the investigation), he met with Cohen, who related the extortion story. Caudle was highly indignant. He called Nathan on the phone in Cohen's presence and excoriated him. Caudle apparently knew who Teitelbaum was, according to Cohen, since he didn't have to go into any special explanation with Nathan. Caudle said to Nathan, "A very dear friend of mine has just told me about my name being mentioned in the wrong light in reference to the Teitelbaum case. I am getting off that oil lease I am on with you and Jess Larson." Caudle then dictated a letter to Larson in which he advised him that he wanted to relinquish his interest in the lease. It never occurred to Caudle as one of the chief law enforcement officers of the country to report the fix to the Attorney General or the FBI.

After dinner that night, Cohen was sitting with Caudle in his home. Cohen said that he thought Teitelbaum's story was quite intriguing. He told him about the call from a person with a guttural voice with a deep German accent and suggested that that voice could be traced. To that Caudle replied, "That might be Grunewald. He is a Dutchman."

The principals in the case were examined before the King subcommittee. Nathan and Naster branded the story as completely false. Said Nathan, "That man has made such a dirty, filthy lie it ain't in the book." He admitted the friendship with Caudle, which he said was close. He said that he was a friend of Jess Larson. Larson, former War Assets head and now head of the General Services Administration, made a dramatic appearance. He appealed to the committee. "I will not permit my reputation to be ruined by this sort of thing and with the help of Almighty God and you gentlemen in Congress, won't you please give us some legislation that will help us stop this sort of thing." There was great applause. He branded Frank Nathan as "a man who has hung around this town for four years to my knowledge, selling names, selling reputations, trying to put himself in a favorable position, and any businessman who falls for that sort of thing should have himself examined as a fit subject for an institution." He said that he had no business relationships or social relationships with Nathan. He said that in 1948 he had put Nathan on the "referred" list in the War Assets Administration, meaning that transactions in which he was involved would have to be closely examined.

The evidence, however, threw a good deal of doubt on Mr. Larson's version. Nathan said that he did not have the slightest idea that he was being socially ostracized until Larson testified. Nathan had appeared in public with Larson and, in fact, had paid for a room that Larson had occupied in the Waldorf-Astoria in New York. His name was on an oil lease with Larson's and Nathan testified that he spoke to Larson constantly about oil deals. Larson himself admitted that Nathan had called him at least thirty times at home and at least thirty times at his office. A telephone record shows that Nathan called Larson in Los Angeles in 1949 from the Waldorf and that the call lasted seventeen minutes. In June 1951, just a few months before Larson's testimony, telephone records show calls to Nathan from Larson's private number, four in June and four in July. Nathan said it must have been about oil deals. Nathan, moreover, had made a lot of money acting as an intermediary in deals with the War Assets Administration. In a sale of the used electrical equipment at the former

Alcoa Aluminum plant in Torrance, California, Nathan got a fee of $57,000. In a disposal of an oil refinery, he received $10,000.

Caudle testified that he asked Larson several times about Frank Nathan, in connection with an oil lease in Alfalfa County, Oklahoma, and that Larson replied that Nathan was all right. It appeared later that Larson was a good friend of the fixer, Henry Grunewald.

Caudle fraternized with Nathan even though he was well aware of Nathan's shady reputation. In fact, while Caudle was head of the criminal division of the Department of Justice, Nathan had been indicted and tried for a federal offense and Caudle himself had ordered retrial.

Burt K. Naster testified that he and Caudle took to each other immediately. He said that they became "platonic friends," which he defined as "we never talked about business." Naster was a person with a reputation as a fixer. He had been convicted of income tax evasion and sentenced to five years in jail. Although he had broken prison rules, he had been released under parole in the minimum time, a privilege which is accorded to less than one-tenth of one per cent of prisoners in federal penitentiaries. While on trips to Washington and Florida, he was violating parole. Naster said their first meeting was in connection with a passport which Naster wanted and that he went to Caudle's home to talk to him on Nathan's introduction. Caudle, chief tax prosecutor of the United States, was aware of Naster's prison record as a tax offender but it had not affected his friendship. Caudle, with staggering naïveté, said that he thought it was natural for Naster to approach him on a passport application, since the tax division had put him in jail and therefore the tax division might be expected to get him a passport. Naster did get this passport. Caudle said that he did nothing for Naster. However, a report in August 1953 of the Keating subcommittee to investigate the Department of Justice contains this statement:[1] "This application was first turned down by Rogers [parole board member] in September 1950 and was granted two months later in December. Rogers states that the favorable action was induced by a representation to him from Assistant Attorney General Caudle that the Justice Department was of the opinion that Naster's trip would contribute to the National Defense Program."

Nathan supported in part the shakedown story of Teitelbaum. Mrs. Menkin said that she had called Nathan in July at the Waldorf and screamed to him about the extortion attempt. Nathan admitted the call, stating that Mrs. Menkin mentioned a figure of $175,000 and that he had called Naster on his houseboat in Florida. Naster said that he was trying to get for Teitelbaum a lawyer by the name of Paul Dillon of St. Louis. Dillon, who was a friend of the President, was implicated in the paroles for the Capone gangsters, was the lawyer for Naster in his tax fraud case, and was himself convicted of tax fraud in 1954. According to Nathan, he said to Naster, "What are you trying to do? Why are you asking so much money for the case?" And Naster replied, "This is a high class lawyer. He wants a lot of money." Mr. Edlin, who originally had introduced Teitelbaum to Nathan, says that at Teitelbaum's instance, he called Nathan, who said there was no foundation to Teitelbaum's allegations. It was not he, but Naster who was trying to get the money.

Let us now go through the doors of the Bureau of Internal Revenue, into the files and find out what was actually happening to Teitelbaum's case. When Teitelbaum heard in April 1951 that his file was being forwarded to Washington, he immediately connected it in his mind with the threat which had been made by Nathan and Naster. In actual fact, however, the forwarding of the case had nothing to do with outside pres-

1. Report of Keating subcommittee to investigate the Department of Justice (83rd Congress), p. 122.

sure. The Internal Revenue Bureau had begun a drive against racketeers and on April 18 had requested that all tax fraud cases against racketeers should be transmitted to the Department of Justice. The Chicago office believed that the name of Paul R. Simon, with whom Teitelbaum had been connected in real estate operations, should be put on that list and therefore they combined Simon's tax case with that of Teitelbaum. In forwarding the case, the Chicago office expressed doubts and stated that there should be a grand jury investigation before indictment.

Insofar as racketeer cases were concerned, the Bureau had decided to give them expeditious treatment and had decided that such cases would be tried if there were a prima facie case, that is, if the case could get to the jury, without the usual test as to whether conviction was reasonably certain.

Mr. Richard C. Schwartz, assistant head of the penal division, who was handling the case, had some doubts as to whether or not this was a racketeer case. In fact, on the basis of the definition set by the Bureau at the end of April, it would not be so classified. He conducted the conference with Teitelbaum on July 20, which was routine. The "Count of Monte Cristo" hearing that Teitelbaum complained of was a product of Teitelbaum's hyperactive imagination at that point. On July 23, Mr. Schwartz received a call from his boss, Charles Oliphant, general counsel of the Bureau, in which Oliphant asked Schwartz what was the status of the Teitelbaum case. It was the first time that Oliphant had discussed the Teitelbaum case with Schwartz. Schwartz told Oliphant that after his conference with the taxpayer, he had decided there were certain matters that should be reconsidered in the field and that he had doubts as to whether or not this was a racketeer case. Schwartz then prepared the file to be sent back to Chicago.

On July 25, the file had been initialed and had gone out of the chief counsel's office mail room to be mailed. Mr. Schwartz then received another call from Oliphant, who inquired again as to the current status of the case. Schwartz replied that he had written a memorandum and started the case back to Chicago. Oliphant said that the memorandum should be recalled and the file sent to his office. The file was finally located either on its way to the post office or in the post office. It was then sent back to Oliphant's office. On July 30, the file was sent back to E. Riley Campbell, head of the penal division. He made a notation: "CO [Oliphant] directed me to look and advise on this matter. Specifically, is this a racketeer case to be processed as such." Mr. Schwartz considered the action of Mr. Oliphant as nullifying his memorandum. He then completely reconsidered the case and on November 2, transmitted the case to Oliphant with a letter addressed to Mr. Caudle's division of the Department of Justice, recommending prosecution. The intervention of Mr. Oliphant had therefore resulted in expediting the Teitelbaum case for prosecution.

Mr. Oliphant resigned the day before Schwartz's testimony. In his letter to the President, Oliphant said, "I find it beyond the limits of my endurance to protect my name and reputation and the prestige of the office I hold in the face of baseless and scurrilous charges." He appeared before the committee and testified that his action in the Teitelbaum case grew out of a request that had been made of him casually by his friend Henry Grunewald at a lunch on July 23. He stated that he had made the inquiry because Grunewald had asked him to, and he had informed Grunewald that afternoon that the Teitelbaum case would probably not be considered as a racketeer case. Mr. Oliphant could not remember why he had asked for the files to be recalled to his office on July 25. Mr. Oliphant was asked, "At the time you handed them back to Mr. Campbell [on July 30], you knew did you not, that the case would not go back to Chicago but would be considered for prosecution?" Mr. Oliphant replied, "I may well have."

In disclosing to Mr. Grunewald the fact that Teitelbaum was not on the racketeer list, Oliphant appears to have disclosed information which was so highly secret that when the names had been submitted to a Congressional committee, a few months earlier, they were not printed on the record. This was the first time Grunewald's name had been discussed before the investigating committee. Grunewald had gone to Oliphant's home, asking him not to mention him; but Oliphant said there was no choice.

On July 15, the night before Caudle left for Europe, he admits that he received a call from Burt K. Naster; he said that Naster begged him to call Henry Grunewald, but he refused because Grunewald had a shady reputation. That factor, as committee counsel abundantly emphasized, had not prevented him from having a close relationship with Nathan and Naster.

As stated previously, Teitelbaum told of a telephone call from a Mr. Watson, a guttural voice with a German accent, a collect call from Palm Beach, Florida. Nathan admitted that he knew an Arthur Brevaire of the Brevaire Engineering Company, which had its offices in room 424 of the Hotel Washington in Washington, D. C. Mr. Nathan said that Mr. Naster was closely connected with Mr. Brevaire in business. Mr. Brevaire, he said, came from Palm Beach, Florida. This engineering company, apparently, consisted of only Mr. Brevaire and a secretary. Mr. Brevaire was a Swiss who had a guttural voice with a thick accent. During the investigation, he went to Cuba and stayed there, so he could not be questioned.

There was a complex of calls with the Washington hotel as the hub. On July 22, a Sunday, telephone records show that at 11:20 A.M. Mr. Nathan received a collect call from a Mr. Watson, calling from Washington to Nathan in Miami. At 9:58 that morning, Nathan had called the Washington hotel. There were many calls in that period from Nathan to room 424 in the Washington hotel. On July 23, the same day that Grunewald talked to Oliphant about the case at lunch, at 12:15 P.M., Frank Watson called collect from the Washington hotel to Abraham at the phone of Mrs. Shyrl Menkin in Miami. That night, another phone call was made by Frank Watson from the Washington hotel to Abraham, collect person-to-person. On Wednesday, July 25, there was a call from the Waldorf to the Washington hotel, a person-to-person call to Mr. Brevaire.[2]

Mr. Henry Grunewald lived at the Washington hotel. Hotel bills for room 424 in the same hotel in the name of A. A. Brevaire were submitted to the committee, marked "to H. Grunewald, P. O. Box 244, Washington, D. C., paid September 19, 1951."

These are the facts in the case of Mr. Teitelbaum.

The testimony in this case presents some fascinating problems. That there was a shakedown attempt seems overwhelmingly probable. It also seems likely that Teitelbaum was in on the fix at some point and that the negotiations broke down over the amount. The Bureau had a record of the fact that in July 1951, Teitelbaum's lawyer, Bernstein, was saying in Chicago that the case was going to be fixed. Teitelbaum was no lily, and, in fact, he was subsequently indicted for income tax evasion. However, the fact that Teitelbaum was no lily was precisely the factor which might make him a "good touch."

The allegation that government officials were in league as a combine to shake down income tax evaders was, in the words of the Scotch verdict, "Not Proven." The intriguing question is why on July 15 Caudle refused point-blank Naster's request to call Grunewald. Did he balk at something he was expected to do? Caudle must have felt the need for an explanation because months later, before the Chelf committee, out of the blue he furnished a reason for Naster's call. "He

2. See also testimony of Henry Grunewald before Kean subcommittee on the Internal Revenue Laws (83rd Congress), pp. 1287-92.

heard from some source that my job was in danger, and he wanted me to meet Mr. Grunewald; that Mr. Grunewald was very close to higher-ups and he wanted me to meet him, that he could help me."[3] Ten months of deliberation had at least produced an ingenious reason.

About the black side of the case there could be little dispute. Two of the highest members of the Truman administration, Theron Lamar Caudle, chief tax prosecutor, and Jess Larson, head of the War Assets Administration, had held the dignity of their offices so cheaply that they had associated with shady or underworld characters in such a way as to make possible a shakedown or influence peddling of the most vicious type, whether or not it occurred or they were aware of it. Another high-ranking member of the administration, Charles Oliphant, general counsel for the Bureau of Internal Revenue, for no reason connected with the execution of his responsibility, had, after a contact with a tax fixer who was his close friend, Henry Grunewald, personally intervened in the case, an intervention which had acted to the detriment of Mr. Teitelbaum.

3. Testimony of Theron Lamar Caudle before Chelf subcommittee to investigate the Department of Justice (82nd Congress), p. 1340.

## · XI ·

# OF TAX-FIXING AND TAX-FIXERS

> *Mr. Keating. They would say, Well, this first attorney has no influence with the Department, so we will get one with more influence?*
>
> *Mr. Caudle. Yes, sir.*
>
> *Mr. Keating. And that was encountered repeatedly?*
>
> *Mr. Caudle. We repeatedly encountered that and the Bureau of Internal Revenue ran into the same thing. Mr. Oliphant ran into it.*
>
> *Mr. Keating. They would get one attorney whom they figured had pressure over in the Internal Revenue Bureau, and they would then switch to another attorney whom they figured could fix you fellows up?*
>
> *Mr. Caudle. That is right.*
>
> —THERON LAMAR CAUDLE, testifying before the Chelf subcommittee to investigate the Department of Justice.

### Theron Lamar Caudle[1]

AFTER President Truman dismissed Theron Lamar Caudle from his post as assistant Attorney General in charge of the tax division, Caudle said that he was "shocked to death." He put on a performance which adequately proved the point. A

1. All matters discussed concerning Caudle are taken from testimony before King subcommittee on the Internal Revenue Laws (82nd Congress) pp. 919-1904; Caudle's testimony before Chelf subcommittee to investigate the Department of Justice (82nd Congress), pp. 1159-1386; report of Chelf subcommittee to investigate the Department of Justice (82nd Congress); report of Keating subcommittee to investigate the Department of Justice (83rd Congress); Charlotte *News*, December 12, 1951.

person may be shocked when he is fired for three reasons: First, because of the direness of the event, whether expected or unexpected; second, because he was singled out for such treatment even though it may have been deserved and it was therefore unexpected; or, third, because he was personally blameless. Insofar as Mr. Caudle professed to be shocked for the third reason, his public exhibition was one of pretense, sham and ham. Analyzing the Caudle stream of consciousness, there is no doubt that he was genuinely "shocked to death" for the second reason.

As Caudle had meandered along the path of government service, he had foraged in convenient cabbage patches along the way. Caudle, however, took his cue from the world about him. He was repeatedly called on to fix cases. The atmosphere in which he worked was one of looseness, laxness and license. On the day he was fired he said that "regardless of tremendous pressures, like the gyroscope on the battleship, I have steered straight down the course." A month later in December 1951 before the King committee, he changed his story. No one had asked him to take an action that was improper. "I do not believe that I can ever remember of a single instance—not a single instance." In September 1952 before the Chelf committee, he talked of the "terrible pressure, which spreads out like a spider web in all directions." From the cases that were narrated, it was obvious that by that time Mr. Caudle had made a career of responding to pressures.

To those who watched Caudle testify, the big question was, how a man of his caliber ever reached such a commanding position. It was even more puzzling that he was chosen to discharge the post as head of the tax division. He had never handled a tax case in his private law practice. He had had no law practice in making out tax returns; he had never prosecuted a single tax case when he was U. S. attorney in North Carolina; yet he had been made chief tax prosecutor in this country to oppose the most skilled tax practitioners of the nation. When he became head of the tax division, he had appointed as his assistants two of his associates in the criminal division, Turner Smith and James McInerney, who also had no experience in tax work. The appearance that Caudle gave of limitedness was not illusory—he was limited. For example, in the Roy E. Crummer case, which arose when he was in charge of the criminal division, involving mail fraud against a bond dealer, an attorney working for Caudle stated that Caudle "didn't know a coupon from a bond" and four of his attorneys had to spend a day in Caudle's home trying to explain the case to him.

What Caudle lacked in ability, he tried to make up for by capitalizing on his undoubted Southern charm, his unsurpassed ability as a raconteur and his agreeableness. He was "on the make." By his own account, he was a wearied elbowbender on the Washington cocktail circuit and his new-found friends would be visiting him "always wanting something." He was often out making political speeches. He was given some credit for saving North Carolina for Truman in 1948, and he claims the Democratic National Committee listed him as one of the five who did most for the party in 1948. He courted the President's favor. In October 1951, less than three months before Caudle's dismissal, after Truman had returned from a visit with Caudle to Wake Forest, North Carolina, the President wrote to him: "Men like you and Jess Larson make it possible to carry on in this job." Only three weeks before his dismissal, the President thanked him for the gift of a handsome cigarette case which Caudle had brought back from his expense-paid trip to Europe, in a note which began "Dear Lamar." Caudle tried to ingratiate himself with Presidential assistants, Dawson and Connelly. However, he never became a member of the inner circle, and the President discarded the tool fast when it became soiled.

Caudle was a protege of Tom Clark, who now sits on the

Supreme Court. He was a small-town lawyer who became U. S. attorney for the western district of North Carolina in 1940. He became acquainted with Clark, who, as assistant Attorney General, headed various divisions in the Justice Department; Caudle entertained him in North Carolina on a deer hunt. In 1945, when Clark succeeded Biddle as Attorney General, he was responsible for Caudle's appointment to head the criminal division. An FBI report was submitted on Caudle to Clark, in which Caudle admitted he was "indiscreet" and said that "somebody kept putting presents in his automobile" while it was in a parking lot. Clark reviewed the report. One of the tests that was reputedly made in the Hannegan era of the Truman administration was "Is he a ball player?" Clark subjected Caudle to a more exhausting test. In a conference in the Justice Department with two FBI agents from Charlotte, he asked, "Will he embarrass me, does he know his way around?" Caudle passed the tests and so the appointment went through. It should be noted that Caudle was, politically speaking, an asset in the Justice Department, because he was a Southerner, and the Truman administration was anticipating southern opposition to its civil rights program designed to solidify its political strength in the North.

In reviewing some of the cases in the Caudle record, particular note should be paid to the attorneys in the case, since, as Caudle candidly stated to the Chelf committee, they might be the key to an attempted fix.

1) Caudle, together with Tom Clark, did fine service for the administration in suppressing the investigation of the Kansas City vote frauds following the 1946 election which purged Truman's foe, Roger C. Slaughter. Caudle closed the case in January 1947 after a very limited investigation. He was rewarded a few months later with the tax division job. His assistant, Turner Smith, who had helped him in the Kansas City case, was also permitted to move over.

2) In Housatonic Dye, as we have seen, the attorney, Wallace Cohen, operated under the good offices of David Niles in the White House; Joseph Sherman was from the Democratic National Committee.

3) On December 1, 1955, Caudle was indicted in St. Louis along with the appointments secretary to President Truman, Matthew Connelly, and Sachs' attorney, Harry Schwimmer, for conspiracy to fix the tax case of Irving Sachs and Shu-Stiles Company.

Sachs had no defense to speak of against the criminal tax charge. Nonetheless, the case was kept locked up in the Bureau of Internal Revenue for two years. Despite pressure from within the Justice Department, Caudle refused to give the signal to prosecute. In September 1952, Caudle told the Chelf committee of the intervention by Connelly. He gave an horrendous picture of Sach's physical condition to the Chelf committee and then stated "Personally, I did not want to send that case out ... but when that thing broke out in St. Louis and Mr. Drake Watson [the U. S. attorney] wanted to send the case to the grand jury, we just sent him a wire and told him to send everything to the grand jury and that case was sent to the grand jury and Mr. Sachs was indicted and later he pleaded guilty."[2] Caudle neglected to tell the committee that he had previously ordered the prosecution to be quashed and that as to the wire to Watson, he had no choice by that time in the matter. Recorded telephone conversations show that Caudle's assistants, Rothwacks and Smith, had discouraged the grand jury investigation and that Caudle himself talked to Watson with a good deal of asperity.

Although Caudle claimed that the decision to send a man to St. Louis was that of Peyton Ford, deputy Attorney General, he testified that he did choose Ellis Slack, his assistant, as the man to go. Slack, whose mission is discussed in Chapter

2. Testimony before Chelf subcommittee, *op. cit.,* p. 1331. For Caudle's testimony on the St. Louis grand jury, see pp. 1236-72.

Five as part of the story of the McGrath regime, was named in the indictment along with Caudle as a co-conspirator in the Sachs case but was not indicted. As for the whitewash or "partial report" approved by Slack over the phone, Watson in a letter of May 1, 1951, to Caudle stated, "You may recall that prior to the submission of the partial report referred to by the court, the report was submitted to and approved by your office, after which it was submitted to the grand jury which filed it." The indictment alleges that Caudle continued to work in behalf of Sachs after his indictment in order to prevent him from being imprisoned and that he sent a report to a probation officer.

According to the St. Louis *Globe-Democrat*, Caudle, while he was being interrogated by the grand jury, told a reporter that an oil royalty had been given to him by Schwimmer, but that this was without his knowledge and he had canceled it when he found out. Presumably Caudle gave this testimony to the grand jury. The indictment contained no charge that Caudle received anything but, legally speaking, that would not prevent such proof at the trial.

4) In the Ripps-Mitchell case in Alabama to be discussed in the next chapter, the lawyers mentioned as representing the defendants included Will Bankhead, a famous name in Alabama; W. M. Nicholson, Caudle's former law partner; Morris Shenker of St. Louis, connected by friendships with the President; and Caudle's often-present friend, I. T. Cohen. A large campaign contribution to the Democratic National Committee was involved.

5) In the Freidus case to be discussed in the next chapter, the lawyer was John Caffey of Greensboro, North Carolina, a long-time friend of Caudle.

6) While Clark was Attorney General and Caudle was in charge of the criminal division, two indictments were dismissed against a bond dealer named Roy E. Crummer.[3] At-

3. For Crummer case, see report of Keating subcommittee, *op. cit.*, p. 39.

torney General McGranery in 1952 said the case against Crummer was "one of the biggest mail fraud cases ever to be filed by the government." The Keating subcommittee in reviewing the case, stated in 1953: "There is not the slightest question from the full record that the indictments were improperly dismissed. . . . one of the most striking features about the case is that the subordinate officials who knew the case best are persuaded even now a decade later that they should have been pressed to trial and could have been won." The indictments were highly technical in nature, involving the so-called Crummer plan to finance Florida municipalities which were in shaky financial condition. An investigation by the Securities and Exchange Commission began in 1941 and culminated in two indictments in August 1944. Crummer sought a defense, and according to the Keating committee "the weak spots he sought and found seemed clearly to be the offices of Attorney General Tom Clark and Clark's protege, Caudle."

As an attorney, Crummer hired James Laurence Fly, who had been chairman of the Federal Communications Commission and was well-known in official circles in Washington. Fly arranged a conference with Clark in November 1945 during which certain letters and material were presented. "It was improper for these attorneys to offer them and for the Attorney General to accept argumentative material of this sort in a pending case." Political pressure was also brought to bear notably from Senator Pat McCarran. The negotiations opened with Caudle. Caudle, who was learning about stocks and bonds for the first time, was full of doubts about the government case. Beginning in February 1946, conferences were held in which Caudle attacked the SEC officials who were urging prompt prosecution. Caudle was acting on all kinds of unsworn letters and charges which were being made by defense witnesses. Caudle, in testimony before the Chelf committee, reflected an attitude towards the government's case the same as in the Housatonic Dye case. "I was completely convinced that this thing was a conspiracy." In May, the Justice Department advised the SEC that it was going to drop the prosecution. The files were referred to Clark and shortly thereafter the dismissal was authorized.

Assistant U. S. attorney Davis from Topeka never concurred with Caudle's staff and maintained throughout that the case could be won. "Furthermore, though none of his subordinates openly challenged him at the time, Caudle alone seems to have been the prime moving party—except to the extent that he too was following the lead of his superior, Attorney General Clark." On the basis of Caudle's testimony, the Keating committee reported that while Caudle was aggressive in dismissing the case he was "shockingly ignorant" of the government's case, and that he had allowed himself "to be used as a mere tool to serve the ends of Crummer or his counsel, or Attorney-General Clark, or both." In 1952, Attorney General McGranery, reviewing the case before the Chelf committee, stated that in view of the position of the SEC and the local U. S. attorney, "I say to you, Mr. Congressman, in all due deference, that you cannot dismiss matters under these circumstances without leaving some real suspicion and a cause and reason for the suspicion."

7) As the Chelf committee described it, Caudle played a part in a successful effort by Norman E. Miller to keep a criminal and civil case against him from reaching the trial stage until, in the words of one disgusted government attorney, "they had become enfeebled with age."[4] Miller, who had served a jail term for robbery, established a company, Norman E. Miller and Associates, Inc., during the war, which rendered engineering services for businesses which were working on government cost-plus contracts. The indictment against Miller alleged that he charged his clients for hours of service never performed. He was indicted in Detroit in July 1944. Attorneys were frequently changed. The head of the Detroit war fraud

4. For Miller case, see report of Chelf subcommittee, *op. cit.*, p. 69.

unit said these were "attempts to buy influence." Clark as head of the criminal division and as Attorney General received the attorneys and Mr. and Mrs. Miller. In August 1945, a year after indictment, Caudle wrote to Detroit asking that Miller's attorneys be given a chance to be heard. Then another attorney came in, E. C. Bevan, Democratic national committeeman from Michigan. Another conference was arranged with Clark. Months dragged by while Bevan was given a chance to file more information. In the fall of 1946, Bevan sought a further conference with Caudle in Washington and Caudle agreed to give Bevan and his client "every opportunity to be heard."

Bevan continued to play Washington against Detroit. Every time the U. S. attorney wished to schedule a trial, Bevan claimed that he was negotiating with Washington. In December, Bevan wrote to Caudle referring to his "recent conversation with the Attorney General in Washington" and enclosed a check for $7,500 as settlement for the criminal prosecution and Miller's civil liability. Caudle kept the check even though this was improper since criminal offenses except for certain income tax violations are never compromised for money settlements. In the meanwhile, the witnesses were disappearing. The U. S. attorney had planned to build his presentation around three chief witnesses. "One of these died in the interim; one was confined briefly in a mental institution; and one was ensnarled in a bigamy charge." It is strongly implied that Miller framed the man who was incarcerated and conducted the investigation which exposed the bigamist. Other witnesses, after being offered employment and entertained by Miller, disappeared. Early in 1947, the criminal prosecution was suspended altogether and the whole matter together with the check for $7,500 was referred to the claims division. J. Edgar Hoover sent several memoranda to Caudle protesting the delay, referring to the shady maneuvers of Miller and pointing out the unfavorable publicity. Caudle replied that the matter was in abeyance, pending some action by the claims division. This incredible saga came to an end in 1950 and 1951, when both the civil and the criminal actions against Miller were dismissed.

8) In the Shapiro case the attorney was Scott Lucas of Illinois, majority leader of the Senate until 1951.[5] Lucas came to see Caudle twice, each time preceded by a phone call from Attorney General McGrath. Mrs. Shapiro was considered the chief culprit in a tax liability of over $500,000 involving her husband. For some reason the case had been kept for three and a half years in the Internal Revenue Bureau while the statute of limitations barred prosecution for two years, but there was finally an indictment in Milwaukee. The effort was to get Mrs. Shapiro off on the health ground, that a trial would endanger her life. Caudle said he explained to Lucas, that after an indictment, that decision was up to the local U. S. attorney and the judge. Nonetheless, Caudle sent his trouble-shooter, Ellis Slack, to Milwaukee. According to Caudle, "Mr. Slack told the judge that from what had been represented to us, the woman was very ill and was likely to die. . . . if the court felt inclined to dismiss the indictment against her to save her life, it would be up to the court and the Department of Justice would have no objection to it." The indictment was dismissed against Mrs. Shapiro after Mr. Shapiro pleaded guilty. Rumors of a fix abounded.

9) On one occasion Caudle was swift in prosecution. Caudle got a case from Oliphant against the rum-runner of prohibition days, Niggy Rutkin, three days before the statute of limitations was to expire and by heroic efforts got an indictment. This is the story as Rutkin's lawyer told it: Rutkin had given another rum-runner, Reinfeld, his start and contended that Reinfeld owed him $20,000,000. Reinfeld's lawyer was Joe Nunan, former internal revenue commissioner. When Rutkin kept insisting on payment and

5. For Shapiro case, see testimony before Chelf subcommittee, *op. cit.*, pp. 1229-36.

started suit, Nunan turned Rutkin in to his friends in Internal Revenue and Justice, for prosecution.[6]

Let us now examine the activities of Theron Lamar Caudle in behalf of Theron Lamar Caudle.[7] An FBI complaint on Caudle before he came to Washington was in part connected with an association with a friend, Keith Beaty, and lack of proper prosecuting zeal growing out of that friendship, in the case of law violations. He continued his friendship with Beaty after he went to Washington. Beaty was being investigated by the Bureau of Internal Revenue in connection with tax evasion charges of a very substantial sum. Of this Caudle was aware. He took an expense-paid trip to New York with Beaty in 1945. In 1947 he got a new car through Beaty by exchanging his 1942 car. In 1949, Caudle spoke to Oliphant about Beaty. His version was that he orally disqualified himself from the case. This seems absurd, since the case had not yet come to the Internal Revenue Bureau in Washington. The deduction from the evidence, as drawn by the King committee counsel, is that he told Oliphant that the charge against Beaty was only a spite charge brought by the chief of police of Charlotte, who was trying to get at Caudle. In any event, the tax fraud investigation was dropped.

Caudle accepted gifts. An I. T. Cohen was associated with a Jacob Landau in a law practice in Washington, which was largely devoted to tax cases. Landau got a mink coat for Mrs. Caudle in New York, which was appraised at $3,500 or $4,000 for a payment by her of $1,500. There were two mouton coats valued at $563 which were bought, one for Caudle and one for Turner Smith, his assistant, the cost of which was chalked up as a deductible business expense by the law firm. Turner Smith sent a blank check to Cohen, which Cohen tore up.

6. For Rutkin case, see testimony before Chelf subcommittee, *op. cit.,* p. 1240.

7. These activities are contained in Caudle's testimony before King subcommittee, *op. cit.,* pp. 919-1654.

Caudle claimed that his wife had sent a check but Cohen had no record of a payment or a proferred payment and Caudle had no canceled check. Cohen gave Caudle a gift of a television set worth $350.

The assistant Attorney General was grubbing for small change on the outside. He sold an interest in an oil well operated by a Mr. Robert Fletcher, whom he possibly met through Frank Nathan, to Landau and received from Fletcher a commission of $1,000, which was twenty per cent of the sales price. Through Caudle, I. T. Cohen was persuaded to buy an interest in oil leases from Fletcher. Cohen made a total investment of over $13,000, but the promised royalties started dropping to nothing. In the course of the transactions, Fletcher gave Cohen a rebate of $1,250, saying "he was able to get the boy (or the fellow) to waive his commission." To whom could he have been referring except Caudle?

Caudle enjoyed a really juicy trip to Europe in 1951 as a companion of Carmen D'Agastino, president of the Renault Champagne Company. Not only were his expenses paid, but he also obtained a loan of $2,000. Why D'Agastino was willing to pay this money is not clear. Caudle said that D'Agastino wanted him to help in straightening out his father's estate. It might possibly have been in connection with a matter of getting some lira released so that they could be exchanged into dollars. At any rate, D'Agastino was willing to pay for the use of Caudle's prestige if not his company. Caudle got approval for the trip from Attorney General McGrath. He might have told McGrath about the payment of expenses but he did not mention the $2,000. To McGrath, who was a prominent Catholic layman, he said he was going abroad to make a survey of communism. To the Chelf committee he said "the real purpose of that trip was communism." Actually, Caudle spent only ten days in Italy, almost all in Rome, and as much time in Paris and London. This is how he reported his investigation of communism:

MR. DEWIND: Is communism rampant over there?

MR. CAUDLE: Oh my golly, they have a communist school over there, they have a regular trunk line to the Kremlin at Frascotti and back. I never did see anything else like it.

MR. DEWIND: Where else did you find outcroppings of communism?

CAUDLE: I tell you in Rome—you see we did not get up to Milan, it was too hot to go down to Sicily, but I tell you that country is in a bad shape, Mr. DeWind. I was just a pygmy to try to do anything for Italy, but I think we have accomplished something for Italy.

Mr. Caudle received a fee of $5,000 as commission on the sale of an airplane to a Mr. Knohl. It was the disclosure of that transaction which was the immediate cause of his being purged out of the Justice Department. We shall discuss that in relationship to the Freidus case in the next chapter. Mr. Caudle's life as assistant Attorney General was a gay one. It included expense-paid trips on many weekends to Florida or on fishing trips or to the Gulf of Mexico. In 1947, he arranged two parties for fishing trips on a boat called the "Naughty Lady" in which the host was Mr. Troy Whitehead, a friend of his from Charlotte. (Caudle did not testify to that effect, but the pilot of the plane was quoted in the *Charlotte News* as saying that Attorney General Clark was a guest.) Among his guests on one or the other of these trips was Charles Oliphant. Mr. Whitehead was under investigation for tax fraud and a fraud case was jacketed in the intelligence unit on June 25, 1947. Subsequently, Mr. Oliphant was in a position to reciprocate Mr. Whitehead's hospitality.

## Charles Oliphant[8]

Charles Oliphant, who resigned while under fire as chief counsel of the Bureau of Internal Revenue, was the bearer of

8. All matters are from testimony of Charles Oliphant before King subcommittee, *op. cit.*, pp. 1794-1875, and from testimony of Henry Grunewald before Kean subcommittee on the Internal Revenue Laws (83rd Congress), pp. 987-1323.

a fine name. He was the son of Herman Oliphant, a professor of law at Columbia and the general counsel of the Treasury Department in the early years of the New Deal, in the forefront in the formulation of New Deal legislation. Undoubtedly, the Oliphant name helped in the son's rise in the Treasury. He did not add luster to the name.

On March 23, 1948, Henry Grunewald called on Commissioner Schoeneman in connection with the case of Hyman Harvey Klein. Schoeneman on that occasion introduced Oliphant, the counsel for the Bureau, to Grunewald. The two men, the young government career attorney, and the wily, hardened operator almost twenty years his senior, seemed to find an affinity immediately. They had lunch together frequently, sometimes with Schoeneman, and visited in each other's homes. Undoubtedly, Oliphant was a useful man for Grunewald to cultivate in Grunewald's line of work. On the other hand, Grunewald with his world of contacts in Washington might be useful for an ambitious young man like Oliphant. Grunewald gave Oliphant many gifts, including a television set, an air conditioning unit, a train set for his children; he gave a Chrysler car to Oliphant on which he did not receive payment until after Oliphant's resignation; he took precautions that the bill of sale would not reveal his name. Congress set up twenty-five positions in the higher salary range of $14,000 and over, and Oliphant, who was making less than $11,000, hoped to get one of these jobs. Grunewald contacted Louis Johnson, the Secretary of Defense, in order to get a favorable recommendation from the President. Oliphant did get that salary boost. All this was really small change for the cynical Grunewald, who must have regarded with contempt this hardworking bureaucrat who was content with so little, while his own income was well up in the six figures.[9]

Oliphant was willing to do favors for Grunewald. His disclosure of the racketeer classification for Abraham Teitelbaum

9. For gifts, see Grunewald's testimony before Kean subcommittee, *op. cit.*, pp. 1009-18; for salary boost, see Grunewald's testimony, p. 1264.

could be construed as a violation of the secrecy rules. Oliphant admitted that he had talked to Grunewald in connection with the Hyman Harvey Klein case and also that Grunewald had introduced to him a Mr. Halperin in connection with the Patullo Modes case. There are further cases that we know of which go beyond Oliphant's admissions. On March 25, 1949, the Oliphant log shows that Grunewald introduced Walter Duke to Oliphant on an excess profits tax case. On March 31, the file shows that an attorney who was assigned the case in Internal Revenue stated: "Mr. Oliphant has directed that this case be advanced for consideration." On April 1, the attorney reported to Oliphant: "In compliance with your telephonic instructions, I transferred the case to Mr. Mathis yesterday and asked him to advance it to the head of the list." This expeditious treatment given to the Consolidated Electric and Gas Company enabled the company to get a refund of about half a million dollars in about two months. Grunewald got a fee of $25,000 from Duke.

Grunewald acknowledged receiving fees totaling $10,000 from taxpayers for whom he claimed he did nothing other than introduce them to a tax attorney. In most cases, it appeared that he did more. He received $3,750 from a J. R. Jordan. This was a criminal tax fraud case on which prosecution was declined by Mr. Oliphant's office in 1948 on the basis of a doctor's advice that Jordan was ill. The investigators found that after the case had been closed the Bureau received additional information to the effect that Mr. Jordan was not sick at all. By that time, the case had been closed out and could not be reopened.[10]

Oliphant, like Caudle, was an energetic freeloader.[11] He occupied a position in which he had the last word in the Internal Revenue Bureau as to whether or not a prosecution should

10. For Duke and Jordan cases, see Grunewald's testimony before Kean subcommittee, *op. cit.*, pp. 1131 ff. and 1222 ff.
11. For following activities of Oliphant, see Oliphant's testimony before King subcommittee, *op. cit.*, pp. 1794-1875.

be undertaken. Naturally, he was a person in high demand socially. He was an official with a relatively small salary, but a shake of his head could mean the difference in several hundred thousand dollars for the taxpayer. He nonetheless accepted entertainment from persons who had or might have matters before the Internal Revenue Bureau, and he was in no position to reciprocate.

Oliphant had a friend, Poncet Davis, for whom he constantly reiterated his high regard. Mr. Davis was under investigation for tax fraud. Oliphant was his guest in private plane trips to Florida, to New York and for the World Series, for the Ray Robinson fight, for the Belmont Stakes. He went with Edwin W. Pauley to the Kentucky Derby; Pauley had pending a tax case with the Department. He went in a private railroad car to a football game in Philadelphia, and met Arthur McBride whose son, Edward McBride, was said to own Continental Press, the wire service for bookies. McBride was probably the host. Internal Revenue was investigating Continental Press, which was the glue for the underworld. Oliphant said he insisted on paying for his hotel room on these trips, with a reimbursement to his host in cash. He says that he bumped into Frank Nathan on several occasions.

Mr. Oliphant disqualified himself in the case of Poncet Davis, who was indicted in 1952 for tax evasion of close to a million dollars. However, as Congressman King commented to him, disqualification under such circumstances would not be enough. "By so doing, the [the government official] is depriving the government of his services . . . second, the person supplying the entertainment when dealing with officials, associations or subordinates can give color to a claim that he was a good friend of the official he entertains. Tangible or intangible benefits of such claims are difficult to measure."

In one case, Mr. Oliphant appeared to confer a substantial favor on his host. He had been a guest, on a fishing trip with Lamar Caudle, of Mr. Troy Whitehead. At that time, there was a tax fraud investigation pending against Whitehead, a fact which Oliphant said he did not know. In October 1948, Whitehead called Oliphant and said the deputy collectors were at his plant with notices of seizure on the liens which might enable him to operate but would discredit him in the community. The local collector felt that the seizure should go through because Whitehead had never kept prior agreements in connection with payment of taxes and he felt if they did not seize the plant, the government might lose out. Oliphant prevailed on the collector to take Whitehead's agreement and remove notices of seizure. Later, Oliphant commented to Caudle that he had certainly rubbed Robertson (the local collector) the wrong way.

One of the companies which showered bounty on Oliphant was American Lithofold. Cecil Green delivered to him one of their expensive Polaroid cameras. James P. Finnegan gave Oliphant two suits and an overcoat; Oliphant said he got them at a discount. A Mr. Walter Wolfner gave him a couple of suitcases. He also received case lots of liquor.

Oliphant put great premium on friendships. In the Washington Beef case discussed in the next chapter, he seems to have been influenced by friendship with a congressman. When the investigation of Caudle began he advised Caudle that his income tax returns had been requested, an improper divulging of information. Oliphant said that he had done things for Grunewald because Grunewald was his friend. Grunewald did not put the same premium on friendship. When he appeared before the Kean subcommittee in public testimony and was reminded of some Oliphant testimony, Grunewald replied, "Mr. Oliphant's testimony I wouldn't give a hoop for. . . . I wouldn't give you anything. First of all, he is an alcoholic, and, secondly, they had to put him in the George Washington hospital for a mental test."[12]

12. Testimony of Henry Grunewald before Kean subcommittee, *op. cit.*, p. 1002.

### *Henry W. Grunewald*[13]

The Kean subcommittee said: "Henry W. Grunewald personifies the decay of the tax system during the period following World War II." As soon as Oliphant mentioned Grunewald in the Teitelbaum case, Grunewald got into a hospital bed, and thereafter was an elusive object. He refused to testify on the ground of illness. Then when he disappeared the FBI had to be turned out to uncover him and found him on a farm in Virginia. When he appeared before the King subcommittee, he refused to testify and was thereafter convicted of contempt. To lighten the sentence, he finally testified evasively before the Kean subcommittee in April 1953 and drew a suspended sentence which he served for violating the conditions imposed.

All the while the press had a field day with the mystery man known as "The Dutchman." While not exactly a television celebrity, Grunewald was far from being unknown in Washington. He had lived at the Westchester Apartments for seventeen years and had educated two daughters in Washington. He also had a circle of friends and acquaintances which might have been second to none in the city. His distribution of Christmas ties alone to government officials cost him over $1,000 a year.

Grunewald knew Commissioner of Internal Revenue Schoeneman well enough that Schoeneman's office record shows forty-five personal visits from him. Schoeneman's house was built on a lot that Grunewald acquired and sold to the commissioner at cost as a service to him. Grunewald also arranged financing for the home. Grunewald was a friend of Jess Larson and gave him a television set. Harry Woodring,

13. All matters discussed concerning Grunewald, except where otherwise noted, are from his testimony and that of William H. Vander Poel before Kean subcommittee, *op. cit.*, pp. 987-1323.

the former Secretary of War, shared Grunewald's Washington hotel suite, went to Germany on a deal for Grunewald and was paid by him. Louis Johnson, Truman's Secretary of Defense, was familiar enough that Grunewald could ask him to intervene with the White House for a pay raise for Oliphant.

Grunewald knew some senators well enough that "he could walk into their offices without taking his hat off." Former Senator Gerald Nye borrowed money from him; former Senator Worth Clark paid him. He talked business with Max Gardner, the former Under Secretary of the Treasury. He asked Gardner before he left as Ambassador to Great Britain to get him an agency for Scotch in this country. By his own account, he could get J. Edgar Hoover on the phone to discuss a personal problem. An investigator, Edward Gill, walked into the office of Leo Crowley and asked him about Grunewald, saying that he understood he worked for Crowley. Crowley was then Alien Property Custodian and later was the head of the Foreign Economic Administration. Crowley said that he didn't know him. The investigator then obtained the personnel file and learned that he was not only a special employee hired over the objection of the Civil Service Commission, but there was a letter from Crowley that Grunewald should act as director in his absence.[14]

Grunewald had been born in 1892 and came to this country from South Africa when he was fifteen. After a term in the Navy, when he acquired the nickname of "The Dutchman," he was an FBI agent and investigator for the alcohol tax unit. After he was dismissed by the Treasury, he was indicted in 1923 for conspiracy to defraud the United States by falsely issuing customs permits and fraudulently removing cases of champagne from the customs' bonded warehouse in New York. Afterwards, he was employed as a confidential secretary and investigator for Henry Marsh, the wealthy head of Marsh and McLennan. Through this connection, Grunewald became

14. Testimony before King subcommittee, *op. cit.,* p. 2293.

acquainted with many important and influential men in both the public and business life of this country. He thus obtained access to various sources of information such as those maintained by banks and insurance companies and became intimate with officials in most of the federal agencies which collect information on individuals.

Marsh died in 1943 leaving Grunewald $50,000. Grunewald set himself up in Washington as an investigator and public relations man specializing in the collection of uncomplimentary information on the past life of his subjects. He was hired, for example, by John L. Lewis to investigate the personal life of the late federal judge, T. Alan Goldsborough, at a time when Goldsborough was considering a contempt case against the United Mine Workers. His income tax return shows a fee of $16,000. He was hired for investigative work by Tommy Corcoran, the Roosevelt braintruster who, incidentally, gave him the name of "Captain Henry," which Grunewald often used. Corcoran once told him that an investigative assignment was for President Roosevelt. He was also hired by numerous corporations whose officials were being subjected to lawsuits, and in each case, as far as the Kean committee could find, Grunewald obtained sufficient derogatory information about the plaintiff to persuade him to discontinue the suit. He was employed by corporations as a strike-breaker. He was publicly mentioned in connection with wire-tapping in the Howard Hughes-Pan American fracas.

His income was tremendous. He had an apartment in the Westchester, a suite in the Hotel Washington, a home in Spring Lake, New Jersey, and a home in Florida. The telephone installations in his Florida home to enable his guests each to have a private wire for long-distance calls cost $10,000. He owned three corporations, Henry Company, Hendrick Inc. and Metropolitan Import and Export Corporation. He got $75,000, he says, from the Chinese government for one hundred fighter planes which he got by lifting the phone and calling Charles Kindleberger of North American Aviation. His income tax return did not break down his receipts too carefully and there was a large sum listed as commissions and expenses. For a five-year period, he said that $220,000 represented winnings at the race tracks. These were the winnings from sums bet by his chauffeur, Charles Burke, who, conveniently, had died in 1952. Burke under questioning had sworn that his only function for Grunewald was as a chauffeur.

Grunewald expanded his operations from investigating to fixing. An investigation of black market operations of the American Distilling Company uncovered Mr. Grunewald in the middle of a deal for $500,000 of liquor in which Grunewald was always referred to as "the Prince." He started dabbling in surplus property deals. He introduced Walter Duke to his friend Jess Larson and collected a fee of $25,000.

Tax fixing was a line of activity in which his talents could be pre-eminently and remuneratively employed. Admissions which were drawn from him as to individual fees showed that he operated on a contingent basis, collecting only if successful, and his fees were high. He obviously discussed cases with Schoeneman, since the Oliphant log shows that in discussing one case he opened up with Oliphant, saying, "Since George is not here. . . ." Grunewald became acquainted with Daniel A. Bolich years before, when Grunewald had been working for Marsh and Bolich was special agent in charge in Brooklyn. Bolich, Oliphant, Schoeneman and other important internal revenue officials were frequent visitors in Grunewald's business suite in the Washington hotel, as well as his various other residences.

William H. Vander Poel testified before the Kean subcommittee and gave some insight as to Grunewald's method of operation. He was an executive of Union Carbide and Carbon, and had become acquainted with Grunewald in World War I while he was a special agent with Grunewald. Grunewald approached him in 1940 and said that he understood that the estate of Mr. Billings was having some tax trouble with a trust fund in Washington. Grunewald said that he thought he could help, and asked for a fee of fifteen percent of the tax saving if he was successful. Advised that there was nothing to lose, Vander Poel told him by phone to go ahead. The issue was whether an *inter vivos* trust set up by Billings for his daughter-in-law should be included in Billings' estate. Mrs. Vander Poel would inherit from Billings' daughter-in-law.

A case was pending before the Supreme Court, and normally the Bureau of Internal Revenue would not have closed the estate until the Supreme Court decision was handed down. In this case, obviously due to undue influence, the Bureau ruled for the daughter-in-law. Grunewald walked in a month later and said, "Well, we won the suit and I want my money." Vander Poel offered him a check, but Grunewald said that he handled only cash. So $60,000 in hundred dollar bills were obtained from a bank wrapped up for him. Four months later, the Supreme Court ruled the other way.

## Daniel A. Bolich

On August 10, 1949, William E. Mould, a revenue agent, visited the Munsey Trust Company of Washington to inspect Henry Grunewald's account. He acted on a tip. He was shortly afterward told by his group chief to do nothing more on the case. The group chief had acted to relieve Mould because he had a call from a higher source, which had, in turn, been relayed through the Commissioner's office. His penciled memo of the conversation has these notes: "Grunewald"—"Called the Commissioner"—"Bank had called taxpayer"—"Willing to surrender records."

In September 1949, agent Moll was given Grunewald's returns to audit. He called Grunewald who said he would call him back later. Grunewald never did. The next day his group chief told him to take the returns up to the office of the assistant deputy commissioner of the income tax unit; the case was taken away from him. The group chief was told later by Stowe, the assistant deputy commissioner, that there had been a mistake and Mould had been confused with Moll, who apparently was considered too much of an eager beaver. Stowe's diary record shows that he had gotten a direct call from Bolich.

Agent Leese, who was then assigned the audit, finished his audit by October 25 and found no change in the tax liability for the four years 1946 through 1949. He was told to send in his report directly to Mr. Bolich, which he did. This was an extraordinary procedure, since the regular routine would have been to send it to the Baltimore office for further review and audit.[15]

On examination, Grunewald admitted that he had complained to Daniel Bolich, assistant commissioner of internal revenue, when the agent had visited his bank.

Daniel A. Bolich resigned as assistant commissioner of internal revenue on November 19, 1951, on account of ill health. He was aware at the time of his resignation that he was the subject of an intensive investigation. Since the time when he was twenty-two years old, he had held responsible positions in the Bureau of Internal Revenue. When he was only thirty years old, that is in 1930, he had been appointed revenue agent in charge at Philadelphia. In 1946, he was appointed special agent in charge in New York and in September 1948, he became assistant commissioner. He was a close friend of Joe Nunan, who resigned as internal revenue commissioner in 1947. At the present time, Mr. Bolich is under sentence of five years for tax fraud.

Mr. Bolich's financial position, even on the very surface seemed remarkable for a man making around $10,000 a year. He supported a wife and five children. Three of the children went to college. He owned a home in Brooklyn and Spring

15. Testimony before King subcommittee, *op. cit.*, pp. 3327-39.

Lake. While working in Brooklyn, he lived at the Bossert hotel for $150 a month and while working in Washington, he lived first at the Hotel Washington, a first-line hotel, and then at the Westchester Apartments, a luxury apartment house. These were the homes of Henry W. Grunewald. In August 1951, Mr. Bolich was given a net worth questionnaire of the Treasury Department to be filled out, which he completed in October 1951. It showed that for the period 1945-1950, the total family income was under $54,000. During that time, he listed expenditures of $82,000 and an increase in net assets of $15,000. Two revenue agents made as careful a check as they could of his actual expenditures during that period. It was admittedly incomplete. For example, for clothing expenditures, the agents circularized stores in the neighborhood, and since there was an indication that Mrs. Bolich did a lot of shopping around Fifth Avenue, stores were circularized around Fifth Avenue. The stores circularized were few in number and many of them kept no records because they were cash sales. Nonetheless, clothing expenditures were found to be at least $6,000 more than the amount Mr. Bolich swore to. Bolich bought monogrammed handkerchiefs at $3.50 apiece, shirts at $31.50 each, neckties at $8.50 each, cuff links at $47.50, pajamas at $20 each. They were bought in quantities. According to the check the agents found the actual expenditures were $33,000 more than Mr. Bolich had sworn to on his net worth questionnaire.

Mr. Bolich accounted for $50,000 of excess expenditures and increase in net assets in the form of gifts which were given to him plus gambling winnings. A Mr. Routzahn, who had been a collector of internal revenue in Cleveland when Mr. Bolich was a deputy collector in 1922, said that he gave him $10,800. The reason for giving him this sum was that Mr. Bolich told him he could not afford to stay in Washington so Mr. Routzahn agreed to give him $400 a month. There were also other substantial cash gifts. He gave it to him out of the goodness of his heart because Mr. Bolich could not support his large family. He took the money in cash out of a safe deposit box, so none of these amounts appeared in his records, nothing appeared in his checking account, nothing appeared in any of his personal records which would establish any of these payments. He claimed that he had accumulated this money over a period of 15 years, but when the agents examined the safe deposit box, they found only a few hundred dollars in fresh bills.[16] Another donor of gifts to Mr. Bolich could not testify because he had passed away. Grunewald testified that he knew Routzahn well enough to give him a new Chrysler.

Mr. Bolich lived at the Hotel Washington in Washington from September 1948 through April 30, 1951. During a period of that time, he occupied a suite which was registered in the name of Harry A. Woodring, a former Secretary of War. Grunewald said that Bolich lived in his suite until he was scared by the publicity in the Howard Hughes affair and moved into a room of his own. The records for the period June 22, 1949, to June 22, 1950, are missing. Mr. Everett Harding, assistant manager of the Hotel Washington, gave this version of their disappearance. Around June 1950, Mr. Bolich came up to him in the lobby and asked him if he could get him his records for approximately a year back. Mr. Harding collected them, brought them down to his office and the next time Harding saw Mr. Bolich, he told him he had the records. Bolich replied, "Well, all right." Bolich came by his office sometime later and picked them up.

It was rather unusual to give a guest original records, but Harding thought it was all right for a man in Mr. Bolich's high position. Mr. Bolich did not return the records. In December 1951, investigators of the King subcommittee visited the hotel and asked to see the records. Remembering that Mr. Bolich had taken away the records for that year period,

16. Facts on Bolich's financial status from testimony before King subcommittee, *op. cit.*, pp. 3427-81.

Mr. Harding sent him a letter on December 14, stating that the records were now under subpoena and would he please return them. Mr. Bolich called him from New York and said he didn't have them. Mr. Harding reminded him of the circumstances under which he took them, saying, "I recall you had your hat and coat on when you entered the office." Mr. Bolich replied, "I don't remember a thing about it." Mr. Harding was staggered by Mr. Bolich's statement to him, and immediately made a memo about the conversation in which, incidentally, Mr. Bolich made a point of saying that he had paid the bills for his room.

Records which were produced by the committee showed that payments made to the Washington hotel during 1950 in connection with the hotel bills on Suite 419-20-21, occupied by Bolich, were all paid for by Henry Grunewald.[17]

17. See testimony before King subcommittee, *op. cit.,* pp. 3340-58.

# · XII ·

# SOME REMARKABLE TAX CASES

## *The Freidus Case*[1]

LARRY KNOHL was a Broadway character straight out of Damon Runyon. He had an allergy to the word "prison" and always used the word "incarcerated." As a matter of fact, Mr. Knohl had been "incarcerated" on a federal charge of embezzlement. He was a friend of Theron Lamar Caudle, who exhibited his usual fastidious taste in his choice of friends. Larry Knohl probably needed a private airplane, in the Runyon vernacular, "like a hole in the head," but he bought a plane, Mr. Caudle received a commission of $5,000, and thereby hangs the tale. The cause-and-effect relationship between the $5,000 and Mr. Caudle's conduct in the Freidus case is circumstantial. The congruence of circumstances was sufficiently strong, however, to propel Mr. Caudle out of the federal service.

Jacob Freidus and his stepfather, Samuel Aaron, were indicted for tax fraud in New York in February 1949. When the case was first referred by the Bureau of Internal Revenue, there was a letter attached from the revenue agent, warning that the defendants and their counsel would practice delaying tactics, and that is what happened.

1. Unless otherwise noted, all matters discussed are from testimony before King subcommittee on the Internal Revenue Laws (82nd Congress), pp. 472-1507; 1071-1175; and 1634-52.

In April 1949, a delay was arranged by the tax division in Washington to permit a Mr. Wright, a new attorney, to familiarize himself with the case. Then in September John Caffey of Greensboro, North Carolina, a friend of Caudle's, entered the case, and Caudle called Tom Murphy in the U. S. attorney's office in New York, who granted a six-weeks delay. The strategy seemed to be to get a new lawyer every time the case came up for trial. After Caudle's assistants had submitted to him a memo that the case should now go to trial, on March 30, Caudle's assistant, Ellis Slack, called U. S. attorney Irving Saypol in New York to request a postponement till May 15. On May 4, Caudle had sent a wire to a new lawyer, Charles Margiotti, that the Justice Department would have no objection to a further delay and he had sent a copy to Saypol. On May 12, Meyer Rothwacks stated to his boss, Caudle, that there should be no further delays; but that same day Caudle had called Saypol in regard to a delay.

Since the case was in the hands of Saypol from the time of the indictment, the tax division had no right to intervene in the case. On July 19, 1950, Saypol called Caudle and complained to him about "the apparent circumvention of this office." At that point, it was apparent that Saypol would consent to no further delays.

Caffey had been hired by Larry Knohl, who was intimately connected with Freidus. Knohl was vice president of one of Freidus' companies. He said that in the two years 1949 and 1950, he was paid $100,000, and worked for Freidus as an investigator. He became a close friend and business associate of Frank Nathan and their children became engaged. Knohl had met Caudle in early 1950 in a conference in Washington on the case. A memo on January 20, unsigned, by some Justice official states, "From my slight acquaintance with Mr. Knohl with the first Ambino case where I questioned Knohl as to disposal of assets, Knohl is a shady character." Knohl, with Caffey, met Caudle several times publicly thereafter at a Jefferson-Jackson Day Dinner and on one occasion at, of all places, a dinner of the American Bar Association.

This friendship led in time to a purchase by Knohl of an airplane owned by Caudle's friend, Walter Stonnell, for $30,-000. In September 1950, Caudle collected from Stonnell a check for $5,000 as a commission for arranging the sale. Caudle had met Stonnell on weekend jaunts for fishing trips to Florida with Harry Payne, who had flown them down in his plane. Knohl said that he needed a plane because he had oil properties in Kansas, but it is difficult to see how inspecting them could make the oil gush any faster. He had been in the oil business only a few months. Said Knohl, "I was interested in getting a plane for my company because I had future vision in the oil business and going to many places concerning my business in oil." At any rate, the $100,000 he received from Freidus would have adequately covered the cost of the plane. Knohl had never approached any plane dealer to get a plane. Nonetheless, he says that he heard from Caudle that Stonnell was hard up and had to sell his plane and so called up Caudle from Kansas about it. If Stonnell were hard up, it is difficult to see how Caudle would have taken $5,000 from a friend. Caudle was asked if it was not true that the price was $25,000 and that he was told by Stonnell he could collect anything above that.

Caudle said that he had cleared the commission with Attorney General McGrath, but may not have been accurate. McGrath said[2] that Caudle called on him at his home at night and at the end of the conversation waved the check in front of him as a *fait accompli;* it would have been hard for McGrath to tell him to tear it up. Caudle testified he told of Knohl's connection with Freidus and Aaron, who, he told McGrath, were already indicted. McGrath's recollection is different. He said that Caudle assured him only that neither of the parties

2. See testimony of McGrath before King subcommittee, *op. cit.,* p. 1663. Also his testimony before Chelf subcommittee to investigate the Department of Justice (82nd Congress), p. 23.

to the sale, Stonnell or Knohl, were involved in prosecutions. He was not told about Freidus and Aaron.

There was now a new tactic in the case. The lawyers for Samuel Aaron claimed that he should not be prosecuted under the health policy in tax cases; that is, no criminal trial would be held if the trial ordeal might endanger the life of the defendant. The federal court in New York appointed a doctor who made a medical examination in September. His conclusion was, "Because I have personally observed many patients with even more serious heart disease undergo dramatic and strenuous situations (including emotional courtroom procedures) and come out unscathed, I am reasonably certain that Mr. Aaron can stand the trial without seriously jeopardizing his health. I must reiterate, however, that although I cannot calculate on a percentage basis the risk involved—this possibility does exist."

Although somewhat wishy-washy, Caudle agreed that this medical report did not meet the test that would exempt Aaron from criminal prosecution.

Under the health policy, after an indictment the question as to the physical capabilities of the defendant was entirely in the hands of the local U. S. attorney. It was no longer within the jurisdiction of Washington. The medical report did not come to Caudle through official channels, but must have been relayed to him through Caffey. Since a doctor had been appointed, the defendant's rights in any event had been protected and there was no basis for Washington to intervene. Caudle received his plane commission on September 18. On October 4, Caudle called Oliphant and discussed the medical report. Oliphant was agreeable. He was in Lynch's office and said to Lynch's secretary, "Will you make a note that I talked with Caudle? We went to some length on the testimony of the physician and both agreed that he should not stand trial." Richard C. Schwartz in the penal division wrote, "Messrs. Oliphant and Caudle had agreed that Aaron should not be prosecuted."

On October 6, Turner Smith, Caudle's assistant, sent a letter to Saypol in New York which stated, "On the basis of Dr. Hitzig's letter alone, this office is of the opinion that if the matter of health had been presented prior to transmission of the case to the United States attorney's office, prosecution would have been declined as to Mr. Aaron. The Bureau of Internal Revenue is of a similar opinion as indicated by its letter of October 5."

Caudle, Smith and Rothwacks could not explain why the letter was sent. It was purely gratuitous information. But it could have influenced the court and it was a letter that defense counsel could use to advantage as in a plea for a rehearing. Caffey must have been furnished a copy of the letter, since on January 13, 1951, Caffey wrote to Caudle regarding a case against Freidus and Aaron in Brooklyn: "It would be perfectly in order upon request of taxpayer to give the same opinion regarding Aaron as was submitted to the Southern District attorney."

Federal Judge Weinfeld and U. S. attorney Saypol both ignored the letter. The trial went on and both Freidus and Aaron drew jail sentences.

A trial of Larry Knohl for income tax evasion was held in the eastern district of New York in January 1956. Freidus testified that his payments to Knohl were not $100,000, but that they totaled close to a half million. His testimony included the following points (U. S. v. Knohl, indictment number 43642, eastern district of New York):

Knohl had called him when he had read of his tax trouble, and "he said also that he could help kill my case," pointing out that he knew people and procedures in the Justice Department. The sum mentioned initially was $50,000. Knohl had given a show of his influence by getting liens lifted from Freidus' property. Knohl said he had met Caudle through

Frank Nathan. In the late summer of 1949, Freidus, Caudle, Knohl and Nathan were in a hotel room in the Waldorf, and Nathan said to Caudle, "I want you to do all that you personally can for this boy."

Freidus had hired John Caffey because he was told, "Mr. Caudle preferred to have an attorney he could deal with." He hired Margiotti because "Mr. Caudle was recommending a competent trial attorney." (Margiotti is Caudle's defense attorney in the pending St. Louis indictment.)

Money that Freidus paid, he was told, was for the benefit of Caudle. Knohl showed him a pocket watch and lady's broach which cost Freidus $2,800. Knohl said he went to a race track with Caudle, bought tickets on every horse running and then pulled out a winning ticket in every race and gave it to Caudle. That cost $1,200. Knohl said he was sent by Caudle to help out in a primary in North Carolina and Freidus sent him $18,850. He was told that some of the money he was asked for was for Frank Nathan. Money went, too, for campaign contributions—$30,000 for tables at a Democratic dinner and $10,000 in a local campaign.

## Washington Beef[3]

On April 20, 1948, a case against Washington Beef and Provision Company and Witt & Company, involving an understatement of income of $200,000 was submitted by Internal Revenue to the Justice Department with a statement that "convictions may reasonably be expected." No one ever disputed the assumption of guilt or that the case at the outset was strong. There was an unusual feature in the case—the revenue agent investigating the case had joined the law firm representing the defendants.

The offense covered three years, 1942, 1943 and 1944. Rufus

3. All matters discussed are taken from testimony of King subcommittee, *op. cit.*, pp. 1530-51; 1775-94; 1815-28.

189

McLean, handling the case for Justice, decided that the year 1942 was critical, and the statute of limitations must not be allowed to bar prosecution for that year. A complaint was filed which extended the statute for 1942 from March 15, 1949 to August 30. McLean several times reminded Oliphant that 1942 was critical for the case. In April Congressman Morrison of Louisiana intervened for the defendants and asked that the case be referred back to Internal Revenue for a consideration as to whether prosecution was barred because there had been a voluntary disclosure. (If taxpayers made a voluntary disclosure of facts before investigation there could be no prosecution.) The case was referred back even though the attorney for the defendant had in March 1947 admitted that there had been no voluntary disclosure in this case.

Oliphant now took personal charge of the case. He undertook to get testimony on the voluntary disclosure issue. The vital testimony was that of Simpson, the revenue agent who was now working for the law firm on the other side. Simpson was in Washington so a phone call would have been enough to summon him. However, instead of picking up the phone a letter was drafted to Simpson on June 28, asking him to appear. Oliphant's office claimed it was lost so the same letter did not go out till July 28. Simpson said he was going on vacation and so the meeting was put off till August 18. Simpson admitted that there had been no voluntary disclosure, but refused to put it in writing till a conference on August 24.

The impression in Internal Revenue which Oliphant must have shared was that the statute for 1942 had been extended only till August 23. E. Riley Campbell, head of the penal division, had written to Oliphant on August 22, urging immediate action, but his letter to Justice was not sent by Oliphant.

Then it appeared that the statute would not run out until the 30th. Oliphant let the date pass without giving the authorization for an indictment. He told Justice that he had promised Congressman Morrison a conference and that Morrison would not return to town until September 10. So the case for 1942 was now destroyed. Oliphant seems to have violated instructions from Commissioner Schoeneman. When Oliphant told him that Morrison was out of town and that the next day would be the last to present the case to the grand jury, Schoeneman said, "Don't you think that you should tell his administrative assistant that the situation is such that you must go through with it?"

The statute of limitations would expire for the year 1943 on March 15, 1950. It was vital in the eyes of Justice and Internal Revenue attorneys that what was left of the case be presented for a grand jury indictment before that time, if any case were to be made at all. Weeks passed and Oliphant did nothing, ignoring reminders of the need for action. On March 8, Campbell made another plea for action with a proposed letter to the Justice Department. In that draft of a letter was the sentence, "It is accordingly believed that a strong prosecution case exists. . . ." On March 14 Oliphant finally transmitted a letter which did not contain that sentence. He enclosed the testimonies on the voluntary disclosure issue, all of which had been completed in August 1949, six months before. The letter was received by Justice only a few hours before the statute of limitations expired on March 15. Because of the problems of processing the case and getting it before the grand jury, it was impossible to follow through on getting any indictment. Mr. Oliphant was quite cavalier about the case. In a conversation with Caudle on March 14, he said, "It may be you will figure for trial purposes it won't do but that is all right with me, even for 1944. I have to call Jimmy." (Congressman Morrison.)

The last year, 1944, had to be ditched because, as Oliphant had been informed, the case was now thinned out to a shadow. Thus, the result of the delays was that a strong criminal case had been killed.

Since it was Mr. Oliphant's sworn duty to prosecute violation of the law where violation existed, where was there justification in this case for allowing the statute of limitations to expire where repeated warnings had been given that otherwise the case would be lost? In his letter of resignation to the President, Oliphant had written that he was ready to "defend every action I have taken in public office as being in the best interest of the Government. . . ." Oliphant was asked by the committee how his actions conformed to that statement.

## *Ripps-Mitchell*[4]

In 1945 a revenue agent walked into the offices of a firm in Alabama, the Gulf Coast Tobacco Company, to make a routine audit of the company's books. His practiced eye suspected fraud immediately. He closed the books and hurried out to get a special agent of the intelligence unit to be assigned to him. There was a delay and it was not until three days later that both of them returned. The books and records were gone—gone forever. This was the beginning of the Ripps-Mitchell case, known widely in the Justice Department as the Alabama case.

Joseph Mitchell and Sam Ripps had made a fortune in the wholesale jewelry business, selling principally to Army post exchanges. The technique for the tax swindle was simple. The bookkeeping system was the so-called intact system of bookkeeping—that is, all receipts went into the bank account and it was necessary that all receipts be deposited to keep the books in balance. Mitchell and Ripps would stash away a lot of small checks and cash, until a big check came along. They would then deposit the small checks and cash, while the big check went to a check cashing agency in New York. By this method, the understatement of income amounted to nearly $750,000.

4. Matters discussed taken from testimony before King subcommittee, *op. cit.,* pp. 1177-1297.

The Bureau of Internal Revenue from the start was firm about prosecution. In November 1947, it transmitted the case to the tax division of the Department of Justice. In March 1948, the case was assigned to a highly able Justice attorney, John H. Mitchell. In August, he prepared to go to Birmingham to confer with the U. S. attorney there. Congressman Frank Boykin called him and said that Caudle had indicated to him that Mitchell would enjoy staying at Boykin's place at Mobile Bay where there was good fishing and boating. Mitchell not only declined the invitation but said he went into Caudle's office and reproached him since there was no secret in the fact that Boykin was very much interested in the case. "I got the impression they had probably contributed very generously to Boykin's campaign," said Mitchell. On September 21, Mitchell recommended prosecution.

Mr. Caudle did not show any signs of enthusiasm. He had a talk with the U. S. attorney from Alabama, Mr. Hill, from which Mr. Mitchell seems to have been excluded. On September 27, the case was sent to Mr. Hill with a letter asking him to evaluate it. Customarily, the case would have been sent with a recommendation for prosecution. Around the same time, Caudle wrote a memorandum in which his only comment on the merits of the case was, "There are many proclaiming the innocence of these people."

It was most difficult to try the case since there were no books. The statement of the bookkeeper for the firm could not be relied on too heavily. The department considered having one of the defendants turn State's evidence against the other. Then there was consideration to developing a case on the net-worth theory. Finally, by June 1949, Mitchell was convinced that prosecution was impracticable and so acquiesced in a return of the case to Internal Revenue.

In November, Internal Revenue resubmitted the case and made reference to an audit report. This sparked a thought in Mitchell's mind. If there was an audit report, there must be records of some kind and the taxpayer's accountants must have them in their possession, so why not subpoena the taxpayer's accountants. Peyton Ford, deputy Attorney General, approved a presentation of the evidence to a grand jury which would be impaneled in Mobile instead of Birmingham, where U. S. attorney Hill was averse to the prosecution of the case. When Mitchell told Turner Smith, Caudle's assistant, of the step that was being taken, Smith's reactions were immediately recorded by Mitchell in a memorandum. He wrote: "Mr. Turner Smith then stated that Mr. Caudle would not like such a recommendation; that he had always had the distinct impression that Mr. Caudle did not want this case prosecuted and that he knew Mr. Caudle had been pleased when U. S. attorney John Hill had recommended that the prosecution be declined." A few days later Smith advised Mitchell that he should not play ball with Peyton Ford, because Ford was leaving the department, Mitchell recorded in a memo.

Before Mitchell's departure for Mobile, he received a call from Congressman Boykin in which the latter discussed point by point the various matters that the prosecution intended to raise. It was evident that he had been well briefed on all that was transpiring in the Justice Department. A call from Peyton Ford reached Mitchell in Mobile to the effect that no further information was to be given to Mr. Caudle and that he was to advise Caudle that Mr. Ford was handling the case. Mitchell's strategy was successful. The grand jury was impaneled and indictments were returned against Mitchell and Ripps and their wives. Mitchell and Ripps pleaded guilty and received heavy sentences. Mrs. Mitchell was a suicide.

Mitchell did not expect to be treated like a conquering hero on his return to Washington, but was unprepared for what was in store for him. Mr. Caudle refused to see him. He was given no further work to do. Mitchell heard that there was a memorandum to that effect by Caudle. Caudle testified that the reason for the cold shoulder was that he had lost confidence in Mitchell. Mitchell's change of heart in regard to prosecution had coincided with a visit by Drew Pearson in which Pearson reported rumors about a fix in return for a campaign contribution. Caudle felt that Mitchell lacked a fixity of purpose in being swayed by a newspaper reporter's complaint. (As a matter of fact, Caudle and Pearson were good friends.)

In any event, it was obvious that there was no longer any place for Mitchell in Caudle's department. Mitchell went to Peyton Ford, who arranged for a transfer to the criminal division, after Mitchell had been inactive for weeks in the tax division.

What was the explanation for Caudle's attitude? Rumors were rampant of a contribution to the party. Caudle testified, "And I remember this was sometime in 1948 when I got rumors that these men might try to make some contribution to the Democratic Committee. Mr. Joe Blythe was the Treasurer then, Mr. Chairman, and I know the Democratic Committee was hard up and did not have anything, if you will remember, and I called up Mr. Blythe and told him under no circumstances accept a contribution from these taxpayers because of rumors I have heard about this case." When Mr. Mitchell returned from Mobile the first time, he referred to the prevalent rumors that a substantial contribution had been made. According to Mitchell, Caudle stated: "I advised them not to do it, but Frank went ahead and took the money." Caudle admitted that he had received a call from the Democratic National Committee from a Mr. Carraway on the case. The contribution was rumored to be between $50,000 and $75,000.

### Hyman Harvey Klein[5]

On March 3, 1948, Hyman Harvey Klein admits that he got

5. Unless otherwise noted, all matters discussed are from testimony of King subcommittee, op. cit., pp. 3005-3310.

one of the worst shocks of his life. He had been looking forward with relish to a Caribbean cruise the following week, with his girl friend, according to Henry Grunewald. Two men walked into his office and identified themselves as internal revenue agents. The exact words exchanged were etched in Mr. Klein's mind. They laid down on his desk tax assessments for over $7 million. "Will you please inform me as to what this is all about?" he said. "We don't know," they answered. "All we are here for is to collect money." Klein replied, "That is rather unusual."

It was Klein's Caribbean cruise which had resulted in the assessment. The Internal Revenue Bureau got a tip that Klein was leaving on a round-the-world cruise. It was known that he had several million dollars worth of government bonds, and it was feared that the money might depart with Klein. Internal Revenue therefore slapped on him what is called a jeopardy assessment to protect the interests of the government.

During the war, there was an extensive black market in whiskey in which millions of dollars in currency changed hands. Klein, a Baltimore liquor dealer, attempted to circumvent the OPA price regulations on liquor through a series of complicated maneuvers involving the creation of a number of foreign corporations, principally in Cuba. Essentially, his operation consisted of buying whiskey in Canada, invoicing that whiskey to his Cuban corporation, which then resold the whiskey to his United States enterprises at a substantial markup. The purpose of the alleged transfer to the Cuban corporation was to justify the price markup under OPA ceilings. The whiskey, in fact, never left the United States, and the transactions were simply matters of form designed to evade OPA regulations. On a paid-in capital of $4,000, Klein made a profit of $5 million between April 1944 and January 1947. He paid a tax to the federal government of twenty-five percent, or over $1,200,000, as a capital gain. When he paid the tax, he thought that he was in the clear.

As soon as the jeopardy assessment was imposed, Klein hired legal counsel, originally the Root, Ballantine law firm in New York, and then two young lawyers who had left that law firm, E. Gayle McGuigan and Richard Kilcullen. It was a big case to these two lawyers and they poured hundreds and hundreds of hours into it. Feverishly they worked on letters and briefs, many times burning the midnight oil. By December 1951, the jeopardy assessment despite their best efforts, had not been lifted. To their astonishment, during his testimony in the Teitelbaum case, Charles Oliphant revealed that he had discussed the Hyman Harvey Klein case with Henry Grunewald and with a lawyer, I. Alfred Levy, whose son Oliphant had placed on his legal staff through Grunewald's efforts. McGuigan and Kilcullen demanded to know from Klein how Grunewald had come into the case. Klein, returning from California, said he had not the slightest idea. In indignation, at a luncheon at Longchamps Restaurant in New York, he, reportedly in anger at the unauthorized intervention, had pounded the table so hard that the silverware flew into the air.

Mr. Klein was an excellent actor and had been throughout the case. McGuigan and Kilcullen had also been acting, but in their case they had been completely innocent. Their performance was a sham one, a mock play before the footlights, while the real action transpired behind the curtain. For all their efforts mattered, they might just as well have gone fishing. It was not until the testimony in the Klein case before the King subcommittee that they learned of the machinations that had been going on in Washington and New York to fix the case, and that their actions were guided as if by an invisible hand which reached out from behind the curtain.

The first record of Grunewald's intervention in the case came twenty days after the jeopardy assessment. On March 23, 1948, Commissioner Schoeneman called Oliphant at 9:40 A.M. "I have a visitor coming in this morning. The same one that asked me about the Klein case. Can you find out about it?"

Grunewald visited Schoeneman at 10:15. At that time, Grunewald was introduced to Oliphant, a meeting that was to result in disaster to both. I. Alfred Levy, a friend of Klein, admitted speaking to Oliphant and Grunewald about the case. He says that he spoke to his law associate, William Power Maloney, who was an attorney for Grunewald, saying of Klein, "Bill, this poor devil is really being crucified." It was an act, he said, purely out of the goodness of his heart without any request by Klein.

Klein says that he did not know at the time of the jeopardy that he was under investigation. As a matter of fact, there was an intensive investigation by both the alcohol tax unit and the Internal Revenue Bureau, of which Klein must have been aware. This was the biggest black market investigation being carried on by the alcohol tax unit. Fifty-three of Klein's bank accounts had been collected for study and all of his movements were being reconstructed.

Even before the jeopardy assessment, Daniel A. Bolich, special agent in charge of the intelligence unit in New York, was showing unusual interest in the Klein case. In December 1947, four months before the jeopardy, Bolich advised agent Thomas J. Victory that criminal prosecution of Klein would be impossible, even though the investigation was in the early stages. The alcohol tax unit was in a prime position to unearth the facts since the unit was familiar with the liquor industry, who has or are seeking licenses, how liquor is merchandised, invoiced, transported, and so forth. Bolich took the position that he was against any co-operation with the alcohol tax unit on the ground that it would be a violation of the United States-Canada tax convention, but when that problem was cleared away, Bolich was still against such co-operation. In March 1948, when the case was becoming hot, the same month of the jeopardy assessment (which was imposed by the Washington office, not Bolich's New York office), Bolich, over the protests of Victory, took him off the case for two months to attend advanced training school. Without Victory, the Klein investigation was suspended, since he was in charge of it.

On August 24, 1948, McGuigan and Kilcullen were called over to the revenue office in New York and told that the special agent in charge, Mr. Bolich, was leaving New York to become assistant commissioner of internal revenue in Washington and wanted to close the Klein case before he left. Would they file a brief by August 27. The two lawyers protested the short time but having no choice worked continuously for the next seventy-two hours to file a brief. They could have spent the time to better avail because no one bothered to look at the document. On August 24, Victory was told by Bolich that he should file a report by the 26th and that no prosecution was to be recommended. Thus, the decision was made completely independent of any brief by the Klein lawyers. It was a nice thing, however, to have on the record.

The criminal prosecution angle had now been disposed of. Bolich didn't waste any time as assistant commissioner in Washington before taking his next step in behalf of Klein. He now moved to scuttle the investigation by the alcohol tax unit. On September 9, Carroll Mealey, alcohol tax unit chief, asked for a report as to the progress of the Klein case from Dwight Avis, indicating that it was at Bolich's request. On September 16, Avis finished his memorandum, a long document, and that very same day got an order from Mealey to close the probe. On that date, there was a call from Oliphant to Bolich in which Oliphant stated: "As I understand, you told White [a secretary's error for Dwight] this is not an ATU case, get out of it." This call was at noon, two hours after Avis had submitted his report.

This last step was to get rid of the jeopardy assessment that hung around Klein's head, making it impossible for him to conduct business. This was most difficult since there were so many lawyers in the Internal Revenue Bureau who knew and understood the issues involved and particularly the inflexible requirements of the statute governing rules of jeopardy assessments.

On September 16, Schoeneman said to Oliphant, "I think I will suggest they have the attorney write to Feidt for a conference. Then I think I can tell Buddy about it." (Buddy was Aubrey Marrs, head of the technical staff.) On September 18, two days later, Klein's attorneys did, in fact, write and request a conference. They claim they acted independently, but this is only the first case of what would be an astounding series of mental telepathy phenomena. On March 1, 1949, in a conference in Commissioner Schoeneman's office about the jeopardy, Oliphant noted in his summary, "The Commissioner advised them to address a letter to me [Oliphant] setting out the hardship and asking for a conference." On March 2, the day afterwards, Klein's attorneys did write a letter to the Bureau asking for a conference. Again, they thought they were acting independently. In November 1949, McGuigan and Kilcullen went to Washington and made an offer of settlement with the Bureau for $1 million. It was their judgment that they had arrived at that figure by long hard calculations and ratiocination. They were astounded to learn from the testimony that the offer of settlement for $1 million had been made long before. On June 20, 1949, in a conference of Bureau people the record states: "CO (Oliphant) says taxpayer will settle for an additional million dollars to settle 1944, 1945, 1946 and 1947."

The negotiations were being carried on by Grunewald.[6] In April 1949, the Bureau prepared interrogatories to be submitted to Klein. Grunewald asked Oliphant to hold them up. They discussed what was presumably the million dollar offer together on June 10, 1949. Oliphant said, "I am still thinking about that," and Grunewald said, "Fine, you take your

6. Testimony of Henry Grunewald before Kean subcommittee on the Internal Revenue Laws (83rd Congress), pp. 1260-66.

time." On July 8, Grunewald said, "I was talking to that fellow we met [presumed to be Levy] and you haven't got a chance to sell that question, have you?"

On December 20, 1949, revenue agent Barnes was examining Klein's books at the office of his accountant Maurice Haas. Grunewald was impatient for action. A few hours after Barnes left the office, Grunewald phoned Oliphant "that fellow Burns has that all written up or all investigated. . . . he said 'there is no hurry about it. I will write it up after the first of the year.' " Oliphant replied, "You are getting some double talk. I have got an expedite on it."

In early 1949, Aubrey Marrs, head of the technical division, was called into Bolich's office. "He recited briefly to me the horrible wrong that had been done to the taxpayer and that some way should be found to lift those liens. Mr. Bolich has a booming voice and he stormed around the room for some little while and I got my orders. I was head of the technical staff and any head of the technical staff ought to find some way to lift those liens." Marrs says he simply ignored Bolich's orders. The problem was highly complex. Marrs says of Oliphant who was cognizant of the complications, "Oliphant was probably a little solicitous about the taxpayer but very definitely he was trying to explore the settlement field trying to figure out if there wasn't some way or basis for settling the case." A decision to reject the million dollar offer was made on February 3, 1950, but Klein's lawyers knew nothing about it. Their hopes grew bigger as months elapsed. The Bureau prepared a letter for them in June 1950, but didn't bother to mail it until May 1951. Further efforts to lift the jeopardy were interrupted by the King investigation.

In the end, all these efforts came to nought when Klein was convicted in 1955 and sentenced on September 23, 1955, together with his two associates, to long jail terms for income tax evasion.

## Gotham Beef

Commissioner Dunlap, in November 1951, appointed a special board to review the criminal cases that had been closed in the New York office including the period in which Daniel A. Bolich had been special agent in charge from the beginning of 1946 until September 1948, when he became assistant commissioner of internal revenue. Of 509 cases that were closed the board found that 39 had been improperly closed. There was a case closed without prosecution, for example, of an olive oil dealer who had paid no income tax whatever, though his civil liability was $300,000. A case was closed of an estate with a tax of $10,000,000 and a fraud penalty of $5,000,000. There were abuses of the health policy of the Bureau—it was amazing how fast a man threatened with criminal prosecution developed grave circulatory disorders. Under the voluntary disclosure rule, the Bureau would not prosecute if the taxpayer came forward with the facts. Thus, there was often a race between the taxpayer when he realized that the Bureau was on his trail, and the Bureau to build up the case before the taxpayer made disclosures on his own. This disclosure rule could be the loophole through which a case could be readily fixed by a corrupt official.

The tax returns of the partners of the Gotham Beef Company, a New York partnership, were audited by the Bureau in 1945.[7] The agent on the case recommended criminal prosecution of the partners for income tax evasion. While this case was pending in the New York office of the intelligence division, the taxpayers decided to retain new counsel. They hired the firm of Schopick and Davis and offered to pay them $25,000 if prosecution could be averted. Their counsel tried to arrange a conference with the special agent in charge

7. For Gotham case, see examination of principals before Kean subcommittee, *op. cit.*, pp. 1066-1111.

in New York about the case, Bolich, but were unable to do so. It was thereafter suggested to them that a conference could be arranged with Bolich through the intercession of Henry Grunewald, and that the case could be fixed for a payment of $60,000.

The payoff was to be $60,000 to be transmitted to Schopick and Davis for transmittal to persons unknown. On September 15, 1948, a bundle of $52,000 in currency was taken to the office of Schopick and Davis. Irving Davis and Max Halperin were there when the money was counted. Two weeks later, the remainder was brought over. The accountant of Gotham, Leo Greenstein, and Max Halperin of Schopick and Davis, took a safety deposit box together, the former being escrow agent for Gotham and the latter for the Washington associate in the case, Henry Grunewald. The money was to be kept there in the Trade Bank and Deposit Company until the taxpayer was notified that he was not to be criminally prosecuted.

Halperin and Davis met Grunewald at his suite in the Hotel Washington, where Grunewald called Bolich in his presence, using the name of "Captain Henry." Grunewald told Davis to see Bolich, and lo and behold, he walked in on Bolich without an appointment the very next day. Bolich referred him to his technical adviser, and Davis told Gotham's accountant that the case was fixed.

A conference was arranged in the office of the intelligence unit at 253 Broadway so that Gotham's man, Tobias, could hear with his own ears, on October 28, 1948, that the fix was on. The word was then given that it was all right to release the money from the safe-deposit box to give to Halperin. Halperin and Hoffman went to Washington together. Halperin carried two bags and transferred one, which contained cash, to Grunewald who met him in Washington. Schopick and Davis got a check for $5,000 for their services.

That is the story as the Kean subcommittee had it. It was obtained from intermediaries in negotiations by the lawyers for immunities. The principals all refused to answer questions, pleading the privilege against self-incrimination.

## The $100,000 Sturgeon

Patullo Modes, Inc., a New York corporation engaged in the dress manufacturing business got into the internal revenue clutches when its tax returns and those of its officers were audited in 1944, and prosecution for criminal violations were proposed by the special agent on the case. Through the brother-in-law of Milton Hoffman, associated with Schopick and Davis, the taxpayers retained that law firm.[8]

On October 1, 1948, Irving Davis met with officers of Patullo Modes and advised them that Mr. Halperin had a friend in Washington. On October 8, Patullo Modes was advised that the cost would be $125,000. A couple of weeks later by negotiation it was reduced to $100,000. Hoffman and Davis told them to get busy and raise cash, but to be careful. They must not include the cash on the books of the corporation, nor should they sell securities, since that would leave a record; a safe deposit box was obtained at the Bowery Savings Bank, $72,000 was put in it during October by charging fictitious expenses for travel and entertaining of the corporation and then from personal sources another $3,000 was added. The remainder came from a loan from a Mr. Al Jacobs, secured by hypothecating nonregistered government bonds. On October 29, this cash was taken to the offices of Schopick and Davis. Following instructions, the money was in $100 bills in an envelope. "Here it is," said Morton Marks of Patullo Modes. They counted the money and found it a few hundred dollars short. So Schopick and Davis asked them to make it up, please. Davis had met Grunewald previously in his office in the Munsey Building in Washington.

8. For Patullo Modes case, see examination of principals before Kean subcommittee, *op. cit.,* pp. 1153-89.

This was a heftier case in size than Gotham Beef; the tax liabilities considered for prosecution ran to about a quarter of a million dollars—and so added precautions were taken. To give the appearance that negotiations were being conducted through regular channels, another law firm was brought in, Schwaeber, Quinn and Saver, who were to be paid a fee of $3,500. According to their records, Patullo Modes paid a total of $107,500 in fees to Schopick and Davis, who, in turn, paid Halperin a total of $7,700.

James D. Saver was an expert on tax prosecutions, having prosecuted all the tax cases for the eastern district of New York from 1935 to 1947 as a member of the U. S. attorney's office, so it was a good firm for Schopick and Davis to hire for the record.[9] Saver handled the case strictly on the merits—he went to Baradel who was the New York agent in January 1948, and later took up the case with Bolich, who was special agent in charge at the time in New York. Baradel, who succeeded Bolich as special agent in charge, rejected the argument on November 4, 1948. The claim that was made on behalf of the taxpayer was that no prosecution could be undertaken because the taxpayer had made a voluntary disclosure to the Bureau. An accountant, Maurice Smith, claimed that he had discussed the case with revenue agent Scherm and that Scherm had admitted that Smith on behalf of Patullo Modes had made a voluntary disclosure. Smith was indicted on a charge of filing a false statement. The record stated "Mr. Baradel advised the taxpayer's representative that the case did not qualify as a voluntary disclosure." Saver then advised Irving Davis that the defense would not be accepted and that the case would go on to prosecution.

Grunewald had introduced Halperin to Oliphant (it was this disclosure at the time of the Teitelbaum case that had first brought the finagling to light). That contact didn't mate-

9. For testimony of Schwaber and Saver, see testimony before King subcommittee, *op. cit.*, pp. 3390-3413.

rialize into anything for Patullo Modes. It was Bolich who produced results. After Saver told Davis the case was hopeless, Davis suggested that Saver should go to Washington to see Bolich. Saver said he could see no reason but "he continued to request that I go down and try again, put my point before the Assistant Commissioner." Saver said, "We have already been turned down." Davis replied, "Well, go down and try." Saver did go down in December 1948, had dinner with Bolich whom he knew, and saw him in his office the next day. Everything worked out fine. The case was dropped for a reason with no legal standing. "While the case might not technically be considered a voluntary disclosure case, nevertheless, if the taxpayer continues to co-operate in every way completing the investigation and rendering every possible assistance toward that end, the case would be given no prosecution consideration." Saver on his return notified Davis of the gratifying denouement in the case, and Davis registered no surprise. Bolich advised the New York bureau that there would be no prosecution. The report states: "In view of the commitment by higher authority for no prosecution consideration of this case, criminal prosecution is not recommended."

When Halperin and Hoffman came to the Truman inauguration, they brought a package, wrapped in brown paper. Grunewald swore that it was sturgeon that Halperin brought down from a place famous for sturgeon on 68th Street in Manhattan. Grunewald had a fine sense of humor. Halperin, who in the hearings refused to answer almost all questions on the grounds of self-incrimination, did swear that he had never brought down sturgeon. The package which Grunewald picked up in Union Station was believed to be $100,000 in currency.

This is the story as the Kean subcommittee had it. The principals refused to testify on the ground of self-incrimination.

On June 25, 1954, Grunewald, Bolich, Schopick, Halperin and Davis were indicted on a charge that $60,000 was paid in one case (Gotham Beef) and $100,000 in another case (Patullo Modes) in small bills that could not be traced, for fixing the two cases. On October 26, there was another indictment for conspiracy to avoid detection. On March 29, 1955, in the federal court for the southern district of New York, Grunewald, Bolich and Halperin were convicted. Davis and Schopick pleaded guilty and testified against Grunewald and Bolich, who received terms of five years.

## · XIII ·

# ROMAN HOLIDAY IN LOCAL
# TAX OFFICES

*There is an honest graft, and I am the example of how it works. I might sum up the whole thing by saying "I seen my opportunities and I took them."*
— GEORGE WASHINGTON PLUNKITT,
Sachem of Tammany Hall.

GEORGE WASHINGTON PLUNKITT died a millionaire. In this chapter we shall see how collectors and revenue agents throughout the country emulated Mr. Plunkitt. Many did not make the grade. During the Truman administration, nine revenue collectors were fired in connection with tax frauds. Between January 1, 1951, and April 10, 1952, a period when Internal Revenue, under severe pressure, was moved to act to cleanse itself, a total of 177 internal revenue officials were fired—72 for "irregularities" involving their relations with taxpayers; 18 for "embezzlement"; and 87 for "improper activities" not desirable in the service. More than two dozen had been jailed for shakedowns, connivance with racketeers, and for accepting fees and bribes. The loss of revenue to the United States Treasury is beyond calculation.

Much of the ill-gotten gains were hard to trace. Committee investigator Dowling of the King committee said,"We discovered a case where the agent put in the fix for the contractor after the latter weatherproofed the agent's house; another builder over the barrel built a garage for the tax collector. Sometimes the tax agents picked out a TV set or a washing machine in the stores owned by their intended victims. One fellow had a dozen tailored suits ($125 apiece). We learned that he had processed tax returns for a clothing maker . . . one tax clerk making $6,000 a year had an elaborate Chinese art collection. Another leaned to historic documents, including letters of Presidents. Still others bought costly furs and jewelry."

Local tax collectors were often beyond the control of the Bureau headquarters in Washington. The reason was simple. Everything was weighed in the balance of politics and, politically speaking, many local tax collectors were more potent than those in Washington who were supposed to give them directions.

### Politics and the Choice of Collectors

Mr. James B. E. Olson gave a graphic description of how a collector was chosen. The post at issue was the Brooklyn and Queens post which had just been vacated by Joe Nunan when he moved up to commissioner of internal revenue. It was dinner time at Toots Shor's in New York.

> I went over to speak to Mr. Kelly [county leader of Brooklyn] to ask him how he was and he said, "Fine." And he said, "Is that Hannegan with you and Nunan, Jimmy?" And I said, "Yes." And he said, "I would like to meet him." And so I got Mr. Kelly and brought him over and introduced him to Mr. Hannegan, and Mr. Hannegan was the National Democratic Chairman and Mr. Kelly then asked to speak to Mr. Nunan, and Mr. Nunan went over to Mr. Kelly's table and came back to me and he said, "You are out. It is Marcelle." [Testimony before King subcommittee, p. 89.]

And that is how Mr. Marcelle was chosen to be collector.

The politics was elementary. Olson was a Queens man and Kelly insisted that the job should rotate and should belong to Brooklyn this time, hence Marcelle. Mr. Marcelle's qualifications for the job were irrelevant. In the investigation that was made prior to submission of Marcelle's name to the Senate, at least two prominent citizens recommended against the appointment. But the investigation was rushed. Kelly called Hannegan and said he was getting impatient. The request for an investigation was made on March 14, and the report was made by the 24th, a period of ten days.[1] The probe of even a low-grade government employee takes three months or more. Mr. Irey, chief co-ordinator of law enforcement for the Treasury protested against the haste. Nunan said he would go to New York personally and submit a further report, but nothing was done about that. A few days later Marcelle's name went to the Senate.

Mr. Delaney, the collector for Boston, who wound up in jail, had a little more trouble with his investigation.[2] The probe lasted from August until November 1943. Delaney had filed a petition in bankruptcy in 1934 and had not been discharged by the time of the appointment. He claimed that he had not been discharged because of an oversight of his attorney. This argument was accepted, even though the general counsel's office of the Treasury reported that the argument had no validity. Actually, the trustee in bankruptcy had made many charges against Delaney, such as the receipt of unaccounted-for sums, incorrect schedule of assets and liabilities, and other charges. It was difficult to check thoroughly on the case in 1943 since somehow the bankruptcy file had disappeared from the federal district court.

Charges of larceny had been filed against Delaney in 1933 by an insurance company and the court had put him on pro-

---

1. Testimony before King subcommittee on the internal revenue laws (82nd Congress), p. 911.
2. Testimony before King subcommittee, *op. cit.*, pp. 767-81.

bation. In his application form for the revenue job, Government Form 57, he denied that he had been involved in any court action, but he had not sworn to the application as he was supposed to do.

None of the derogatory facts appeared in the summary which the Assistant Secretary of the Treasury had prepared for the Secretary. That summary had only two paragraphs. The first, in full, read: "He has the necessary political support."

Delaney proved to be a dynamic public servant, politically. A memorandum of February 25, 1946, to Mr. Delaney, from his chief office deputy, John E. Burns, reads: "In considering promotions in the field, I thought you might like to have the list of employees who purchased dinner tickets for the Hannegan reception." Frank Kraemer, collector of internal revenue for Connecticut, was threatened with indictment for violation of the Hatch Act for collecting political contributions from his employees. Delaney wrote to Matthew Connelly, secretary to Truman, "It does appear a shame that one of our boys is being penalized for doing what comes naturally. Will you let me know what I can pass along to Kraemer?" Kraemer was indicted, convicted and removed from office, but was pardoned by Truman.

Mr. Finnegan of St. Louis was so popular with the administration that it would not let him go. Three times he submitted his resignation, and three times it was declined, twice by Matthew Connelly, the last time by President Truman himself who asked him to stay on.

There were distinctly unfavorable reports on collector Smyth of San Francisco which had no effect in halting his appointment. When he was appointed a deputy collector in 1935 and again in 1941 there were adverse reports from the intelligence unit. In 1945 Elmer Irey, chief law-enforcement co-ordinator for the Treasury, wired as to his appointment as collector: "My reactions to proposal are not favorable."

The derogatory information applied to his income tax returns, his filing record and his drinking.[3]

## *The Marcelle Story*[4]

Joseph P. Marcelle, federal collector of internal revenue for the first district of New York, covering Brooklyn, Queens and adjacent counties on Long Island, was frank in speaking to the committee about the personal tragedy of his being fired from his job on October 23, 1951. It had deprived him of his long-cherished dream of becoming a Supreme Court justice in New York.

He had been the Democratic leader of the nineteenth assembly district in Brooklyn. He said he had cleaned it up and made it a "lovely, lovely district." When asked if there had been racketeers in his district, he said, "I wonder if they were really racketeers or just hoodlums." He longed to become a Supreme Court judge but the policy of the Democratic leadership, because of severe criticism of Tammany, was to deny these plums to district leaders. By getting a federal job as collector, he said he could retire "as undefeated champion," disavow politics by wrapping himself up in the Hatch Act and thus build up his stature to a point where he could get the Democratic nomination, tantamount, of course, to election.

But the prize eluded him. As he testified: "I was pretty much heated up. The last 10 years I was a nominee each year, and I was supposed to be nominated and something would always happen. The county leader would die or somebody else would die or there would be a change in the organization." By 1949, it looked as if he would be a cinch—then that damnable tax trouble arose. He tried to get the investigation killed

3. Testimony before King subcommittee, *op. cit.,* p. 1996.
4. All matters discussed in this section taken from testimony before King subcommittee, *op. cit.,* pp. 818-909.

by talking to various people, including the commissioner of internal revenue, George Schoeneman, former deputy commissioner, C. B. Allen, and the former commissioner, Joe Nunan. He tried to make a deal to delay the investigation until after the judicial nominations, but as Marcelle complained to the committee, he got clipped when the prize was only inches away.

When Marcelle was fired, he was told that there were irregularities in his tax returns, that he owed $30,000 to $60,000 more than he had paid. A return had been submerged by a very simple device. His 1948 return which showed a gross income of $135,776 and after deductions $65,000 (his salary as collector was around $10,000) had been labeled as a "collector's return," which was a classification for a return under $8,000. Such a return never went over to the internal revenue agent's office and is never audited. Had it not been for Marcelle's investigation, it probably would never have been seen.

Marcelle made lots of money by private law practice while he was collector. For six hours work in a guardianship case, assigned by a court, he received $17,500. He became part owner of the Eastern Electric Vending Machine Corporation and on an investment of $5,000 he and his wife got $175,000 return in a period of less than three years. This company did a big business with Abner (Longie) Zwillman, a notorious gambler.

Marcelle, as collector, often went to the race track. He explained that he wanted to check on the deputies who were assigned there for checking on tax evaders. "I hated to be caught in the rush, but many Saturdays I have gone out, until I decided golf was healthier." For several years, always on January 27, by a peculiar coincidence he was stricken with a strep throat and notified the commissioner in Washington that he needed sick leave. He would then go to Florida where he would take treatments by attendance at Hialeah race park. These sick leaves always came at the busiest time for the internal revenue offices when they were making out tax refunds. He went to Europe and charged expenses off on his tax return. He was no longer counsel for the man whom he claimed to represent. He charged off the cost of running his car as an expense and explained on his state tax return that the cost was for visiting local revenue offices. As a matter of fact, he never went inside any of these offices though he testified that he did drive by in his car. "I didn't go in because I didn't want the fellows, they would think I was butting in there or going over the field deputy's head."

This was the man who was charged with the duty to collect each year $1 billion of government revenue.

## The Delaney Story

Denis W. Delaney, collector of internal revenue for the Boston district, was responsible for collecting $2 billion of federal revenue. He was a popular figure in Boston—an Elk, a member of the Ancient Order of Hibernians and a Legionnaire. He was a popular figure in charitable causes, but a little careless.

In the Republican 80th Congress in 1947, a subcommittee of the House Appropriations Committee, headed by Representative Canfield of New Jersey, turned over to the Department of Justice evidence of a "condition which may embrace criminality," in the Boston office. An amount totalling $1,911 in change from the March of Dimes had turned up in a file cabinet in his office, and he was accused of drawing on the March of Dimes to pay for a champagne cocktail party. He was charged with disregard of trust funds, improper handling of collections for charities and political organizations and violations of the Hatch Act. Democratic leaders claimed it was a Republican smear. Representative John W. McCormack, House Majority Leader, said, "The hearings have shown Collector Delaney to be a fine, public-spirited citizen who has made a great collector."

A Mr. Shapiro, who owned the Maxwell Shapiro Woolen Company, owed the Government $142,000, which he was unable to pay.[5] A Mr. Daniel Friedman and a Mr. Hugh Finnegan, the latter the brother of collector James P. Finnegan of St. Louis, whom we shall later encounter, visited Mr. Shapiro in April 1949 and said that they could shave down the liabilities to $40,000. They asked for a fee of $10,000. Mr. Shapiro called up Mr. Delaney and said, "Are these fellows all right?" Delaney said, "It is all right to give it to them." Referring to Mr. Finnegan, he said his brother was "scheduled to take the place of Mr. Schoeneman, and he is going to be the head of the collectors." Shapiro gave them a check for $5,000. Ten days later, Mr. Friedman returned and said Shapiro's offer had been taken favorably. Shapiro called Delaney and said, "Is it all right for me to give them the check for $5,000?" Delaney answered, "He is all right."

Friedman seemed to know all about Shapiro's tax problems. He said "Everything is all right. It takes just a little time, that is all." He tried to sell him insurance and wanted to look over his business. Nothing happened, and Shapiro continued to pay his taxes as they accrued, as usual. At the end of 1950, Friedman suggested to Shapiro he should send in $40,000 to Delaney as a settlement for his liabilities, which Shapiro declined, since there were no documents, no letter offering a compromise, nothing to go on.

At a luncheon with Delaney in January 1951, Shapiro said, "Denis, I am beginning to think these guys are fakers," and Delaney replied, "You must have patience."

Checks were offered in evidence. Two for $2500 each were made out by Estate Research Bureau dated a few days after the two $5000 payments by Shapiro. Another for $2500 was

5. Matters discussed in this section as to Delaney are taken from testimony before the King subcommittee, *op. cit.*, pp. 595-645; 709-81.

dated a few days after a $5000 payment by a Mr. Hellman, a client for Estate Research Bureau recommended by Shapiro. Testimony was also given that Mr. Delaney in 1949 directed that accounts outstanding in the warrants stage against Maxwell Shapiro, which would enable the government to get out levies on his property, his bank accounts, and so forth, were taken out of the file. Delaney advised the deputy collector that he was going to handle the case himself.

Another person to whom Friedman paid a call was Morris Boorky, secretary of the Massachusetts Steel Treating Corporation. In 1949, this company had outstanding liabilities to the government of $100,000 and the Internal Revenue Bureau had put liens on the corporation to that extent, which, of course, made it extremely difficult for them to do business. Mr. Friedman walked in, introduced himself as a tax expert and gave as a reference Denis W. Delaney. He was very familiar with the case and said that "If it were presented through the proper channels" that something could be done. Boorky, overawed by his peculiar knowledge of the case, gave him checks totaling $5,000 and, sure enough, in a few days the Worcester office called and said that the liens had been removed. Mr. Friedman returned and asked for another $10,000. He said that he would arrange to have the debt of the company, now reduced to $80,000, cleared up. Boorky objected to the amount asked and Friedman replied, "You don't think that I get it all?" It was obvious now to Boorky that this man was not a tax expert but was engaged in something that wasn't according to Hoyle. So he refused to give the $10,000. Sure enough, shortly afterwards, the liens were put back onto the plant. Proof was shown that the liens of Massachusetts Treating had been removed by direct order of Denis Delaney.

Martin P. Higgins, chief field deputy, testified that Delaney had illegally lifted many liens, and Higgins frequently protested. On one occasion, Delaney reminded him that he was the boss. On another occasion, when Higgins reminded him that lifting a lien was particularly dangerous, Delaney said to him, "I don't wish to have that type of memorandum." On another occasion, Delaney had said to him, "What can I do to tie these people up?" and seven days later he ordered the lien discharged.

Mr. Thomas E. Scanlon, supervisor of the New England division, says he found the office in fearful shape. There were close to 2,000,000 unfiled case cards and a backlog of 80,000 warrants. The total of liens personally discharged by Delaney amounted to half a million dollars. When he found that De-laney had been discharging tax liens illegally, he walked into his office and bluntly told him off.

> I found Delaney with his feet up on the desk and contentedly smoking a cigar. Delaney was not the least bit upset until I informed him that he could lose his $100,000 bond, his automobile, his home and all his assets unless he obeyed the law in regard to the discharge of liens. Then his feet came down from the desk and he said, "I didn't know anything at all about that."

Like many other collectors, Delaney "seen the opportunities" for making money by furnishing his personal services. Take the case, for example, of Jo-Jo. An outside cafe in Boston had a performer named Jo-Jo, who had a juke box behind him and played drums and sometimes he changed his hat. A federal amusement tax was assessed against the cafe. If he had sung, it would have been clear that the cafe was taxable, but he did not sing, only engaging in pantomime. The cafe owner had numerous conferences with Delaney, who referred the matter to Washington. The tax liability was $15,000. On a trip, Delaney stopped over in Washington and discussed the matter with the Bureau, which decided that prospectively the tax would be imposed, but it would be assessed for the period for which the assessment was made. Delaney later said he had a virus and the owner of the cafe thoughtfully provided Mr. Delaney with a rent-free cottage at the beach equal to $1500.

Delaney received $2,000 as a fee for introducing a friend to important personages in Washington like Schoeneman and Connelly in connection with a license for a new radio station. He picked up a Cadillac in a very easy way. The dealer came out of a conference with Delaney and told his son, "They know we are in trouble, and they know Uncle Reuben is in trouble, and he wants to get a new Cadillac for his car and $250." After he was dismissed, Delaney sent them a check.

Mr. Delaney was indicted; one indictment had six counts charging acceptance of bribes; the second indictment had three counts charging corruption in the filing of false certificates and the lifting of liens. He was convicted on three of the six counts of the first indictment and all three counts of the second indictment. The conviction was reversed by the Court of Appeals on the ground that he did not get a fair trial because of the charged atmosphere in Boston at the time. Mr. Delaney then pleaded guilty to tax evasion and bribery and was sentenced to a year in jail.

### The Finnegan Story[6]

John Martin Brodsky was a young man who had just entered the insurance business, but he had a world of confidence. He drove up with insurance broker Richard V. Clark, Jr., to the offices of the Valley Steel Products Company. Brodsky said that he was going to go in and sell them insurance. Mr. Clark said, "I think you are wasting your time, Marty." Clark said he had solicited this account over a period of years and, in fact, had given his last sales pitch two months ago. Brodsky said to Clark, "Oh, no." He walked in and in no time at all he had sold them a packet of insurance.

This man, Brodsky, was a fireball. He sold insurance all

6. All matters taken from testimony before King subcommittee, *op. cit.*, pp. 326-566.

over the lot to prospects who were considered by the best insurance salesmen to be unsellable. The more amazing evidence of his virtuosity was that the sales resistance of his prospects crumpled almost immediately after he entered the door.

Mr. Brodsky, as you readily may suspect, had a secret weapon. It was not too secret, because he babbled about it to several people. When he visited Valley Steel Products Company with Mr. Clark, he said cryptically, "They are in trouble on 12th Street," which is where the office of the collector of internal revenue is located. The firms that he visited had sizable tax delinquencies. Mr. Brodsky merely walked in and said, according to a witness, "I am from Mr. Finnegan's office." According to insurance agent Donald D. Kelly, "He told me that he had formed an association with Mr. Finnegan in an insurance agency and that time there were a great many firms in St. Louis who had tax delinquencies, and it was his plan to follow these firms and tell them that they should buy insurance to cover these—life insurance on key men to cover these tax deficiencies. As Mr. Clark wrote to him when he brought suit against him for a commission, "Your partner supplied the entree, you were to supply the leg work, and I was to supply the know-how."

His association with Mr. Finnegan was not all clover for Brodsky. Let us consider, for example, his sale of insurance to Valley Steel Products Company. That firm had outstanding tax liabilities of close to $300,000. They were eager to oblige Mr. Brodsky with insurance on key executives, but, unfortunately, all the key executives were uninsurable. They therefore went down the line and found a bookkeeper, Mr. Phillip Muennig, whom they sought to insure. The next snag was that the firm apparently didn't have the cash. So they paid Brodsky $23,886.37, the discounted premiums for ten years, by getting a loan from a bank and assigned the insurance policy to the bank as collateral. Then another complication arose when it was found that Mr. Muennig also was uninsurable for physical reasons. The premiums were returned by the insurance company but only $22,400 was used by Valley Steel to liquidate the loan. A check for $1,486.37 was made payable to Phillip Muennig, endorsed by him and made payable to Dudmar Insurance Agency, which was Brodsky's firm. Brodsky was getting a commission on an insurance policy which had not been earned.

Brodsky, apparently under severe emotional stress, begged insurance broker Kelly to send the first year's commission of $700 to Finnegan, who was staying at the Mayflower hotel in Washington. The best that Kelly would do, since the policy had not cleared up to that time, was to write Finnegan and explain to him why it was not possible to send the $700. After Brodsky got the check for $1,486, he deposited it in the account of the Dudmar Insurance Agency, which was a joint account opened by Finnegan, his secretary and Brodsky, two of whose signatures were necessary. Documentary evidence showed that almost all of this entire amount was withdrawn by Finnegan for his own use. Subsequently, Brodsky sold more insurance policies to Valley Steel, but the premiums were used to pay off the remainder of the bank debt that Valley Steel had, amounting to the check made out to Phillip Muennig. In other words, Brodsky got almost nothing out of the sale. Confirming the hard terms of his association with Finnegan, insurance broker Clark said that on one occasion, Brodsky told him, "If that guy doesn't get off my neck, I am going to drop dead."

Finnegan, after some deliberations, might have decided that the joint account was too risky and it was closed. Subsequently, the commissions were paid directly into the Dudmar Insurance Agency and then paid by check to Finnegan, his wife or son, who received $6,193.11 altogether during 1949-50. Finnegan and Brodsky said the sums were for Finnegan's legal services, but they couldn't agree what the services were.

Brodsky got into a fight with insurance broker Clark about

his split in the sale of insurance to Food Center, the entree for which was supplied by Finnegan. Clark started suit when Brodsky refused to pay. Three thousand dollars in settlement of the claim was paid to Clark by an unknown person. The lawyer who gave the money to Clark said to him, "The party that gave me this has asked me to tell you no matter how Mr. Brodsky insults you or what he accuses you of, don't mention this or his brother will have to pay some $19,000 worth of bills that he [Brodsky] owes over town." At this time, Hugh Finnegan, a brother of James Finnegan, gave him $3,000 in cash to prevent some lawsuit that might cause his brother embarrassment. The Finnegans apparently feared that Brodsky, if he were told who made the payment, might realize the power he had over Finnegan and might take further advantage of it.

James P. Finnegan, whom we have met previously in connection with the RFC and the American Lithofold loan, had become internal revenue collector in 1944. He was a close friend of Harry Truman. He worked two or three hours a day and the rest of the time he practiced law. "Genial Jim" made at least $35,000 a year from the law against $10,000 as collector. He was a close friend, too, of Robert E. Hannegan, the internal revenue commissioner at the time, since they had played football together in high school. He said, "When I was sworn in as collector as successor to Robert E. Hannegan, I was told to give as little or as much time to the job as I wanted. Hannegan told me I could continue with my law practice." He made about the same statement that Joe Nunan later made: "As a collector, I understood that I was to be administrator; that I was not a tax expert and that I was not appointed by the fact that I knew anything about taxes." He made it clear that he took the job because it would enhance his prestige and would enable him to build up his law practice. Finnegan did say that he thought the job was a form of public service. When asked how a collector helps, he said,

"You help folks by getting them a position, obtaining a job here and a job there."

We have previously encountered Hugh Finnegan as a member of the Friedman-Finnegan team which visited Maxwell Shapiro in behalf of the Estate Research Bureau. The collector for the Philadelphia area, Francis R. Smith, testified that James P. Finnegan had phoned him and arranged an appointment for his brother, Hugh Finnegan, and Donald Friedman. The gentlemen visited him and with caution and circumlocution sounded him out on the objectives of the Estate Research Bureau. Mr. Smith was an honest man and after catching the drift of what they were discussing, told them curtly that he was not interested.

At the time that Shapiro paid the Estate Research Bureau $10,000, of which Denis Delaney took a share, a sum of $2,000 was paid to James P. Finnegan. He had no plausible explanation for his receipt of the money. He said that he had been paid by the Hydroplane Company, of which Hugh Finnegan was president. He said his services consisted of telling people whether they should invest their money in Hydroplane. It is hard to see why Finnegan should have been paid money for advising investors to stay out of his brother's project. He was not an engineer. As a lawyer, he was hardly competent to advise Hydroplane on New York law.

One of the charges on which Finnegan was subsequently indicted involved his activities with the Karol Kell Garment Company. This firm had sizable tax liabilities, and Finnegan arranged, contrary to usual practice, to have it paid off on an installment basis of $425 a week. The informal basis on which this whole arrangement was made was evidenced by a note on a letterhead of Karol Kell, which contained this notation: "Joe's firm owes this. Can this be handled $125 a week, social security, General Electric. Who should the following checks be made or sent to." The handwriting was Sam Abromavitz's, part owner of Karol Kell, with Joe Goldberg the other owner. The back tax liabilities of Karol Kell were arranged to be disposed of at $125 a week on the social security liability and $300 a week on the other liabilities, making $425 a week. General Electric refers to representation by Finnegan as a lawyer in behalf of Abromavitz.

In the middle of 1948, the installments were reduced from $425 to $250 a week. By a strange coincidence, in June and for four months thereafter, Karol Kell made a personal check out to Finnegan of $250 a month. By 1949 the back liabilities had increased from $10,000 to $27,000 and pressure by Finnegan's assistants forced a collection from Karol Kell. The monthly checks to Mr. Finnegan then ceased. During 1948, while these payments were being made, Finnegan gave instructions not to file a lien.

Mr. Abromavitz also owed $10,000 personally. In November 1949, Abromavitz paid Finnegan $1,000. It was Finnegan's contention that the money both from Karol Kell and from Abromavitz came to him because of legal advice that he had given to Abromavitz in real estate matters, and that Karol Kell owed money to Abromavitz so it was logical for him to receive money from Karol Kell. The embarrassing fact for Mr. Finnegan was that Abromavitz owed Karol Kell money, not vice versa. Records of the RFC show, moreover, that Finnegan's efforts in behalf of Karol Kell included calls on two occasions to Charles G. Alexander, manager of the St. Louis RFC office, in which Finnegan inquired about its application for a loan. Finnegan also allegedly had a $641 furniture bill paid by Karol Kell.

Finnegan was indicted on five charges. On March 15, 1952, he was convicted of having accepted $5,000 from the Warwick Operating Company in its claim against the government for damages. The charge was that he used his information and position as collector to obtain information for Warwick concerning its claim. A second count on which he was convicted is based on receipt of money from Lithofold in the course of efforts to get Lithofold an RFC loan. He was sentenced to two years in jail.

## New York

The third district of New York, the upper part of Manhattan, was considered the worst in the country. This office was a rich harvest for thieving magpies of the Bureau, since it was the locus of the concentrated wealth of the nation. Revenues increased from $235 million in 1939 to over $3 billion ten years later.

In December 1949, a complete report on the conditions in the office were submitted to Commissioner Schoeneman after which the collector, James W. Johnson, was deprived of all authority over his employees. The charges against Johnson were not of personal dishonesty, but inability to control a corrupt office. For the next year and a half, the office was run by a team of specially qualified Bureau officials sent in from Washington. By 1951, eight of the agents had been found guilty of shakedowns and embezzlements and seven had been sent to the penitentiary. Taxpayers got warrants for taxes they had paid, social security payments were allowed to run delinquent for months until the special committee took over. Commissioner Schoeneman in February 1950 advised Secretary Snyder the time had come to fire Johnson. Truman delayed because the Democratic party was split with the mayoralty election coming up and, no matter who the new choice was, it would precipitate further discord in Tammany. It was not until November 30, that Johnson was asked to resign and not until July of the next year that he was fired. The new collector was Monroe Dowling, who was fired in March 1952 for irregularities in his own tax returns.

Here are some of the typical cases which were considered by the King subcommittee. Let us look at agent Robert W.

Selden.[7] Mr. Selden's net worth when he joined the service in 1935 was $470. In the 10 years until 1945, at an average pay of $3,000 a year, he was paid $30,000. His net worth, however, had gone up to $23,727. He had four brokerage accounts by 1951 and two safety deposit boxes. In one year he had deposited over $12,000 in cash in one brokerage account and $8,000 in another year. He had personal property which was insured for $23,000. Mr. Selden was unavailable for comment.

Agent Hofrichter was put in the embarrassing position of trying to explain expenditures far above his income.[8] On first examination, he answered that he had won $5,000 in horse racing and betting. When it appeared that the unexplained surplus was $13,000, he raised his winnings from $5,000 to $13,000. He explained that he had had a phenomenal run of "hot horses," paying 20-to-1, which he had been tipped on by a bookie named Packy, whom he used to meet on the corner. Packy, he said, had disappeared. He supplied the committee with a list of horses on which he had won commencing with Mah Heavens. Many of the dates had been erased and a date one day earlier supplied. It looked as if Mr. Hofrichter had gone to back files of the *Morning Telegraph,* and it occurred to him only after he made out the list that the horses actually ran the day before the *Telegraph* published the results.

In many tax investigations, a favorite explanation of the taxpayer was winnings at the horse races. Horse racing is about the only method of making money today in which there are no documentary or human witnesses to rebut one's statement. For every investment, there is a record and for any other form of wagering there are human beings involved. The pari-mutuel machines, however, have no eyes or ears and are forever silent. A taxpayer or revenue agent in trouble, however, can claim that he received a gift of money. The favorite source is money from Mother, which Mother always thought-

7. Testimony before King subcommittee, *op. cit.,* pp. 2721-54.
8. Testimony before King subcommittee, *op. cit.,* pp. 2761-2826.

fully provides in cash. The recipient is so overcome by sentiment that he refuses to put it in a bank, he locks it up at home and draws on it as it is needed.

Agent Mordecai Miller was forced to admit that he had four savings accounts and had to stop at that point, because his memory was poor.[9] He went to Florida on vacation, moved from an apartment at $50 a month to one for $108 and sent his children to a summer camp. He explained that he had received from his mother substantial cash gifts which he had kept in a vault. His mother and father had seven children and the question was how they managed to make such substantial gifts. Miller said, "My mother and father preferred me over all the children." A Mr. Charles Hagopian supplied another explanation. He says that Miller investigated his tax situation, then invited Hagopian to go out to a restaurant. He said to Hagopian, "Are you an Armenian?" Hagopian said yes, and Miller said, "I am, too." They got into a car together and Miller told him that if he gave him $1500 everything would be all right. Negotiations broke down.

Adrian Ash, the agent in the Universal Pictures case (the case which involved Secretary Snyder) had a preference for stocks.[10] He examined the books of a textile company and the vice-president in charge of sales made a loan to him of $8,500 and gave him a check for $1,890 with which Mrs. Ash opened a brokerage account. In an examination of the books of Gimbel Bros., Mr. Spar, assistant treasurer, "stated that he had purchased some Dumont stock. Mr. Ash replied that he was interested in getting some stock in Dumont; that since he did not have a brokerage account would Mr. Spar buy him 100 shares of Dumont. Mr. Spar complied and bought 100 shares of Dumont stock for Mr. Ash through his brokerage account." Spar said he was repaid by check; Ash said he repaid him with cash; there was no record of such a withdrawal from his

9. Testimony before King subcommittee, *op. cit.,* pp. 646-74.
10. Testimony before King subcommittee, *op. cit.,* pp. 2831-86.

account. The stock was kept in Spar's account till the completion of the audit when it was transferred to Mrs. Ash.

## San Francisco

The San Francisco office liked to run things its own way without interference. Stanley V. McKenney came to San Francisco in 1935 as assistant to the supervisor of collections and accounts, which plays the same role in collectors' offices as bank examiners do to banks. The collector said to him, "Do you know what we do to supervisors out here that we don't like? We throw them out the window." That was the tone of his relationship with the office for the next fifteen years, during which he became supervisor, one of continuous hostility, lack of co-operation and contempt from the office.[11] He didn't get much help from Washington. He wrote a letter of complaint to Assistant Commissioner Schoeneman and received a reply in which Schoeneman urged him to co-operate more closely with the staff. Since 1940, Washington had been told that the San Francisco office was a bad one, but nothing was done about it. In 1944, Commissioner Nunan asked McKenney on a visit to Washington, what he thought of the office. McKenney gingerly replied that Collector Smyth liked to run his office without interference. Nunan cut the conversation short by saying, "Mr. Smyth is a fine person."

The San Francisco office was an important one. In 1950, collections ran over $1,850,000,000 from 2,580,000 returns. From an administrative viewpoint, it was a bad office, second to that of New York. Backdating of returns was widespread, agents had outside activities and sources of income, backlogs of work piled up and undeposited money orders and checks were strewn around the office. John J. Boland, who was chief

11. Testimony of McKenney before King subcommittee, *op. cit.*, pp. 2081-101.

field deputy till he was suspended in October 1951, had tax-payers' returns, checks and warrants in his desk drawer and in a box at home. The checks totaled $31,000, some dating as far back as 1944 so that when deposited, the government lost thousands of dollars from checks which were no longer good.[12]

The office was as political as any in the country. The collector, James Smyth, had managed Roosevelt's campaign in northern California in 1944. He had managed the campaign of Senator Downey. He had been a candidate for mayor of San Francisco in 1947 and again in 1951 until the tax irregularities arrested his ambitions. The assistant chief of the income tax division was John A. Malone, the brother of William M. Malone, chairman of the Democratic central committee of San Francisco County. The office was ruled by a small clique of about half a dozen individuals who were known within the office as "The Royal Family," and who were reputedly accessible to persons who wanted to fix tax difficulties, or obtain special favors.

The political tone of the San Francisco office is illustrated by the case of George T. Davis,[13] who had been in charge of the Truman-Barkley campaign in northern California. His income tax returns for 1946, 1947 and 1948 came under scrutiny as a result of investigations of passport frauds. The revenue agent found that bank deposits exceeded reported income by an average of $10,000 each year. In referring the case to the special agent in charge, there was mention of Davis' political position and an explanation that Davis might have put campaign contributions through his personal account. "A fantastic thought," said Congressman Kean, but nothing was done about the discrepancies.

The Kefauver committee revealed a new technique for extracting money from taxpayers developed by revenue bureau

12. Testimony before King subcommittee, *op. cit.,* p. 2057.
13. Testimony before King subcommittee, *op. cit.,* pp. 2262-327.

employees in the area.[14] Patrick Mooney, a former chief field deputy, was an officer in Mountain City Consolidated Copper Company, which was a "shadow mine." Elmer "Bones" Remer, a prominent California gambler, who had a tax deficiency of $773,535, bought $2400 worth of the copper stock, deducted it from a check to the government against an outstanding income tax warrant and was not bothered further by tax difficulties. Ernest Mike Schino, another former chief field deputy, was apparently a participant in the scheme. Several hundred persons, many of whom were having tax trouble, bought stock in the mine. There was evidence that Gertrude Jenkins, a convicted abortionist, paid $5,000 to Mooney, half of which was to go to Schino to fix her case. The owner of a large wholesale automobile-parts store, who refused to buy the Mountain City stock, was convicted for tax evasion.

Things started boiling in San Francisco when testimony in the case of Archer Zamloch, a lawyer who had been indicted for bribing a witness in a narcotics case, showed ramifications which aroused suspicions of political collusion.[15] A grand jury in session, headed by Richard A. Seward, handed down indictments against two agents whom Schoeneman after many delays had fired. Schoeneman, however, consistently belittled the allegations of corruption. On November 23, 1950, he said, "It takes more than the idle rumors and unverified mumblings of a disgruntled former employee to produce indictments." The federal authorities gave the grand jury no co-operation. It could get no transcript of its hearings, no information from Internal Revenue, and despite repeated pleas to Washington, no help from the FBI. It got no help from the U. S. attorney,

14. Report of Kefauver committee, Third Interim Report of Senate Committee to Investigate Organized Crime, (82nd Congress), p. 99.

15. For matters discussed concerning San Francisco grand jury investigation, see report of Keating subcommittee to investigate the Department of Justice (83rd Congress), pp. 88-105, and testimony before King subcommittee, *op. cit.*, pp. 1929-2667.

Hennessy, who was described by one of his office associates as "a man who believed in live and let live."

A group of Bureau employees, based on their collective knowledge, filed a bill of particulars with sixteen charges which were prepared by deputy collector Thomas J. Doolan. A young U. S. attorney, Charles O'Gara, unlike Hennessy, began to co-operate very actively with the grand jury in its efforts to unearth and punish corruption. O'Gara suggested that Doolan see the new U. S. attorney succeeding Hennessy, Chauncey Tramutolo. He saw him on April 25 and Tramutolo, he testified, said to him, "My God, if this evidence comes out, we won't be able to elect a Democrat in California for 20 years."

The Seward jury instructed O'Gara to present the Doolan bill of particulars to a grand jury newly convened, the Taylor grand jury. May 16, 1951, is known in San Francisco as "Wild Wednesday." O'Gara began presenting the Doolan charges to the grand jury. Chief assistant U. S. attorney, Robert B. Mc-Millan, walked in and ordered O'Gara to stop. O'Gara refused. McMillan went to Judge Louis E. Goodman who was a stalwart in the Malone organization. While O'Gara was still speaking, a U. S. marshal entered the jury room with a formal written summons from Goodman, ordering the jurors to appear in his courtroom. He gave them a sound dressing down for listening to the O'Gara charges and, excoriating O'Gara, he said, "It was a most serious affront to the laws of the United States." Judge Goodman's intercession was the more amazing since Judge Murphy considered himself as the one assigned to the Taylor grand jury and sat throughout the day waiting for it to summon him.

The investigation now switched from the collector's office to Mr. O'Gara. An FBI investigation of the Zamloch matter, which was started in April, was concluded in May, but on May 28, Attorney General McGrath personally reopened the investigation on charges that O'Gara and two others had intimidated a witness. On July 5, charges against O'Gara were presented to the Seward grand jury by U. S. attorney Tramutolo. When the jury cleared O'Gara, the Seward grand jury was summarily dismissed without a chance to make a report. On October 24, O'Gara was interviewed by two FBI agents and on December 8 the third ranking officer of the FBI told him that there were 28 separate charges lodged against him. Tramutolo wrote McGrath urging O'Gara's dismissal—on one occasion he said to O'Gara, "Charlie, it is either you or me." In March 1952, after having been given no assignments since May 16, O'Gara thought that he might as well resign.

In September 1951, the Department of Justice sent Irvin Goldstein with the rank of special assistant to the Attorney General, to assist Tramutolo and McMillan. Goldstein's activities consisted in large part of his interrogation of O'Gara. In November, Doolan was quizzed for three hours by FBI agents. Goldstein took anything but an aggressive part in promoting the investigation. However, on September 27, 1951, shortly after Goldstein's appointment, the President suspended the entire ruling clique in the San Francisco office, not only Smyth but Paul V. Doyle, chief office deputy, John J. Boland, chief field deputy, John Malone, assistant chief of the income tax division, Martin Tierney, chief of the wage and excise tax division, and Ignacius Beresford, assistant chief of the wage and excise tax division. Subsequently, Smyth, Boland, Beresford, Doyle and Malone were removed.

Smyth was indicted on the charge of backdating income tax returns and also on a charge with Doyle and Boland of conspiring to impede the due processes of the government. Doyle and attorney Cosgrove were named in three indictments charged with cheating the government of delinquent penalties in three cases. Edwin M. Furtado, chief of the accounting section in the wage and excise tax division, confessed to backdating receipts of tax returns to obviate interest penalties and was sentenced to ten years on a charge of embezzlement. The case against John Malone collapsed when Furtado refused to testify against him. Deputy collector James Christman was indicted for disclosing confidential information received in the course of an income tax investigation. Assistant field deputy William B. Anater was fired on a variety of charges, including conducting four different businesses while he was working for the government.

There was one new wrinkle in this office. There was an internal revenue employees' welfare fund established in the office. $10,400 was collected from 1944 to 1948. The fund was administered by Doyle and John Malone. They kept no record of how they disbursed the fund, nor were there any checks to be found. It was charged in the Doolan bill of particulars that money was collected from brewers, bookies, operators of houses of prostitution and others with potential income tax trouble. It was proven that taxpayers did contribute to the fund.

In the three months, October through December 1951, after a new collector took over in San Francisco, the rate of tax collections was doubled over the previous three-month period.

# · XIV ·

# TOP TAX COLLECTOR GUILTY
# OF FRAUD

*There is an old adage that politics and liquor don't*
*mix. That is just as true of politics in liquor tax ad-*
*ministration. In my judgment, the present ills of the*
*Alcohol and Tobacco Tax Division can be attrib-*
*uted to politics, the wrong kind of politics.*

> —DWIGHT E. AVIS, head of the alcohol
> and tobacco tax division, testifying be-
> fore the Kean subcommittee on the ad-
> ministration of the internal revenue
> laws, February 1953.

ON JUNE 28, 1954, Joseph D. Nunan, commissioner of internal revenue for the United States between 1944 and 1947, was
convicted of income tax evasion. For violating the laws that
he was charged with enforcing for a three-year period, the former chief tax collector of the country was sentenced to five
years in jail. Nunan's case has a double twist—the taxes which
he was convicted of evading were on income that undoubtedly
came to him from fixing tax cases.

When Nunan left the government, he became one of the
most successful tax practitioners in the country. The net income that he reported from the practice of law between 1946
and 1950 was half a million dollars. The door which led to
Nunan was the investigation of the alcohol tax unit of the
Bureau of Internal Revenue. From the time Nunan entered
Internal Revenue, he was closely associated with liquor interests.

The unit, now known as the alcohol and tobacco tax division, is highly important but not nearly as well known as those activities which have to do with the collection of income taxes. The taxes on alcohol bring in close to $3 billion in federal revenues. The Bureau impinges on the liquor industry not intermittently as in other businesses, but in all of the details involved in the establishment of the physical installations of each liquor plant and its operation. The government operates almost like a partner and collects the lion's share, since the cost of making whiskey runs to less than $1.50 a gallon, while the federal tax is $10.50 a gallon.

## Carroll E. Mealey

A highly important function is screening the applications of those who seek to go into the liquor business in order to keep out undesirables. The alcohol tax unit somehow failed to exercise its responsibility of keeping undesirables out. For example, Joe Fusco, a friend of Al Capone, managed to control a vast liquor business. In 1946, the alcohol tax unit in Washington overruled its field office and issued a license to Lou Farrell, a gambler with a record from Des Moines, Iowa. Wolf Riman, who was a slot machine boss of Kansas City (shot to death in March 1949), had been given a liquor license. One of his friends was Sheriff J. A. Purdome of Jackson County. Riman was actually a deputy sheriff to Purdome and used his badge for supervising his slot machine operations. Members of the Mafia also held liquor permits in Kansas City.[1]

Carroll E. Mealey was a well-known name in New York State. He had been chief of the New York State tax commission and commissioner of motor vehicles. He served as deputy commissioner (that is, head man) of the alcohol tax unit from

1. See report of Kefauver committee, Third Report of Senate Crime Committee to Investigate Organized Crime (82nd Congress), pp. 37-43.

1946 through 1949. He was appointed by Joseph D. Nunan, who was then commissioner. He resigned in 1949, giving bad health as the reason.

In November 1951, the Bureau started a check of Mealey's tax returns.[2] His reported income for the years 1946 through 1950 was $50,000. A check revealed that it was at least $92,000. It was discovered that Mrs. Mealey had received a nutria fur coat from a furrier to whom the Mealeys were introduced by one Louis I. Pokrass. The cost of the coat was $1,980 and it was paid for in cash. Mealey lived in style. He stayed at the swank Mayflower in Washington and commuted every weekend to his home in Albany. The extra cost of commuting and maintaining two establishments was estimated, conservatively speaking, at one-half his government salary. He attended, while in the government, a large number of liquor dealer conventions at which his expenses were paid, not by the government, but by the liquor dealers.

Louis I. Pokrass had been engaged in the liquor business since before repeal. His liquor permit had been revoked by the unit in 1944, after the completion of an investigation of liquor tax violations. The basis of the revocation was that Pokrass had concealed the criminal records of himself and his associates in connection with his application for a permit. During the war, when there was an extensive black market of liquor, there was substantial evidence of his complicity in black market operations.

Pokrass was closely linked to the underworld. He built the Flamingo hotel in Nevada with Bugsy Siegel. His firm, Tele-King Television, was owned in part by Frank Costello and Meyer Lansky.

Tele-King got defense contracts during the Korean War period for $2,000,000 and at prices twenty-five per cent higher than bids of competitors, Senator Williams stated to the Sen-

2. All matters discussed as to Mealey from testimony before Kean subcommittee on the Internal Revenue Laws (83rd Congress), pp. 50-134.

ate. He also revealed that Pokrass was given "top secret" clearance on March 20, 1951, which was changed to "secret" clearance on May 20. That gave him the right to inspect our secret work. His vice-chairman of Tele-King, Franklin Lamb, was given a job on Defense Mobilizer Wilson's staff without an FBI check, on recommendation of General Vaughan.

Pokrass made repeated attempts to enter the liquor business but had no luck. Three applications were denied. In March 1946, Pokrass made a new application under the name of Gotham Liquor Corporation. On November 7, 1946, Mealey, who had recently taken office, advised Mr. Wright, assistant supervisor of the New York office, that he was interested in the Pokrass permit and that Wright should give it his attention. On November 19, the following conversation was recorded:

> MEALEY: Did you issue the Gotham permit, yet?
> WRIGHT: No. . . . it is being looked up. It will take the issuance this week.
> MEALEY: Don't want to hold them up too long. . . . Commissioner (Nunan) asked me yesterday if permit had been issued yet.
> WRIGHT: Not yet. You know the background and I want something in our files to show we actually went through regular routine so if anything comes up in the future they will know we did give it consideration. I think that is the way to do on that sort of thing.

On November 1, Mrs. Mealey had selected a nutria fur coat and on November 15, the balance was paid. The permit was issued on November 21. Pokrass made a contribution of $5,000 to the Democratic State Committee of New York shortly before the permit was granted. Four months later, Pokrass purchased a new Pontiac for $1,842.20 and transferred it to Mealey. We shall encounter the Gotham permit again.

Frank Wartur was an employee of Mealey's at the National Safety Council from 1943 to 1946. He later became associated with a manufacturer of wines, in public relations at a salary far higher than he received under Mealey. In that capacity, he represented the Tiara Products Company, when it got into trouble with the alcohol tax unit. Brandy is often used in the fortification of wines to increase the proof of the alcohol and to arrest the fermentation process. A wine maker who fails to use the wine in accordance with regulations can use brandy only on payment of beverage tax on the brandy used. The unit imposed a tax of $33,000 on Tiara. Compromises were often accepted but at never less than ten per cent for the first offender, and Tiara was a second offender. Tiara offered $500 as a compromise. The New York office recommended rejection. Assistant Supervisor Wright had a talk with J. B. Olson, supervisor for New York: "He stated that he [Olson] had a telephone communication from the Bureau [from Mealey] and that the offer submitted by Tiara Products Company, Inc., was being returned from the Bureau to our office and that as soon as it arrived, the offer should be rebriefed and a recommendation made for acceptance." The factual proof was completely rewritten in the New York office and then sent back to Washington.

Carroll E. Mealey was indicted for income tax evasion on April 4, 1954.

### The Cousin—and the Senator

During the Truman administration, decisions on personnel matters at every level of the alcohol tax unit were made solely on the basis of political considerations.

Let us consider the remarkable case of Donald S. Tydings, in which a powerful Democratic politician bullied and hamstrung officials of the government from the Secretary of the Treasury down.[3]

3. All matters discussed as to Donald S. Tydings are from testimony before Kean subcommittee, *op. cit.,* pp. 159-469.

Tydings got a job in the alcohol tax unit on a political recommendation in 1933. From the beginning, he was the center of turmoil, charged with loose gossip. In 1937, he was charged with accepting bribes from bootleggers and was transferred from the Norfolk district. Although he barely escaped discipline, he was promoted to investigator in charge for West Virginia. In 1944, he was sent to the Atlanta office to become assistant supervisor in charge of enforcement. This was an important office since it was the center of moonshining activities; over fifty-five per cent of illegal stills in the country were closed down in the Atlanta region.

Tydings borrowed from agents who were working for him and refused to repay until he was called to book by Washington. One of the agents who lent him money then found it best to get a transfer to another office at a lower grade. Tydings, a married man of 50, started what he called a friendship, and others a notorious affair, with a girl in the office who was 18. He showered gifts on her. He borrowed $3,000 from a bank in 1946 and the note was endorsed by a Georgia bootlegger who, shortly before, had been charged with violations of OPA regulations to the extent of overcharges of $648,000. Tydings had the investigator's report on the bootlegger, Garner, rewritten, refusing to show it to the original investigator. The U. S. attorney, on the basis of the report, declined prosecution, telling the investigator that the charges of which he had informed him were not in the report. The Justice Department agreed that the bootlegger would not be prosecuted if he would give information on other violators—Tydings did not secure that information, but Garner got off. The case for a $648,000 overcharge was settled for $3,000. Shortly afterwards, Garner's name appeared as guarantor. It was widely rumored in the area to be a pay-off. When Garner was questioned, he said, "Well, I can tell you this much, I ain't the only one that he put the bite on."

Tydings said that Garner should pay the note since "he had

helped him get his case settled." By 1949, Garner had gotten a judgment against Tydings on the note and the judgment was still unpaid. Tydings said the money went as a loan to his brother-in-law, who had since died. His sister did not know about the loan, Tydings said, because he had cautioned his brother-in-law not to tell her. It was proved that two days after Tydings received the loan, he bought an expensive ring for his girl friend. A few months later in 1947, Tydings wrote to Max Cohen, a nightclub operator and former bawdy house operator from Baltimore, who was then residing in the penitentiary in Atlanta for tax evasion:

> Dear Max . . . I need $2,500 badly. Any part of that amount you can let me have will be greatly appreciated. . . . there are pretty persistent rumors around that I am to return to Baltimore soon as the big chief.

Since these facts were well-known in the Atlanta office, everybody expected that Tydings would be disciplined, if not dismissed. He was called to Washington twice for explanations, but nothing happened. Everybody knew why. Tydings often boasted that he was related to a powerful figure in the Democratic party, and he was right. He was the first cousin of the senior senator from Maryland, Millard Tydings. The senator had fought for his cousin every inch of the way. He had gotten him his job. He had protected him against discipline in 1937. He intervened with the top men in the Treasury to get him promotions.

In early 1949, the supervisor in Atlanta, W. D. Hearington, resigned, disgusted because Tydings had escaped discipline. As soon as Hearington announced his decision, Donald Tydings wired his cousin, the senator, that he was to get for him the job "even if it is necessary to go to the President." The cost of the wire he charged to the government.

As it happened, the ATU had by that time mustered up its

courage and had sent to the Secretary of Treasury for his approval an order shifting Tydings out of Atlanta into New Orleans. While this was sitting on the desk of Secretary Snyder, he was notified by Senator Tydings that the senator wanted his cousin appointed as supervisor of the Atlanta region. That held up the transfer. At the same time, three other southern senators notified Snyder that they were backing Tydings for the job.

In April, a conference was held of all the high brass on the question of Donald Tydings. Included besides Donald Tydings were the senator, the Secretary of the Treasury, the assistant Secretary of the Treasury, the Commissioner of Internal Revenue, the chief of the alcohol tax unit and some other officials. Donald Tydings, when confronted with the proof against him, offered no effective rebuttal and even the senator was reported disgusted, though he fought hard for his cousin. The upshot was that the acting supervisor, W. G. Malsie, who had been transferred from another post, was to be given the supervisor job and Tydings would be transferred to New Orleans at a higher salary.

The senator did not give up. He called assistant deputy commissioner Avis to his office on August 16. He said that "there were people in administrative positions in the government service who were guilty of more serious misconduct than Donald Tydings . . . he was carrying a heavy burden for the administration, that he had asked for nothing and received nothing, but that he was going to insist on Donald Tydings' appointment as District Supervisor in Atlanta and that if he did not get satisfaction from the Secretary, he would carry the matter to the President." As a result, a compromise was worked out. Tydings would not be disciplined, he would not be transferred to New Orleans. He would be promoted to a higher grade in Atlanta. He would get the next district supervisor job that would be open. Avis discussed the possibility of a job in Baltimore for Tydings with the senator, but the senator was unenthusiastic. Tydings remained on in Atlanta and got into a fight with Malsie when he was accused of leaking inside information to a bootlegger. The department wangled out of the commitment to make him a district supervisor since the senator was defeated at the polls in November, an event that was accompanied by the shedding of many tears that a gentleman had been ousted by the activities of a ruffian like Senator Joe McCarthy.

Mr. Hearington, who resigned as district supervisor in Atlanta, relates that before he retired, he was confronted by Carroll Mealey with an ugly charge. It had been reported to J. Howard McGrath, national chairman, by anonymous letters (probably from Tydings) that Hearington was a Republican from Mississippi. Hearington said to Mealey, "You tell Mr. McGrath that that is a falsehood. I am not a Republican from Mississippi. I am a Republican from Tennessee." He then announced that he had enough and that he was going to retire.

## J. B. E. Olson

James B. E. Olson was, like Carroll Mealey, a close friend of Joe Nunan and a fellow New Yorker. He had been in the real estate business as an appraiser and in the shipping and insurance business. In 1934, he got an appointment as chief of the income tax division of the Brooklyn collector's office and became chief assistant to Nunan. When James P. Marcelle got his appointment to succeed Nunan, Olson went into business at handsome compensation, as we shall see. In 1947, he was appointed by Nunan head of the New York alcohol tax unit office. Testimony showed that Olson used this job as a means of feathering his nest.[4]

4. For Olson's relationship with Lithofold, Gotham, J. B. E. Olson, Inc., and other activities, see testimony before King subcommittee on the Internal Revenue Laws (82nd Congress), pp. 1-265.

As we have seen, Louis I. Pokrass had gotten his permit for the Gotham Liquor Corporation in 1946 under orders from Carroll Mealey, who stated that Commissioner Nunan was interested. The order for the permit was given prior to investigation. Under the statute, Gotham had to start operations within a two-year period or it would lose its license. Gotham met an unexpected obstacle when the New York State liquor authorities would not give a license to Gotham by the expiration date of November 21, 1948. The federal license, however, was not revoked. Instructions were given by J. B. E. Olson, as supervisor of the New York office, to do nothing to revoke the permit until further orders. By 1951 it was still unrevoked—an advantage to Gotham, since it might at some future time manage to get the New York State permit and then it would not have to go through the difficulty of wangling a federal permit.

Pokrass was associated in business with the notorious gambler, Frank Costello, in Tele-King Television Company. Olson had become acquainted with Pokrass in 1948. From that time on until August 1951, Olson had discussions with Pokrass about obtaining a distributorship from Pokrass for distributing his sets in South America. At the time he was discussing the deal, he had the right and, in fact, he was under the duty to revoke the permit for Gotham, a duty which he disregarded.

As supervisor of the alcohol tax unit in New York, Olson worked in his government job only two hours a day. He did not work the other hours because "I would probably be very annoying to be around for that period of time because I would be just butting in because my men were so efficient they could do it." Between 1947 and the end of 1950, Olson received in government salary $33,900. A thorough check by Internal Revenue disclosed receipts during that period of at least $178,-000 and disbursements of $213,000. Olson was admittedly receiving income from activities on the outside but even taking into account such reported income, there was a big discrepancy in the amounts received in cash and the amounts expended by him.[5]

While Olson was head of the alcohol tax unit, he was also head of the board of J. B. E. Olson Inc., an agency selling truck bodies. By a peculiar coincidence, he found a market for his trucks in breweries, one well-known brewery buying over 250 trucks from him. Olson received $25,000 between 1947 and 1950 from this company. Olson was able to use his control over the liquor industry in New York to advantage in another selling operation. In this operation, he allied himself with Joe Nunan, who had left the job as commissioner of internal revenue. The suggestion came from the collector of St. Louis, James P. Finnegan, who introduced him to R. J. Blauner of the American Lithofold Corporation. Olson possibly owed not only the entree but also the sales technique to Finnegan, since it was fundamentally the same technique that Finnegan used in his insurance promotion scheme. It was small change for Joe Nunan with his booming law practice, but it seems that Nunan was unwilling to pass up some easy money.

In early 1949, Olson gave Lithofold's sales representative in New York a list of 20 liquor companies in New York and Nunan gave a list of similar length. Lithofold's man was to contact them in order to sell them continuous printing. He was to tell them that he was being introduced by Olson—he was told by inference that this was all confidential in talking with other salesmen. Olson added further names to the list. Olson was advised by Lithofold that he was now a vice-president, as was Joe Nunan.

To the surprise of none of the participants, many sales were made by waving the magic wand of Olson's name. Nunan actually supplied letters of introduction but few sales were made through him—there was less magic in his name since he was no longer with the government. Olson received $5,851

5. See testimony before King subcommittee, *op. cit.,* pp. 3709-31.

and Nunan $4,055. Originally they were each on a stipend of $750 a month but this was later changed to a ten percent commission. In one case there "was a call in which Mr. Olson asked what business had been done with three liquor dealers on his list, and complained that he had learned of $8,000 or $9,000 worth of business given within the past six months, and yet he had received no commissions."

Olson performed another valuable service for Lithofold. The government used a form 52-B, which as originally prescribed was of a size that could not be readily produced on Lithofold's presses. Olson was shown a condensed form and he authorized Lithofold to quote him in Washington as being in favor of the change. The new form was approved. In citing Olson's endorsement, no one mentioned that Olson was a vice-president of Lithofold.

After Marcelle was appointed to the Brooklyn post left vacant by Nunan, Olson left the government service to become a public relations man for Joseph Applebaum.[6] This was a handsomely paid job. Originally he received $25,000 a year and then, after three months, he was given a fifteen percent ownership. The business liquidated at the end of 1946. In all, in a two-year period, Olson received $94,000 plus $19,100 in loans. What were Mr. Olson's duties? Applebaum owned a winery and he says that he hired Olson to act as his liaison with the alcohol tax unit, which oppressed him because they were anti-Semitic. If so, Olson paid only one call to the alcohol tax unit where, according to Applebaum, he raised the roof in protest about their attitude towards Applebaum.

Otherwise, Olson's duties were supposedly promotional. His salary was $25,000; he was also given a promotional fund of $19,100. In his income tax return Olson deducted $8,065 promotional expense from his promotional fund. We thus

6. For facts on relationships between Applebaum, Olson and Nunan, see testimony before King subcommittee, *op. cit.*, pp. 115-201; pp. 3617-3707.

have a situation, to restate it, in which Mr. Olson was deducting sums for promotion from an amount which he received for promotion, which was in addition to his salary that he got for promotion. Now, the interesting feature of the situation is that Applebaum was not interested in promotion but in depromotion. Instead of producing wine, he was selling the sugar he got under OPA rationing to Pepsi-Cola in the form of syrup. He did not want more customers because their needs would subtract from the amount of syrup he could sell to Pepsi-Cola. As a matter of fact, the whole business was liquidated in 1946, because Pepsi-Cola bought it in order to get hold of its sugar ration. Mr. Olson was unable to explain what he did for promotion except attend a couple of dinners.

Mr. Olson reputedly has an attractive personality and is a great story teller. It is probable that Mr. Applebaum was generous to Olson for other reasons. In 1942, the permit of Geffen Industries owned by Applebaum was revoked for violations, including underpayment of alcohol taxes. When Olson was in the Brooklyn collector's office, he met Applebaum and they became chummy, visiting in each other's homes. Olson introduced Applebaum to his boss, Joe Nunan. Applebaum decided when his friend, Joe Nunan, was placed in the exalted post of commissioner of internal revenue that he would like to get back into the liquor business again. He went down to Washington to visit with Nunan. Nunan personally came to New York with the deputy commissioner of the alcohol tax unit, Mr. Berkshire, to discuss Applebaum's case with the New York supervisor and Applebaum was invited to sit in on the discussions. Dr. Rhees, the supervisor in New York, was dead set against the permit. Nunan told Applebaum that he couldn't get him a permit now in face of the opposition of the New York office, but that if he acquired a minority interest in a plant and if after a few months of operation there were no violations, it might be possible to get him a permit for a plant in which he had a majority interest. So in March 1944, Applebaum secured a 48 percent in San Gabriel winery and then applied for a wine permit to produce wine at Canandaigua, New York.

Applebaum had been told quite definitely by the New York office that a permit was out. But in May 1944, on a Saturday afternoon, James A. Wright, head of the licensing section of the alcohol tax unit office in New York got a call from Washington from Kennedy, the assistant deputy commissioner of the alcohol tax unit. After being told that the investigation on Applebaum's permit was not completed, he called again and "said that he wanted me to get in touch with Dr. Rhees, the supervisor in New York, and tell him that the Commissioner wanted that permit issued and issued immediately." Kennedy, the deputy commissioner, told Wright that "we should not let this incident weaken our morale but to carry on like we had been carrying on." The investigative report recommended refusal of the permit, but the permit was issued the same Saturday as the phone call.

In October 1944, Applebaum made an application for another permit, this one with a majority interest for him. The investigative report recommended decline and Wright wrote a memo to Dr. Rhees in which he said, "Joseph Applebaum in view of his past record of violations is not likely to maintain operations with respect to the proposed bonded wineries in conformity with Federal law and existing regulations." But in a letter of October 28, addressed to Dr. Rhees, Commissioner Nunan personally ordered that the permit be issued.

James B. E. Olson was indicted for income tax evasion on February 3, 1955.

### Nunan

Many men get their significant start in life by marrying the boss's daughter. Joe Nunan started his career by marrying the boss's niece, the niece of Charles F. Murphy, who was the boss of Tammany Hall. Nunan served as a state senator from Brooklyn for several terms, but when Wendell Willkie ran unexpectedly well in New York in the 1940 elections, Nunan was swept out of office. The post of collector for the area, including Brooklyn and Queens, the first district of New York, was offered to him and he accepted. He worked at the job a couple of hours a day. The Brooklyn office under his regime was in sad shape. Joseph B. Marcelle, who succeeded him, says that when he took over the office, he found it a mess. When he met Nunan, who had just been promoted to the top job in the nation, he told him that he was going to demand an audit of the whole office. Nunan said to him "Do you want to get me fired?"[7] It was kidding between friends, of course.

In 1944, Robert E. Hannegan, who was leaving the position of internal revenue chief to become national chairman offered his position to Nunan. In testifying before the grand jury which indicted him in 1953 for tax evasion, Nunan said that he was not a tax expert. He said that when he took the job, he understood from Hannegan that it was a political job. He continued his law practice after he became commissioner. He says that he worked on Saturdays. His legal fees from the New York firm with which he was associated were $27,000 for 1945, $57,700 for 1946 and $77,400 for 1947, the year in which he resigned to go back into private practice.

Carroll E. Mealey, who was physically unable to appear for testimony during the tax investigations but who did supply answers to questions, states that the license for Gotham in 1946 was granted on direct order from Nunan, who told him that the New York State Democratic Committee advised him that the permit should be granted in return for campaign help that had been given.[8] Another permit was granted at the

7. See testimony of Joseph P. Marcelle before King subcommittee, *op. cit.*, p. 846.

8. For facts about Nunan, see testimony before King subcommittee, *op. cit.*, pp. 3733-79.

same time—the Somerset permit, and Mealey said that the order for Somerset was on the same grounds as for Gotham. The diary maintained by Mealey shows that on November 27, he was to see the commissioner with Dwight Avis "Re: The Somerset permits." And later the same day he called New York to issue the Somerset permit. On November 21, there was a note in Mealey's diary "Called the Commissioner re Reinfeld case, time Somerset permit was issued." Pokrass and Reinfeld were interested in the Somerset permit. In the fall of 1948, Nunan got a retainer from Reinfeld for $7,500 a year.

As we have seen previously the lawyer for Niggy Rutkin who was convicted of income tax evasion claimed that Nunan had turned him in to the tax authorities after Rutkin kept insisting that Reinfeld repay him $20,000,000 and started suit.

Permits were granted by Nunan under strange circumstances. There was a beer permit issued on October 12, 1944, to Mr. Roy Spaulding. Nunan had called the Baltimore office and had been advised by Mr. Tuttle that they were investigating Spaulding because they suspected that the holder of the license that had been revoked was providing the funds for handing it a new license and that Spaulding had a bad record. On October 11, 1944, Nunan spent the day at the Laurel race track with Spaulding and a Mr. Duncan, and the three invited the investigator on the case to meet them at the Annapolis hotel in Washington when they returned. The investigator declined. The permit was issued on Nunan's orders the next day.

Nunan as commissioner played ball with the top Truman hierarchy. It was revealed in 1952 that in 1945 after Bill Boyle was hired, a $38,000,000 tax claim against William Rhodes Davis was settled for $835,000 or three cents on the dollar.

Nunan used the contacts that he made as commissioner to good advantage when he left to go into private practice. There was, for example, the application for a ruling on a closing agreement made by Charles Ward, president of Brown and Bigelow in 1946. The transaction, completely above-board itself, was a highly technical question concerning the tax treatment of amounts Ward would receive for giving up his repurchase options on stock.[9] Nunan collected a fee of $25,000 for his services in the case shortly after he left the commissionership. In fact, most of the services were rendered while he was in that job. In 1946, the attorney for Ward held numerous conferences with Nunan, and, after suggested changes, Nunan gave a favorable ruling. The file had a note: "Commissioner interested." Another ruling was required in November 1947, along the same lines as the 1946 ruling. The Ward attorney was encountering delays and went to Nunan, who had by then resigned, to expedite it. Nunan called Schoeneman, the new commissioner. The favorable ruling was then expedited. The $25,000 was paid to Nunan for these services, in the opinion of the Brown and Bigelow people in St. Paul, and not for services with the SEC as Ward's attorney claimed. Nunan's intervention was a direct violation of the law. To represent clients before the Internal Revenue Bureau, he would have had to appear for enrollment with the Committee on Practice of Treasury. No consent would have been given since no former employee of the Department can appear in a case with which he had any former connection.

In 1946, Nunan gave $11,253 in cash to buy stock of Gaylord Container. Nunan refused to discuss the transaction in testimony before the King committee or to give the source of the cash. Nunan bought stock at the brokerage house of Eisele and King, Libaire Stout and Co. In a two-day period in 1946, he deposited 160 $100 bills and 14 $50 bills for a total of $16,700. Like Grunewald, Nunan seemed to have a preference for cash. For a fee of $2,997 in 1950 given Nunan by Unexcelled Chemical Company, the president, Carlton B. Waller, told a revenue agent that Nunan wanted stock not in his own name but in the street name, that is, the name of the broker.

9. For Ward case, see testimony before King subcommittee, *op. cit.*, pp. 3561-3616.

Nunan had gone into law practice with John P. Wenchel, the former counsel for the Bureau. They obtained 102 waivers to represent taxpayers in cases pending while they were with the Treasury. One of the waivers was to represent Jacob (Jack) Udell of a poultry processing plant in Delaware. According to Senator Williams, on December 31, 1948, the case was sent by Oliphant to Justice for prosecution. Seven days later, Oliphant recalled it. Udell began a series of physical examinations. Oliphant then suggested to Caudle in March 1949 that the case be dropped under the Bureau's health policy. Udell's health improved later.

Nunan was able to produce remarkable results as Senator Williams pointed out in public statements. For a brewery in Indianapolis, Williams claimed Nunan turned a government claim of $812,000 into a refund of $35,000. In four other cases he undertook at the same time, the government did not collect a cent on its claims of $2,000,000.

Nunan during the period of his law practice was reported to have been very close to nightclub interests in New York. He admitted that while he was commissioner he attended a dinner given by Frank Costello. He drew Bolich into the same associations and it was commented at the time of the ceremony when Bolich was sworn in as assistant commissioner that there were so many flowers that it looked like a gangster's funeral.

An examination of Nunan's income tax return showed $90,000 of unreported income for the time while he was commissioner of internal revenue.[10] For the 6-year period 1944 to 1950 there were unexplained income items of $161,000. Nunan had no check stubs or bank statements. He said he had destroyed them immediately after receipt. When the tax probe began, Nunan hastened to file amended returns for 1949 to include sums received from American Lithofold. After indictment, he admitted in a voluntary statement that he had

10. See testimony before King subcommittee, *op. cit.*, pp. 3533-60.

not reported receiving an election bet in 1948 for $1,800. At his trial, Frank Erickson, the bookmaker, testified to Nunan's winning that bet on Truman's election and also that he paid a $1,500 fee to Nunan for advice given to Erickson during the Kefauver investigation. Nunan's defense was that his wife had received $90,000 from Tammany boss Charles Murphy and that he had kept $100,000 in a strong box at his home in cash. The jury evidently did not believe him. He was convicted of tax evasion on June 28, 1954, and sentenced to five years. He is presently free on bail.

When Nunan resigned as internal revenue commissioner in 1947, President Truman wrote to him: "I desire to assure you of my deepest appreciation and that of the Nation whose interests you guarded with such vigilance."

# · XV ·

# GANGSTERISM AND MACHINE POLITICS

*Underworld characters do not engage in politics for the good of the community or the Nation. They do so for the purposes of increasing their power and wealth and gaining greater protection for their illegal activities.*

—The final report of the Senate Committee to Investigate Organized Crime in Interstate Commerce, August, 1951.

CARMINE DESAPIO, the leader of Tammany Hall, is respectable and august. He is the Democratic national committeeman from the State of New York.[1] Governor Harriman has made him Secretary of State, a fair return since DeSapio made Harriman governor. Carmine DeSapio says that he knows Frank Costello, the underworld czar, only slightly since it is inevitable that they should brush elbows in a city as small as New York. Mr. DeSapio is too modest about his friendships. Frank Costello, who has consistently belittled his role in New York City politics, admits that he knows Mr. DeSapio very well. Mr. DeSapio's predecessor as leader of Tammany, Hugo Rogers, was so well-known to Costello that Rogers stated in private conversation: "If Costello wanted me, he would send for me." During Rogers' regime, DeSapio was on the steering committee of Tammany with three other good friends of Costello, Frank Mancuso, Harry Brickman and Sidney Moses. In 1942

1. Except where noted, all facts concerning crime and politics in New York are from report of Kefauver committee, Third Interim Report of Senate Committee to Investigate Organized Crime (82nd Congress), pp. 109-144.

252

it is conceded that Tammany leader Michael Kennedy got his job only because Costello backed him. Costello admitted that Kennedy "might be obligated to him." When district leaders Dr. Sarubbi and Abe Rosenthal sought to bring about the nomination of Thomas Aurelio for the Supreme Court, they went to Costello, who gave Kennedy orders. When Kennedy wavered, Costello said to him, "My word is as good as my bond. You gave me a commitment. Are you a man, or a mouse?" After Aurelio was nominated, he called Costello on a wire-tapped phone and pledged Costello his undying loyalty. These revelations drove Kennedy out of the Tammany leadership, but Rogers' accession did not seem to diminish Costello's power. In 1948, in order to accomplish anything with Rogers, the man to see was admittedly Frank Mancuso, Costello's intimate friend.

What was the secret of Costello's power? Costello said that he thought it stemmed from the fact that he had lived all his life in Manhattan. "I know them, know them well, and maybe they got a little confidence in me." Mayor O'Dwyer said as to Costello's appeal, "It doesn't matter whether it is a banker, a businessman or a gangster, his pocketbook is always attractive."

Mayor O'Dwyer's bonds with Costello were very close. In 1942 when O'Dwyer was a major in the Army Air Force, he visited Costello in his apartment in New York. His story was that he visited Costello because he had received an anonymous letter charging frauds at Wright Field by Joe Baker, who was supposedly a friend of Costello. He says he did not ask Costello to come to any Army office because he was "no longer a District Attorney with a fistful of subpoenas but just a little Major or maybe a Lieutenant Colonel." James J. Moran, who accompanied O'Dwyer to the meeting, says he arranged it through Tammany leader Kennedy. O'Dwyer never attempted to see Joe Baker nor did he ask anyone else to do so at this time. At the meeting were Kennedy, Judge Savarese, Bert

Stand, formerly Tammany Hall secretary, and Irving Sherman. It was a perfect portrait of crime in politics: the real boss, Costello; the political boss, Kennedy; the go-between, Moran; and the front man, O'Dwyer.

Irving Sherman, labelled by the Kefauver report as a known gambler and intimate of racketeers, was on close terms with O'Dwyer. They kept in touch during the war. In 1945, O'Dwyer told a grand jury that he wouldn't be surprised to know that Sherman had been a collector for Joe Adonis, Costello and Lepke. Sherman kept in touch with James J. Moran, coming frequently to Moran's office, announcing himself as Dr. Cooper. Costello characterized James Moran as a friend intimate enough to drop in to see him for cocktails. Many of O'Dwyer's intimate friends, such as Judge George Joyce, a law associate, were, according to the crime report, also close friends of racketeer Joe Adonis.

O'Dwyer appointed associates of Costello and Joe Adonis to positions in the city government. He appointed Phillip Zichiello, a brother-in-law of Willie Moretti, the New Jersey racketeer, as deputy commissioner of the department of hospitals. When asked why he could not have found someone else for the hospital job, O'Dwyer replied, "There are things you have to do politically if you want co-operation." He appointed Frank Quayle as fire commissioner, although he knew that Quayle and Joe Adonis were good friends. He appointed Joe Loscalzo as a judge, even though he knew he was sponsored by Costello. Loscalzo was the "Joe" referred to in a telephone tap when Aurelio thanked Costello and said that "now we have to take care of Joe." Loscalzo had gone out to a golf course to petition Costello for his help. He appointed Lawrence Austin, a cousin of Irving Sherman, as city marshal, and Abe Rosenthal, a good friend of Costello, as assistant corporation counsel.

Convicted bookmaker Harry Gross testified on May 7, 1952, that he kicked in $20,000 to a special bookies' fund for the election of O'Dwyer in his 1945 and 1949 campaigns. The contributions were handed to James Moran, who told them he was collecting from all the bookies in the city to insure O'Dwyer's election. In 1945, Gross contributed $5,000; in 1949 Moran first wanted $1,000 per "horse parlor" but he settled for a $15,000 lump sum.

In July 1950, Mayor O'Dwyer denounced a grand jury investigation of Gross' $20 million a year bookmaking ring as a "witch hunt." A month later President Truman plucked O'Dwyer out of the imbroglio by appointing him Ambassador to Mexico. A month later, Harry Gross was arrested. At a department trial, seven months later, he named nearly two hundred policemen who allegedly received a total of $1 million a year in protection money. They included close friends and appointees of O'Dwyer. Gross said, "I paid everybody, everybody." Retired police commissioner William P. O'Brien, whom O'Dwyer called "honest as the day is long," received $200 a month. William T. Whalen, retired chief of detectives, was on the payroll for $250 a month. The collection system was patterned on the organizational structure of the police department with which Gross was familiar. In borough, sub-borough and division units standard fees were collected by the unit commander and the offices concerned with gambling activities in that command. In return, Gross said, "I was never raided. . . . I was not molested if any complaints came in. . . . I was notified in advance [about transfers of police personnel] so as to avoid paying double 'ice.' . . . None of my help . . . ever got a day in jail."[2]

The same pattern of alliance between gangsters, mobsters and racketeers and city political machines, predominantly Democratic, was discerned all over the country. In Chicago, the Capone gang had revived under new auspices. Police Chief Dan "Tubbo" Gilbert was named by the Cook County

2. New York *Herald-Tribune*, May 11, 1952.

Democratic machine for sheriff of Cook County in 1950. Gilbert won fame as the "world's richest cop." He admitted accumulating $360,000 while serving on the public payroll at a modest salary. He admitted that he placed bets with a well-known Chicago betting commissioner and explained, "I have been a gambler at heart."[3]

In the 1950 election, Senate Majority Leader Scott Lucas went down to unexpected defeat, and he attributed it in part to the fact that Gilbert's name was on the ticket. He was furious with the Kefauver committee for exposing Gilbert.

Representative Mike Kirwan of Youngstown was chairman of the Democratic national campaign committee and a friend of Truman. In the spring of 1948, he introduced a bill to prevent the deportation of Frank Cammarata who was an important member of the Licavoli mob. Johnnie Vitullo, who was the local Democratic boss, had $125,000 in cash in a safe deposit box it was revealed after his death in October 1948. After Kirwan's bill was introduced, Cammarata was released from Ellis Island. He had filed no tax return from 1936 to 1944, but he was permitted to file belated returns and the case was dropped.[4]

Edward McBride, who bought the Continental Press Service, which distributes racing results and is basic to the underworld, was advised in the negotiations by Miller and Hornbeck, according to *Look* magazine. Ray Miller, a partner, was Cleveland's democratic boss and headed the Ohio delegation that was all for Truman in the 1948 convention. The father of Edward McBride, Arthur (Mickey) McBride, was reported a good friend of Miller.[5]

Miami in the postwar period was a wide-open gambling town, almost wholly owned and operated by racketeers and

3. Report of Kefauver committee, *op. cit.*, p. 61.
4. Speech of Senator Williams before Senate, January 12, 1954; *Look* magazine, "Those Scandalous Years," May 22, 1952.
5. *Look* magazine, *op. cit.*

criminals from all over the country. At one time, fifty-two more or less elaborate gambling casinos operated in Broward County alone. The net reported income of two gambling establishments in 1949 was $599,703. The gross income from the S. & G. bookmaking syndicate was estimated at up to $40 million a year.

Miami abounded with distinguished personages such as Frank Erickson of New York, Joe Adonis, Mert Wertheimer, the Lansky brothers, Lefty Clark, Abe Allenberg and Anthony Carfano.

A $400,000 campaign contribution was made to Democratic Governor Fuller Warren—made by three persons with gambling interests. Warren failed to record their contribution in an affidavit submitted under Florida law in which he accounted for total contributions of only $8,825. A Senate crime committee noted that one $100,000 contributor to his campaign, William H. Johnston, a dog-track operator and old-time associate of Al Capone's legatees "enjoyed immunity from State-level inquiry." Sheriff Clark of Broward County, whom we have encountered in the Ribbonwriter RFC loan, enjoyed a great increase in wealth. He was a partner in the Broward Novelty Company, which operated an illegal bolita and slot machine business. According to the Senate crime report, the gross income of this company from 1945-47 was more than $1 million. Sheriff James A. Sullivan of Dade County (Miami) was found to have increased his assets from a reported $2,500 in 1944 to well over $75,000 in 1949 and one of his deputies made enough money in four years to retire to a farm he bought for $26,000. They did not deposit their money in banks but used old fishing tackle boxes and blankets as hiding places. Governor Warren displayed contempt for the Senate crime committee; he refused to testify before it and reinstated Sheriff Sullivan.

Abe Allenberg, a lieutenant of Frank Erickson, was named Miami treasurer of the Truman-Barkley campaign committee. Ten tickets at $250 a plate were bought by Erickson through Allenberg for a Jefferson-Jackson Dinner at Miami Beach's Roney Plaza. The national treasurer of the Democratic party, George L. Killion, sent Allenberg a note: "Dear Mr. Allenberg: We are grateful to you for participating in the Miami Jefferson Jubilee dinner. Your assistance proved of material help to the Democratic party in preparing for its 1948 Presidential campaign."[6]

In Kansas City and Jackson County, Missouri, the home territory of the President, the connection between gangsters and politicians had been strong since the year of the notorious Johnny Lazia, when Truman started his political career. The gambling business in Kansas City grossed more than $34 million a year. The Mafia was still operating in 1952 and Mafia members held liquor permits from the alcohol tax unit. Rumors were prevalent that Charles Binaggio had contributed sums as large as $150,000 to the campaign that made Forrest Smith governor. The crime report stated: "Smith's assertions under oath that he did not discuss politics with Binaggio or discuss Binaggio's expectations are simply not credible." Governor Smith appointed two commissioners, J. M. Milligan and Sheridan Farrell, who were at least acceptable to Binaggio and who appeared willing to go along with him. On April 6, 1950, Binaggio and his lieutenant, Gargotta, were murdered. Apparently Binaggio had been unsuccessful in opening up the town fast enough. He confided in June 1949 to Commissioner Robert Cohn that "the boys were behind in their schedule and were making it hot for him."

In St. Louis, Governor Smith received a $2,000 campaign contribution from William Molasky, owner of a racing wire service who wanted to name the police commissioner of that city, presumably Morris Shenker. In Jackson County, Truman's home grounds, Wolf Riman was a deputy sheriff and

6. For facts on Miami, see report of Kefauver committee, *op. cit.*, pp. 30-37; *Look* magazine, *op. cit.*

used the services of a number of Sheriff Purdome's deputies in placing his slot machines which were used in seventy-five percent of the county taverns. Hundley, Riman's assistant, testified that on one occasion Riman himself used his badge to threaten a tavern owner who was reluctant to take his machines. Riman was murdered in 1949.[7]

## Indulgence from the Internal Revenue Bureau

Gangsters and racketeers managed to get breaks from the Bureau of Internal Revenue which were unavailable to honest taxpayers. In February 1951, the Senate crime committee reported: "There is doubt as to whether the Bureau of Internal Revenue has been making a real effort to check on the income tax returns of known gamblers and racketeers. . . . returns are being submitted by gangsters and racketeers which the Bureau would not accept from ordinary citizens . . . the Government is losing huge sums in tax revenues from the illegal ventures of gamblers and gangsters." Prodded by revelations of favoritism the Bureau launched a drive to crack down on delinquent taxpayers in the underworld. By the end of 1952, the Bureau had liens of $180 million from 16,800 racketeers. Seven out of ten racketeers checked were found to be in tax arrears.

Jake "Greasy Thumb" Guzik, a former Capone gangster, with a long criminal record, got away with reporting $100,000 as miscellaneous income. (Senator Wiley observed that an humble farmer in his home state would not dare put down as much as $100 as miscellaneous income.[8]) In 1936, a tax assessment of $892,283 was levied against him. He started negotiations with an offer of $5,000. He refused to make a sworn

7. For facts on Kansas City, see report of Kefauver committee, *op. cit.,* pp. 37-43.
8. See testimony before Kefauver committee, part 12, p. 674.

statement of his assets and liabilities. His reported net income from 1936 to 1941 was $249,807. In 1942, he offered $100,000. The Chicago office recommended acceptance on the ground of Guzik's "reduced earning power." This offer was accepted in 1942 on the recommendation of the chief counsel of internal revenue, J. P. Wenchel, who later left the Bureau to become a law partner of Nunan.[9]

Harry Gross reported a total income of only $25,000 for three years before January 1, 1952, the only years for which he filed tax returns. No action was taken against him until his expose started. Ralph Capone owned a cigarette vending machine company, a tavern, a mineral water company and apparently gambling interests, maintained no books or records. He reported and paid a tax on a total income of less than $5,000.[10] Jacob (Jack) Udell was relieved of criminal prosecution after Joe Nunan became his attorney. In early 1949, said Senator Williams, Nunan secured immunity from Oliphant and Caudle on the ground that prosecution might result in Udell's death because of his precarious physical condition and "extreme anxiety." Udell then set up the National Meat and Food Institute in Miami to teach veterans how to cut meat. Between November 1948 and March 1952, he collected $451,559 from the Veterans Administration, exclusive of the amounts paid directly to students themselves. In July 1951, it was revealed that books were padded to show 100 percent attendance; 395 erasures and alterations were needed. The strains of business apparently improved Mr. Udell's health.[11]

Senator Williams told the Senate the story of Big Bill Lias, gambling czar of West Virginia.[12] He was convicted four times of Voltsead Act violations but amassed 14 business interests. Between 1928 and 1932, he filed no returns. In March 1938,

9. See speech by Senator Williams before Senate, May 27, 1952.
10. See speech by Senator Williams before Senate, May 9, 1952.
11. See speech of Senator Williams before Senate, February 28, 1952.
12. See speech by Senator Williams before Senate, October 17, 1951.

he effected a compromise offering to pay $10,400 for all liabilities until 1934. He paid off only $3,000 and then claimed financial inability to pay the rest. In 1939, 1940, 1941, he claimed inability to pay taxes assessed against him between 1934 and 1940.

His returns were finally audited and assessments totaling $2,230,744 were made for the six years through 1947. In November 1948, he pleaded guilty and was fined and sentenced to five years. He appealed on the ground that the judge had double-crossed him; he had expected probation. He was granted a new trial and acquitted. But the assessment was still hanging over his head. He started transferring assets to other members of his family and got rid of $401,900 of stock. No jeopardy assessment of any kind was levied. Not until Senator Williams made a speech on October 17, 1951, did Internal Revenue file a lien the next day. The department had waited, for some reason or another, three years after his conviction to file a lien. In September 1952, the Justice Department got around to a deportation action for illegal entry in 1925.

The Club Forrest in New Orleans charged off as expenses or loss against the club's gross the astronomical sum of $372,-000 in one year, with the explanation that this represented monies lent to players and customers which were not repaid or for bad debts resulting from "rubber" checks tendered by customers. The customers must have been exceedingly bold to give rubber checks to the minions of Costello and Kastel. Equally amazing sums were charged off during the years without apparent action by the tax authorities to question or disallow them.[13]

Frank Costello and his wife in 1934 owed the government over $29,000. The debt was not paid until 1947 when he lost a roll of bills totaling $25,000 in a taxicab. In March 1943, a debt of $344,729 of Phil Kastel for taxes from 1936 and 1937 was written off by the Bureau as uncollectible. Part of it was

13. Report of Kefauver committee, *op. cit.*, p. 83.

later paid off but in 1947 a remaining $258,563 was marked off as uncollectible. Yet during this period, Costello and Kastel jointly owned the Louisiana Mint Company, which owned and distributed slot machines, Crescent Music Co., which owned and distributed juke boxes and the Beverly Club, a plush Louisiana gambling casino. Between 1943 and 1947, Costello's profit from the Mint Co. was $213,898 and Kastel's $255,898; from 1943 to 1947 Costello's share in his wife's name from the profits of the Music Company were $31,-458 and Kastel's from 1944 to 1947, $23,743. Kastel, as president of Beverly Club drew a salary of $62,800. How hard did the Treasury look for assets from these boys?[14]

14. Speech of Senator Williams before Senate, June 20, 1952.

# · XVI ·

# INFLUENCE PEDDLING IN
# DEFENSE WORK*

*I have only one thing to sell and that is influence.
My influence is based upon my reputation and you
will find my reputation to be impeccable.*

> —Col. James V. Hunt, quoted by
> Paul D. Grindle before the Hoey
> investigations subcommittee on gov-
> ernment procurement.

On April 4, 1949, Major General Alden H. Waitt was seated
in the office of Col. James V. Hunt, now a civilian engaged in
advising manufacturers on government procurement. He was
dictating to Col. Hunt's secretary a memorandum for the consideration of the President of the United States. It would not
purport to come from General Waitt since it referred to him
in the third person. The subject of the memo was: who should
succeed General Waitt as chief of the Chemical Corps of the
United States Army?

General Waitt considered individually possible candidates
for the job. Of Officer A, he said, "He would probably not be
generally acceptable to the civilian scientists." Of Officer B,
he said, "He is lacking in imagination." Of C, "His health
record should be looked into." Of D, "His handicap is that he
does not have sufficient drive to carry through projects." Of

* All matters discussed in this chapter, unless otherwise noted, are
from testimony before the Hoey investigations subcommittee, "The 5-
Percenter Investigation" (81st Congress), and report of Hoey investigations subcommittee "The 5-Percenter Investigation" (81st Congress).

E, "He has never exerted himself particularly and generally takes things easily. In fact, he might be accused of being lazy."

As to each officer, General Waitt had considerable misgivings. In addition to the records of eight officers which he analyzed, he had a list of thirty-three other officers and potential candidates. All of them were marked doubtful—in fact, two were marked as dangerous.

Would no one be able to meet General Waitt's exacting standards? Then General Waitt's eye alighted on a familiar name. It was none other than that of Major General Alden H. Waitt. Now his enthusiasm was unbounded. As General Waitt testified, complete candor compelled him to give an honest estimate of his own capabilities. "General Waitt is recognized as one of the leading authorities in the world on the subject of toxicological warfare. . . . it should be emphasized that General Waitt has the unique experience of actually serving under gas warfare conditions in World War I." General Waitt had been involved in the scandals of the Garsson brothers and Congressman Andrew May, chairman of the House Military Affairs Committee, which had resulted in all of them going to jail. General Waitt had gone to Europe carrying a letter that Congressman May wrote in behalf of one of the Garsson's sons who was up for a court martial for refusing to follow orders under fire. Waitt brushed aside the entire matter. "The Garsson case was something General Waitt inherited as he had nothing to do with procurement or production during the war." He wound up by pointing out that General Waitt's re-appointment would be a master stroke in international relations. "The Canadian and British research staffs would be very happy to see General Waitt reappointed."

After the memos were typed, Col. Hunt's secretary, at General Waitt's direction, took them to the White House to General Vaughan's office—except for the memo about General Waitt, which he confesses he did not have the "brass" to transmit.

We are not concerned here with the abominable taste of General Waitt in supplying the derogatory information about fellow officers which might well have undermined their careers, and which was in many instances contrary to fitness reports he had himself written which were full of praise. The questions which concern us are these—what was General Waitt doing in Col. Hunt's office, and how was he in a position to use a powerful and influential person like the President's military aide, General Vaughan, in his behalf?

### Visiting with Colonel Hunt

Paul D. Grindle was the president of a woodworking concern and wanted to get a government contract. Through channels he was introduced to Col. James V. Hunt, who, he was told, had real "drag" in Washington. Surrounded in his office by signed photographs of everybody in Washington who mattered, Hunt gave him his standard treatment. Yes, General Vaughan in the White House was one of his closest friends. In one conversation Grindle said Hunt mentioned Vaughan fifty times. "Have no doubt of it, General Vaughan is Harry Truman's friend, and I am one of General Vaughan's closest friends." Two White House parties had been held in Hunt's honor. The occasion for one was the dedication of a song which he had written in honor of Margaret Truman, of which the Signal Corps had made 125,000 recordings and shipped them overseas. When he visited the White House, Vaughan saved a particular type of brandy for him that was received at the White House, to give to Hunt's wife, and Hunt also received boxes of cigars. Hunt might get Grindle a contract to supply woodwork for renovation work at the White House.

As for getting a government contract—well. He had been a top assistant to General Gregory, Quartermaster General, because he was considered the only man who could unify the twenty-two depots of the Corps. He was a dear friend of General Waitt, chief of the Chemical Corps, and General Feldman, present Quartermaster General. He was one of a group of four that was in the White House the night that Louis Johnson was called in and told that he was the new Secretary of Defense. He was the man to arrange war surplus deals. He was the cause of getting Jess Larson appointed War Assets Administrator, although he had expressed hesitation because of Larson's health.

On a visit to Hunt, Grindle asked him how business was and Hunt replied, "he was now working on a $200 million deal for plane parts and he said that the taxpayers' blood would boil if they knew about this one. I sort of laughed, and he said the deal involved having $200 million worth of new and used airplane parts declared surplus and then buying them back for a syndicate which he said he represented for $18 a ton." Hunt told him of a few coups he had made. He had got permission for construction at the Foxboro trotting track; by working with his friend, Frank Creedon, the housing expediter, they found a loophole in the regulations. There was no limit on the amount of money that could be spent in altering buildings. So they moved a lot of buildings onto the race track, bunched them together, demolished them and then built a club house.

Hunt talked compensation. The fee would be five percent of all contracts he obtained for Grindle. In addition, Grindle would have to pay him $1,000 down plus $500 a month plus out-of-pocket expenses. A person who gets a fee often pays a finder's or a forwarding fee to the person who referred the client, but in this case, Grindle would have to pay $1,000 to the person who referred him to Hunt. Grindle would have to pay for the privilege of being discovered by Hunt.

Strangely enough, with certain embellishments Hunt was telling the truth. He *was* General Vaughan's very close friend, he *was* a guest in the White House, he *was* the close friend of General Waitt and General Feldman, if he did not have them in his pocket. He was known as "The Kingmaker." As we have seen previously, Hunt secured the appointment of Tighe Woods as housing expediter and Woods reciprocated with the permit for the Tanforan race track. In view of Hunt's influence in the White House, government and Army officials were not oblivious to the advantage of friendly co-operation— in fact, they seemed anxious to serve Col. Hunt.

## The Five Percenter

Colonel J. V. Hunt was an example of a type of operator who flourished in Washington during the Truman administration. The five percenter, who was more often a ten percenter, let it be known that he could obtain favored treatment by avoiding the working level and presenting his case directly to the top officials. He indicated directly or by innuendo that he could influence the decisions of these officials. The technique embraced the following methods:

1) The five percenter emphasized that to be successful in dealing with the government, you must know the right people.

2) He would discuss in some detail how he succeeded in other cases.

3) Usually he would apply the social technique to the problem to impress the client, whether at cocktails, dinner or some other social affair.

4) He would charge an exorbitant fee. The retainer would insure him an adequate return regardless of the outcome of the case. The contingent fee impressed the clients with the possibilities of success because it was felt that if the five percenter did not expect to succeed he would not agree to such an agreement. There were some cases where the same five percenter represented several clients, all bidding on the same contract.

In May 1949, Defense Secretary Johnson spoke out against five percenters, saying, "There is no need for anyone to intervene between small business and the government to procure government contracts." The success of five percenters in getting business is a refutation of Johnson's claim. The standard government contract contained a so-called covenant against contingent fees, a warranty that the contractor had not paid a contingent fee to anyone other than a bona fide employee or selling agent, but this was of little value. The warranty was in fine print and besides the only penalty was cancellation of the contract.

Although Hunt deserved star billing as a five percenter, Washington abounded in that species. When General Vaughan was bombarded with questions by reporters after the disclosure of Hunt's activities by the New York *Herald Tribune,* he said, "Why pick on Hunt when there are 300 people in Washington in the same business?"

Hunt, who had been a manufacturer before the war, served as a Congressional liaison man in the Quartermaster Corps and then in the War Assets Administration under General Gregory. Between January and June 1946, he worked as a consultant at $50 a day for General Gregory, for a total of $5,750 in all. He collected his consultant's fee every working day during that period, even though he was then engaged on the outside in the five percenter business; he collected $1,000 from Albert Gross on June 1.

Hunt was, indeed, an intimate of General Waitt. He openly bragged that he was responsible for having General Waitt appointed chief of the Chemical Corps in the first place. They reciprocated favors. Let us consider a case that occurred while the re-appointment of General Waitt was pending.

In the fall of 1948, an industrial textile research organization located at Greenwich, Connecticut, retained Col. Hunt to assist in obtaining research contracts with government agencies, particularly the military services. Dr. Norman Armitage checked on Col. Hunt and one of the references was Dr. John Steelman, one of the President's assistants. Beside his name was the notation made by Armitage, "O.K."

Col. Hunt in lunching with Dr. Armitage said that he had no experience in dealing with a company that wasn't interested in a profit, and so he would be extremely modest in his fee, which would be $800 a month plus expenses plus a bonus at the end of the year up to fifty percent of his fee. Dr. Armitage assured him that they were interested in no profit except to keep the research organization intact. On November 3, Hunt and Armitage together visited General Waitt and correspondence began. By March, the same period in which Hunt was using his good offices to get Waitt renewed in his job, Gen. Waitt, in turn, was doing his best to get a research contract for Armitage, for research in chemically treated cloth which would prevent infiltration by toxic gases.

On March 3, Hunt wrote to Armitage that Waitt "feels sure he can expedite this one to DMRT within two months," and Armitage answered, "Your news from General Waitt that we are on line for a contract at Edgewood Arsenal was very welcome." Conversations between Waitt and Hunt, which were in shorthand and were transcribed by investigators, record that on March 3 Waitt said to Hunt, "Contract going through o.k. It is a long process." On April 21, Waitt said, "Made a special trip to Edgewood for the purpose of straightening out this business." As a matter of fact, when General Waitt advised Hunt in early March that Hunt's client would get a contract, that company was not even being considered. The contract evaluation board was considering four names on a list and the No. 1 name was offered the contract. It was only later that Armitage's firm was listed fifth on a list of nine.

Sometime in March, Major John Frederick Gay was called into General Waitt's office. Waitt told him to go to Edgewood and convey a message to Col. John A. McLaughlin that he was interested in seeing that Hunt's client have a contract with the Chemical Corps. "He asked me to carry a message to Edgewood . . . and I carried that message." Gay quoted Waitt as saying to him, "This organization had influence in the White House that might prove valuable to him later." Subsequent to that message, companies 2, 3 and 4 were not considered at all for the contract but only Hunt's client. It was not until June 3 that a report was made that it lacked the equipment and personnel for the job. Around that time, Waitt switched the funds for that particular project to another project.

Hunt had another close friend, Major General Herman Feldman, who was the Quartermaster General of the United States Army. Feldman may have owed his appointment in some degree to Hunt. Col. Evans of Feldman's office admitted that he had spoken on several occasions to Hunt in connection with Feldman's appointment as Quartermaster General. Evans was cagy in his testimony and admitted only that Hunt reported to him on the progress of the appointment. If Hunt could report on the progress of the appointment, he was capable of stronger intercession. Hunt told Grindle that Col. Evans was his contact man for getting quartermaster contracts.

Armitage was introduced to General Feldman, according to Hunt's diary, at Hunt's office and they lunched together at the Army-Navy club. Hunt later advised Armitage, "For your information, it is possible that within a week or two our friend General Feldman may become the Quartermaster General and that move, if it occurs, will not harm us in the least."

Feldman's friendship for Hunt extended to personal recommendations to prospective users of Hunt's services. On November 19, 1947, Feldman wrote to Brigadier General Wayne R. Allen, purchasing agent for Los Angeles, "I would like to suggest that at your convenience you drop a note to Col. Hunt letting him know what the problems of the county of Los Angeles may be for I am sure he could be of considerable help to you." On February 12, 1948, he wrote to O. L. Cook: "I can advise you that Hunt has been very successful in the past in arranging the necessary conferences resulting in satisfactory deals between parties concerned."

In one case General Feldman, who was then chief of the supply division of the Quartermaster Corps, addressed a letter dated July 23, 1947, to Hunt, in which he enclosed a copy of the proposed quartermaster expenditure program for clothing and equipage for the fiscal year 1948. In concluding his letter General Feldman said: "While the above information is not considered secret, I consider it advisable that it be considered as between us, confidential." Investigation revealed that the data which General Feldman furnished to Hunt was information which had not been made public in the same detail and which should not have been disclosed to Hunt unless made available to the general public.

On one occasion during the negotiation with the Henningsen Produce Company of a proposed contract for milk reconstitution plants in the Orient (turning powder back into milk), the company prepared and submitted a criticism of the program through Hunt to the Quartermaster Corps. This criticism was transmitted to General Feldman by Hunt, and General Feldman had one of the colonels on his staff prepare a memorandum on the subject. In reply this original Quartermaster Corps memorandum—which bore the notation, "This form will remain part of the official file of the Quartermaster Corps"—was transmitted to Hunt. Attached thereto was a longhand notation addressed to "Jim" and signed "Herman." Upon receiving this material, Hunt, in a letter to his client dated November 17, 1947, advised him that he had been in contact with General Feldman concerning their problem and pointed out that the Quartermaster Corps had furnished to him "off the record" a copy of the interdepartmental comment by the Quartermaster Corps. Hunt especially pointed out to his client the personal longhand postscript addressed to him from General Feldman. Hunt prepared a cablegram in behalf of Henningsen for transmission to General MacArthur's headquarters which Feldman sent verbatim. It requested a conference for Henningsen and said, "This office believes Henningsen capable."

In one case Hunt was paid $5,000 by the Cyclic Chemical Co. of Washington, D. C., for a few hours work in assisting that company in returning to the government some 800,000 surplus Aerosol bombs which it had purchased from the War Assets Administration. The Cyclic Chemical Co. had spent several months in an unsuccessful attempt to cancel its commitment for the delivery of the balance of these bombs. As soon as Hunt was retained in this case he promptly contacted Brigadier General James A. Mollison, a high official in the War Assets Administration, and General Feldman in the Quartermaster Corps. These two high officials immediately arranged to have the sale canceled and to have the Quartermaster Corps request that the Aerosol bombs be returned to it. As a result of this action Cyclic Chemical Co. was relieved of its contract responsibilities and the bombs were returned to the Army. There was no satisfactory explanation given as to why Hunt should have received this unusual consideration when the businessman was delayed for months on end in his negotiations.

General Feldman was suspended but after a reprimand was returned to duty by Secretary of the Army Gray. General Waitt's request for retirement was accepted by Secretary Gray, who stated, "That it would not be in the best interests of the Service for him to continue his duties as Chief of the Chemical Warfare Service."

There were others besides Hunt who had considerable influence. Glenn P. Boehm, an industrial consultant was engaged in government contract work besides getting RFC loans for clients. A manufacturer who held the rights for a new type of submachine gun paid Boehm $10,000 to represent him plus a 2 percent cut of the business. Boehm described how he proposed to sell it to the Army.[1] "I would beat down all the doors and tell my story to everybody that I could and show it to everybody that I could." It is doubtful that his clients gave him the deal for that reason. Boehm was a friend of Donald Dawson and seemed to have the run of the White House. He was also a good friend of Bill Boyle. He was a friend of Merl Young and went into business with Herschel Young on war surplus deals.

In the investigation of the Detroit Tank Automotive Center, an official of the general accounting office told of two brothers, John J. and James P. O'Haire who made $138,000 from 1947 to 1951 by getting contracts for an engineering company.[2] They were originally ten percenters but they were downgraded to five percenters when the company complained that they were making more money than the company itself. It is strange that the profit for the engineering company was not greater since on one contract for $182,000 the company did $6.00 (six dollars) worth of work itself and subcontracted or "expedited" the rest.

## Finders and Contact Men

Even with his strong influence in what he always called the "White Cottage" and his friendships with the upper crust of the procurement bureaucracy, Hunt needed men to find him clients and advise him of opportunities. Joseph F. Major succeeded Hunt as Congressional liaison officer for the War Assets Administration. He got his job through General Vaughan with whom he had been in Battery D. Major, incidentally, turned up in the diary of Director Walter Dunham of the RFC, introduced by Donald Dawson in connection with an

1. Testimony of Glenn Boehm before Hoey investigations subcommittee "Activities of Mississippi Democratic Committee" (82nd Congress), p. 463.
2. *New York Times,* July 25, 1951.

RFC deal. Major was active in getting clients for Hunt. On June 8, 1948, he spoke to Hunt about some men who were interested in buying an Alcoa plant. Speaking to Hunt, he said, "I said there is a fellow named Jim Hunt. He gets things done around here. We all do what we can for him. . . . I told them that you clicked better than half the time." He warned them that they should hire a person like Hunt in these words, "I don't see how anybody can talk past the people here and do what they want done." Major got Hunt several other clients.

Another government official who gave Hunt improper assistance was Clarence W. Oehler, a War Assets Administration employee. A series of letters written by Oehler from the Midwest area and sent to Hunt contained unauthorized disclosures of activities and proposed activities of the War Assets Administration expressly made by Oehler for the purpose of aiding Hunt in his private business. In discussing with him a plan for storing machine tools, Oehler told him that private contractors would be used in the storage operations. "Army and Navy will negotiate and pay for this work. As the time for getting into this is ripe, I thought it might be a good idea for you to line up contractors you had represented." In discussing a program for selling spare parts, he said, "We will sell these parts to our regional offices in Zone 3. I will direct this program for Zone 3. . . . I have carte blanche to sell them now on negotiated and bid lot sales. This is confidential information. . . . These matters are heading up rapidly. It looks as though now is the time to strike. . . . A lot of money will be made on above programs."

Oehler, as a service to Hunt, provided him with match boxes on which signatures were printed. Oehler wrote to Hunt in 1947: "Enclosed are samples of match folders as requested. The boys outdid themselves on this deal. They are thrilled to get the assignment. I am shipping to your office sealed two boxes White House, 2 boxes HHV, 4 boxes HST. These are for delivery to the White House." Hunt replied to Oehler:

"Our friend Harry has sent me the autograph of one of our ambassadors and has inquired as to obtaining a reasonable quantity of matches for him." It was the Ambassador to Cuba.

Another interesting connection of Hunt's was with Albert W. Lewitt. In the latter part of 1945, Lewitt was employed as assistant to a senator. While so employed, he referred certain persons, the Seidens, who previously had been the owners of Lido Beach hotel, Lido Beach, Long Island, to Hunt. They were anxious to repurchase this property which had been taken over by the Navy Department during the war. In April 1946, the Seidens gave Hunt a check for $5,000. He did not cash the check because at the time he was still employed by the War Assets Administration. He returned the check at the end of June and received another check for $5,000 on July 12, when he had left War Assets, which he deposited. Hunt made a deal that he would get a $50,000 fee from the Seidens if he got the hotel back for them and a percentage of any amount under $800,000. In November 1947, title was turned over to the Seidens for $635,000 and Hunt's fee amounted to $86,000.

While employed on Capitol Hill, Lewitt made official contacts with the responsible government officials in behalf of the Seidens. The Navy, believing that it was dealing with a senator, pledged that the hotel would not be declared surplus without prior notification. Throughout 1947, Lewitt and Hunt were in frequent consultation, before and after June 30, at which time Lewitt established his own public relations office. On November 19, shortly after title had been turned over to the Seidens, Hunt's diary tells of his statement to Lewitt "that the fee figure would be the figure that he and Mr. Lewitt would have to get together on," and he did get together with Lewitt right after he saw the Seidens. Hunt's diary stated, "On December 8, Hunt called Mr. Al Lewitt and advised him that he was ready to discuss the Lido Beach Hotel matter. Mr. Lewitt said that he would come right over." On the same date, there was a memorandum that J. V. Hunt engaged Lewitt for a monthly fee of $500. This lasted for 10 months so that Lewitt got $5,000. There can be little doubt that this $5,000 consultation fee was a thinly disguised attempt to conceal a fee given to Lewitt for handing the matter over to Hunt while he was an assistant to a United States senator.

One of the arts of being a successful influence peddler was the ability to engage in fakery with a straight face. When Lewitt left the government, he was employed by a leather goods trade association and his primary job for the client was to exert his efforts for the repeal of the luxury tax on leather goods. Lewitt was not registered as a lobbyist from January 1948 until August 1949 when the five percenter hearings began. In one of the letters to the association, he said that there would be tax relief in the next session since he had talked with "the chairman of the House Ways and Means Committee and with the officials of the Treasury Department as well as Senator Millikin of the Senate Finance Committee." In another letter he spoke of his visit with former Speaker Joe Martin. "He feels very keenly about this tax." In a speech he said that he had "contacted practically every member of the House Ways and Means Committee as well as the members of the Joint Committee on Revenue and Taxation."

Under oath Lewitt admitted that he had never discussed the tax with any member of Congress.

Hunt himself was the master of humbuggery. Although he thrived in the Truman milieu, which was made to order for him, he was nonpartisan in the sense that he was ready to jump on any bandwagon. On November 25, 1946, after the Republicans had taken control of the Congress, he wrote:

> To tell you the truth, Ralph, I'm swamped. My Hill and "White Cottage" contacts are still swell . . . and in the new turn of events . . . better than ever.

On October 13, 1948, Hunt wrote as follows:

If Dewey is elected (and the betting is 15 to 1) then I am in even a better position than before. I'm sure you will recall that many of my good friends on the Hill were Republicans.

After the election on November 23, 1948, Hunt wrote:

The White House group has been most kind to me. Though we are nonpartisan in politics, we have been close to and loyal to Mr. Truman personally, so our relationship is even closer than heretofore.

On December 29, 1948, when asked by a client how well he knew and how close he was to President Truman, he replied:

I had a nice assurance after the election. I won't tell you over the telephone. I was in the van, down the line. We went through with him all the way. It's going to be a great thing.

## Maritime Commission

There were enormous profits made in the disposal of the huge merchant marine which the United States built up during World War II. The efficiency of manufacturers like Henry Kaiser in turning out ships off the assembly line gave us a fleet of 29,100,000 dead-weight tons. Total cost of the 1,950 ships which were built was $4,561,000,000. The sales price was $1,719,405,000. The difference represented loss to the taxpayer. The power which the Maritime Commission had in disposing of ships offered the opportunity for some ripe political plums. There is no doubt but that the Commission was amenable to political influence. In 1947 George Killion, who was the treasurer of the Democratic National Committee, was made president of the American President Lines at $25,000 a year. The Maritime Commission held 98 per cent of the stock.[3]

3. See Blair Bolles, *How to Get Rich in Washington,* p. 98.

The important step in getting hold of a ship which could be sold at a profit was to get an entree to the Commission and that entree often came through the Democratic party. There is a story of a former employee of the Commission who made a contribution to the Democratic party and thus was enabled to purchase a T-2 tanker for $2,000,000. After receiving the ticket for the vessel, he had 60 days to make a down payment. During that period, he located a buyer. After paying the capital gains tax of 25 per cent, he had a clear profit of $160,000 in return for a small contribution to the Democratic party.

One of the slickest deals was pulled by former Congressman Joseph E. Casey, who, as we recall, participated with Joseph H. Rosenbaum in obtaining the RFC loan for Central Iron & Steel. In this case, he collaborated again with Rosenbaum. On an investment of $20,000, Casey made a capital gain of about $250,000. Casey testified on this deal when he appeared before the Fulbright subcommittee investigating the RFC. Senator Fulbright, who was intrigued by Casey's enormous financial wizardry, wheedled the story out of him. Mr. Casey was not flattered by Senator Fulbright's interest and at the next hearing refused to discuss the deal further. This is the way Senator Fulbright summarized it to the point where Casey clammed up:[4]

> The American Overseas Tanker Corp. is an American corporation formed in 1947 or 1948 to buy five T-2 tankers from the Maritime Commission. The tankers were acquired for cash. After they had been acquired they were registered in the name of Greenwich Marine Co., a Panamanian affiliate of American Overseas Tanker Corp., and Greenwich Marine Co. chartered them to the Standard Oil Co. of New Jersey.
>
> Purchase of the tankers by American Overseas was financed through an equity capital investment of $100,000 paid in by some 30, 40, or 50 stockholders and through a loan of

4. Hearings before the Fulbright subcommittee to investigate the RFC (82nd Congress), p. 1683.

$10,000,000 which American Overseas obtained from an insurance company. Collateral for the loan consisted of the vessels and also the charter which had been or was being negotiated between American Overseas and Standard Oil.

Joseph E. Casey was the president of American Overseas Tanker Corp. His portion of the $100,000 equity capital investment amounted to $20,000. . . . Among the 30, 40, or 50 stockholders were Robert W. Dudley and Joseph H. Rosenbaum, partners in the firm of Goodwin, Rosenbaum, Meacham & Bailen. Their portion of the total investment was relatively small—it had been allocated to them, at least this is so of Mr. Rosenbaum, as a finder's fee for conceiving the ideas which characterized the arrangement. . . .

The charter between American Overseas and Standard Oil was negotiated by Joseph E. Casey. Its negotiation and the other arrangements between the various parties were synchronized insofar as their timing was concerned because the various elements in the financial arrangements were interdependent. The charter could not be consummated until the vessels were owned by American Overseas. The vessels could not be acquired by American Overseas until the loan had been arranged by the insurance company. The loan with the insurance company could not be arranged until the charter had been negotiated between American Overseas and Standard Oil. The financial success of the various transactions was contingent upon the correctness of the assumptions which the parties made concerning the incidence of Federal income taxation and as a part of the synchronized efforts it was necessary that there be some understanding with the Bureau of Internal Revenue. No formal ruling was obtained from the Bureau in writing, but through one of the interested parties in New York some sort of ruling was obtained. . . .

After holding their investment for 3 or 4 years, the stockholders in American Overseas Tanker Corp. sold out to a corporation which was not the same as the one to which the vessels had been chartered. This corporation acquired the vessels subject to the charter rights of Standard Oil and it assumed the obligation for the unpaid portion of the insurance company loan. During the time that American Overseas held the vessels charter rentals paid by Standard Oil to Greenwich Marine had been applied toward the reduction of the debt.

The stockholders of American Overseas realized a capital gain of about $2,800,000 on disposal of their investment. The capital gain realized by Joseph E. Casey was about $250,000, which would indicate that although he put up 20 per cent of the equity capital investment his pro rata share in ownership of the stock was only 10 per cent.

Neither American Overseas Tanker Corp. nor Greenwich Marine Co. paid any Federal income tax nor did they file income-tax returns. The stockholders in American Overseas paid only the tax on their capital gains.

It was vital, as Fulbright stated, for the split-second timing that American Overseas be certain it could acquire the tankers. A strong selling point that Casey used before the Maritime Commission was that the stockholders were so distinguished, including Edward Stettinius, former Secretary of State and U. S. delegate to the U.N. He held ten per cent ownership. It is interesting that Casey's share which was originally twenty per cent had at the end been reduced to ten per cent.

Casey, Rosenbaum and several others were indicted for fraud in February 1954. Although the indictments were dismissed, the government in December 1955 announced that it had recovered $30,000,000 in the "tanker scandals." The settlements would cover five tankers obtained from the group headed by Casey.

Blair Bolles[5] tells of amazing profits in surplus other than ships. Morris Green purchased 872 trucks from the Philippine government for from $200 to $250 apiece. The Philippine government got them free from the Foreign Liquidation Commission, so that it netted $180,000. The Department of Commerce had forbidden the sale of goods here bought abroad as surplus; Green hired a Cleveland law firm which got him an exemption from the ban for a fee of $95,000. Green sold the trucks here from $3400 to $5500 a truck, selling 348 trucks to the Atomic Energy Commission, and paid a

5. See Bolles, *op. cit.*, p. 98.

finder's fee of $125,000. The profit to Green Brothers Enterprises was $340,000. When Congressman Bonner of North Carolina wrote to Secretary Sawyer objecting to the exemption, Secretary Sawyer replied in a scathing letter, saying that he objected to Congress portraying government employees as "knaves or fools."

# · XVII ·

# STEALING FROM THE FARMER

*Five million in losses against $10 billion in
commodities. Five million can almost slip
through the cracks in the floor.*

—CHARLES BRANNAN,
Secretary of Agriculture,
testifying before the Senate
Committee on Agriculture
and Forestry, January, 1952.

IN FEBRUARY 1951, Loutfy Mansour, an Egyptian cotton
broker of the firm of Huri and Company was in the office of
Clovis D. Walker, chief of the cotton branch of the Department of Agriculture.[1] He stepped out and asked Clovis' secretary to type in the bids on the contract forms, which he had
left blank. Mansour sold thirty-five percent of the cotton
bought by the government in that purchase program for
stockpiling.

Mr. Mansour and Mr. Walker were friends. Mansour gave
Walker a gift of $5,000 worth of Egyptian art objects. Walker
in return gave Mansour a special type of large photographic
printing.

About that time, Dyke Cullum, a commodity trader in
Washington, got a call from Walker inviting him to have
lunch with Walker and Mansour. There was a discussion as to
Cullum's representing Mansour in Washington. An investi-

1. For matters discussed on Walker case, see testimony before Senate
Committee on Agriculture and Forestry, "Investigation of Storage and
Processing Activities of the Commodity Credit Corporation" (82nd Con-
gress), pp. 1147-1297, and *New York Times*, May 3, 1952.

gator testified that "Mr. Cullum told me that he knew that his part in the picture was to relay confidential information from Mr. Walker to Mr. Mansour. He said that he conferred with Mr. Walker by telephone, usually every time he received anything from Mr. Mansour and before he sent anything back to Mr. Mansour, and he said, as he put it, Mr. Walker called the shots."

In April 1951, after Mansour had returned to Egypt, a correspondence began between Cullum and Mansour, and Walker's name was mentioned as advising this or furnishing that information. There was reference to developments in the cotton branch and to bids of competitors. Part of the information was denied to the Senate Agriculture Committee under secrecy rules, which caused Senator Aiken to exclaim, "We had better go to Egypt to hold these hearings."

In November, Mansour returned to the States, and a telegraphic correspondence began with his home office. The information outlined occurrences within the cotton branch never made public. One message read, "Thanks Eula our previous new type approved." Eula was Mrs. Walker's name. Walker had signed himself that way in messages to Mansour. The investigator translated this message, "Thanks to Walker our previous new types of cotton [which required Department approval before deliveries could be made under a new contract] have been approved." Another message reads, "Eula will purchase as before, thank God." Until November 28 there had been a question as to whether the cotton branch would actually handle the second procurement.

In the summer of 1951 the price of Egyptian cotton fell to 60 cents a pound. Walker, answering an inquiry, said that the branch was not interested in buying. By December the price had risen to $1.30 a pound. On November 30, notifications were sent out that offers would be accepted by the cotton branch until December 3, which gave little time for many brokers to submit bids. At that time the cotton branch bought

24,000 bales of which Huri and Company supplied 17,500 bales and six firms sold the rest. The timing of the purchases was the worst possible for the interests of the government and cost the taxpayers $7,000,000.

In September 1952, Walker and Mansour were indicted for conspiracy to defraud the United States. In the trial, the government was unable to prove that Walker profited personally and he was acquitted. Mansour stayed out of the country. Cullum sued Mansour for a commission for the sale of the cotton as Mansour's agent. Cullum, who was under indictment for a stock transaction, had been associated with Senator Elmer Thomas of Oklahoma, formerly chairman of the Senate Agriculture Committee, who conceded that he had played the market and whose wife traded in cotton futures.

Senator Aiken said that two members of the President's cabinet whom he did not name, were aware of these "smelly transactions." The Department of Agriculture reeked with "smelly transactions."

## Storage Deals

In the campaign of 1948, Truman had made an issue of an alleged shortage of storage space for farmers' grain. In a speech at Dexter, Iowa, on September 18, he charged that the 80th Congress had put a "pitchfork in the farmer's back."[2] In the revision of the charter of the Commodity Credit Corporation, he claimed that Congress had banned the further acquisition of private storage space. "They are preventing us from setting up the storage bins that you will need in order to get the support price for your grains." This theme on which Truman harped during the campaign has been given major credit for winning the election, since the price of corn declined from

2. See *Saturday Evening Post* "Did Truman Ever Fool the Farmers," August 16, 1952, containing findings of Senator Williams.

$1.60 down to $1.30 and finally down to $1.00 by November. Because of the alleged lack of storage space, farmers were unable to get support loans at 90 percent of parity.

No one had thought of this obscure clause until someone on Truman's staff had dreamt up the argument. The CCC had been liquidating bin space from the end of the war, when it held a total of 292,000,000 bushels of bin space. In 1946 and 1947, three-fourths was sold as surplus before the 80th Congress had anything to do with it. In 1948 when Congress revised the CCC charter, it merely took cognizance of the liquidation that was taking place. Even in August and September of 1948 the CCC sold bins to the extent of over 2,000,-000 bushels. On the day Truman was speaking at Dexter, the CCC was selling bins at a fraction of their cost to the government.

Congress had authorized the CCC to lend, and make subsidies to farmers, and the administration could have used that authority as it did in 1949. It could lend to farmers to purchase bins, the only restriction being that the storage capacity must be delivered directly from the manufacturer to the farmer. In 1949, the CCC lent at 75 percent of the support price for corn stored on the ground.

There is reason to suspect that the administration during the campaign deliberately kept down the price. Even though government purchase programs for its own use and foreign aid are extensive, the government did not buy a single bushel of corn for six weeks in September and October. But in November with the elections over, the CCC bought 3,850,000 bushels. The loan program was reduced to a trickle. In October 1948, only 997,000 bushels were bought under loan and 353,253 bushels under the "purchase agreements." But in November, after the elections, 30,000,000 bushels went under support and 62,000,000 bushels in December. By December the price of corn was back to $1.35. The administration claimed that the corn was too wet for storage, but as Senator Williams commented "something happened on November 2 that suddenly dried up a lot of corn."

There were storage shortages in 1949 and 1950. During this time, the CCC leased space from private parties for storing government grain. These leases resulted in filling the pockets of people who leased space from the government at a nominal price and then leased it back to the CCC at a much greater price, the difference being a windfall profit. The CCC was authorized by Congress to use whatever means necessary to fulfill its duties, but it was to "utilize the usual and customary channels, facilities and arrangements of the trade." It did not always do this. Let us consider some interesting cases.

On September 12, 1949, a group of five men formed a company called Midwest Storage and Realty Company of Kansas City.[3] This company had never been in the trade as the CCC Act required—it was a paper company. Within a few days after the company was launched, it leased government-owned storage space at Camp Crowder from the War Assets Administration for $11,270, and a short time later, Midwest rented it back to the CCC for a rental of $382,201.

Two of the men were politically potent and were friends of Harry Truman, Dan M. Nee, former collector of internal revenue for western Missouri, and Harry Easley, former WPA administrator for Missouri. Another was Ardeis Myers, who had a back tax assessment for $675,000, which had accrued while Nee was internal revenue collector. There is an argument as to whether Nee had allowed the assessment to gather dust. But there was no argument about the fact that Nee was now Myers' attorney. None had experience in the storage business; according to Senator Anderson, "Myers' business was primarily the running of coin machines in Kansas City."

The transactions had these unusual aspects as Senator Kem

3. For matters discussed about Midwest Storage and V. M. Harris, see testimony before Senate Committee on Agriculture and Forestry, *op. cit.*, pp. 284-860.

pointed out: The lease from War Assets was not a lease but only an option so that Midwest could suffer no loss. At the time the company executed the lease, it didn't have a dime of assets. No financial statement of the company was filed with the CCC even though the regulations required it; an official of the CCC was told to make the file complete without it. The official of the WAA who executed the lease was a business associate of Nee's and he sold trucks to Midwest which were shortly sold at a loss. All in all, Midwest was simply acting as a middleman between War Assets and CCC at a fabulous profit.

Let us examine another interesting case in the same Kansas City area, that of V. M. Harris Grain Company, which stored grain for the CCC from September 1949 to June 1, 1951. Like Midwest, it leased government space from War Assets which it then leased back to CCC. The cost of the lease to it was $16,-713; the rental cost to the government was $290,375. The lease was due to expire in July 1950. Harris testified that he wrote to the WAA for renewal but got no reply. Then he had a meeting in a hotel room in Kansas City with Glenn Yancey, who had been a local War Production Board director and W. B. Smith, a War Assets attorney. Harris said that they said to him, "How much is there in it for us?" The name of E. V. Turney, who was director of the War Assets Administration in Kansas City, was brought in. They finally settled on thirty-five percent of the net profits to go to Harris' new partners, who would be Yancey, Smith and Turney. In a short time after the agreement, the lease was renewed. Harris said that because of doubts as to the legality he didn't make any payment.

It developed, however, there was more to the shakedown story than met the eye at first glance. Yancey, Smith and Turney were by no means strangers to Harris. After Harris had obtained his original lease at Camp Crowder, he had gone into business with Turney, Smith and Yancey in a corporation called Kan-I-Mo, and the purpose of this company was to lease facilities for grain storage. Harris said the company never got off the ground. How Turney could have reconciled the signing of leases of surplus space with his job as head of the WAA was not made clear. Harris testified, "It looked like it was too messed up." That characterization seems an understatement.

Some curious facts came to light about transactions between the CCC and Cargill Inc., the biggest grain dealers in the United States, which collected substantial profits in contracts negotiated with the CCC.[4] An official in the St. Paul office told Washington over the phone, "There are shenanigans here. There is no question about it." And the contract with Cargill might be a case in point. In a purchase of six million bushels of grain from Cargill in the spring of 1949, the wheat was bought ostensibly on a cash basis as if it were going to be delivered within a short time. As a matter of fact, at the very time these deals were going through, Cargill and CCC were arranging to ship the wheat several months later. "It enabled Cargill to purchase at lower prices than the cash prices quoted at the time of the contract for subsequent delivery and at the same time to use any inventory of wheat stock for other trades. As for Commodity, what it did was to require Commodity to pay today's cash price which was 20 cents or so higher than the futures prices when they had no real plan then and there of getting the wheat." The loss to the taxpayers was between $500,000 and $1,000,000.

Of this transaction, a vice president of General Mills said, "It is ridiculous to think that a grain man in private trade would pay a cash premium for grain not required immediately in a situation when futures are quoted at substantially lower prices. If I did it personally, I would lose my position."

One of the most serious fraud cases uncovered was first disclosed by an FBI investigation. In an investigation of the Rice Growers Association of California, Sacramento, California,

4. For matters discussed on Cargill sale, see testimony before Senate Committee on Agriculture and Forestry, *op. cit.,* pp. 1468-1573.

for possible violation of antitrust statutes, FBI agents discovered that in 1949 the association had delivered to CCC under the 1948 rice-purchase agreement approximately 60,000,000 pounds of rough rice, 45,300,000 pounds of which was not the property of the association and therefore not eligible to receive the government support price. Evidence disclosed this fraudulent action had been taken to "bail out" certain California rice mills which found themselves with large stocks of inferior quality rice at the end of the 1949 rice season. Loss to the government is estimated to be $731,221.[5]

## Embezzlements and Shortages

After grains were stored they had a peculiar habit of disappearing. There were two reasons for the disappearance. First, the warehousemen stole the government-owned grain, and, secondly, they used the grain for private speculation hoping to replace it when the market dropped. A *Farm Journal* editorial in March 1952 said that the shortages "inevitably associate the Department of Agriculture with the odorous corruptions in other branches of the Government—corruptions which the Truman Administration has tolerated until disclosures have forced belated action. The shadiest episodes so far revealed are those in which persons with political contacts have gained fortunes."

The conversions were investigated by the Ellender committee in the Senate, the Whitten committee in the House. A Senate report published in July 1952 stated that as of May 1952, there had been embezzlements and criminal conversions of government-owned inventories by 131 warehouses aggregating $10 million. The Department of Agriculture had re-

5. See report of House Subcommittee on Agriculture "Investigation of Warehousing Practices Commodity Credit Corporation" February 4, 1952, p. 13.

verted government property. Although fraud by employees of the government was on a wholesale basis, little was done.

In the Dallas PMA commodity office an investigation revealed that fifteen employees had accepted gratuities from firms doing business with that office. Gifts ranged from boxes of fruit and shrimp, raincoats, Stetson hats, and Mexican belts with sterling silver buckles to $100 gift certificates and trips to expensive dude ranches and fishing resorts for employees and their families. One of the employees, Stephen G. Benit, Jr., was indicted by a federal grand jury at Fort Worth, Texas, for the acceptance of bribes totaling $1,750 from an Oklahoma elevator operator to insure allocation of sufficient CCC-owned commodities to keep his warehouse filled. The subcommittee was astonished to learn that Benit, under indictment for his part in this case, was reemployed by the Office of Price Stabilization.

An official investigation of the relations between the Lone Star Co. of Houston, Texas, and Carl G. Rausch, chief, transportation division, Kansas City PMA commodity office, and his assistant, Willard D. McCabe, revealed that in contract awards for grain bags, these two PMA employees showed official favoritism by (1) informing Lone Star of competitors' low bids; (2) allowing Lone Star to obtain contracts by meeting competitors' low bids; (3) awarding one contract to Lone Star at a bid higher than other bids on file; (4) informing Lone Star of CCC bag requirements in advance of making such information available to other dealers; and (5) permitting material changes in contracts with Lone Star to the apparent advantage of that firm. The investigation also disclosed that gratuities such as binoculars and clocks were received by Rausch and McCabe from the Lone Star Co. As a result of this investigation, Rausch was suspended without pay from duty for one month. McCabe was likewise suspended for one month without pay.[7]

7. See report of House Subcommittee on Agriculture, *op. cit.*, pp. 5-6.

# · XVIII ·

# FHA SCANDALS AND MISCELLANEOUS
# FRAUDS

THE lushest profits, percentagewise, during the Truman administration occurred in the area which would seem at first blush to offer the least opportunities for swindle, that is, the insurance program for housing carried on by the Federal Housing Administration.[1] It was not until April 1954 during the Eisenhower administration that the frauds came to light. Federal Housing Commissioner Guy Hollyday and Assistant Commissioner Clyde L. Powell were instantly dismissed and general counsel Burton C. Bovard later resigned. An investigation conducted by the Senate Committee on Banking and Currency under Senator Capehart unraveled the frauds in a long series of public hearings.

The major method for milking and bilking the government and the public was Section 608, which authorized FHA to insure up to 90 percent of the cost of rental projects. The swindles came to light when Internal Revenue Commissioner Andrews reported to the President that there were large windfall profits in 1,149 rental housing projects disclosed by the income tax returns of the sponsoring corporations. Further investigation showed the extent of individual enrichment. Dr. Daniel Gevinson had an estimated net worth of $50,000 in 1947. Six

1. The following matters discussed concerning FHA scandals are from hearings before the Capehart FHA investigation subcommittee of the Banking and Currency Committee (83rd Congress), particularly testimony of William F. McKenna and report of Capehart FHA investigation subcommittee (83rd Congress).

years later he had given up dentistry when his assets were $2 million. Ian Woodner had a net worth under $40,000 at the end of World War II. In the next 5 years, he built $50 million worth of real estate projects financed wholly by FHA and was a millionaire many times over. The extent of this enrichment should not be surprising when it is considered that the profits under 608 ran rather high for a safe investment. For example, in the Shirley Duke apartments, for an eighteen-month period, the profits to the investors were 36,000 percent.

The administration of the 608 program which was discontinued in March 1950, by which time there were 7,045 projects insured for a total of $3.5 billion, was in the hands of one Clyde L. Powell. Mr. Powell had a very interesting background of which the FBI apprized the Civil Service Commission both in 1941 and 1948. Somehow the records disappeared from the FHA. His contact with the law started at the tender age of nineteen, when he was sentenced to a year in the workhouse for larceny. It continued with a series of worthless checks. When he was summoned for Army service in 1918, he was unable to report for duty because he was being held in jail on a check charge. For breaking Army rules, he was sentenced to a term at hard labor. In 1934, Powell decided to dedicate his career to the public service in Washington. His police record from that point on shows arrests only for misdemeanors.

Between 1945 and his dismissal in 1954, Powell made deposits in the Riggs National Bank in Washington for $218,330, or $138,365 more than he had earned plus travel expenses in the government. In addition, he had two safe deposit boxes. He purchased a lot for $12,000 in the most exclusive section of Washington. He was a heavy gambler, giving notes for $8,900 to John "Blackjack" Keleher, a prominent bookmaker, and $8,650 to Rocco De Grazia, a gambling house owner; one evening he lost $5,000 "shooting craps" at the Dunes club in Virginia Beach.

How did Section 608 become such rich pickings? The transaction is fairly complicated, so we will reduce it to fundamentals.

Under 608 the FHA insured mortgages on multi-family dwellings up to 90 percent of the cost. If the estimated cost was $100,000 that would allow an FHA mortgage of $90,000. Let us suppose, however, that instead of estimating the cost at $100,000, the builder estimated it at $140,000. The mortgage at 90 percent would then be $126,000. If the actual cost were $95,000, the difference between the mortgage proceeds and the cost would be $31,000. If the sponsoring corporation, the mortgagor, put in $1,000 which is not an extreme case, the profit would be $30,000 or a profit of 3,000 percent.

This process was called "mortgaging out." After the completion of the project the sponsors were the owners of the buildings and had in their pockets the excess mortgage proceeds. There was no personal responsibility or liability to repay the borrowed mortgage money. Only the property was liable for the repayment of the debt over a period of thirty more years from the rental income to be paid by the tenants.

In the case of the Shirley Duke apartments, which is a model case since almost every method of abuse and skullduggery was used, $6,000 worth of capital was placed in the corporation and the mortgage proceeds were distributed to the stockholders to the tune of $2,200,000. Even though the sponsors advanced only $6,000, they put themselves immediately on the payroll for $60,000 a year. The financing company of the mortgagee which was supposed to get a fee of 1.5 percent in addition to 4 percent interest, got a 6 percent service fee so that it netted 10 percent or well over $1 million for no risk at all. In the Elizabeth Gregory and Marine Terrace apartments on a $3,000 investment $1,616,000 was withdrawn. In the Patchogue Gardens case, there was an investment of $1,000 and dividends of $155,000. Cases could be multiplied along this line.

The first thing the sponsoring corporation did was to hike up its costs. A five percent architect's fee was allowed in every case even though the fee, in fact, might have been as little as one half of one percent, as it was when projects were of the "garden" type, consisting of a great number of small buildings. All types of expenses were included in the costs. Ian Woodner, who built the magnificent Woodner apartments in Washington, included in the construction costs $87,000 in detective fees and $50,000 in lawyers' fees for his divorce and the expense of a trip to Nassau to recuperate from the strain of his marriage. Travel expenses and entertainment were included in costs to the tune of tens of thousands of dollars.

To widen the profit, costs of construction were lowered by the use of inferior materials and short-cuts. One of the commonest methods was to pay lower than prevailing wages. In an investigation of sixty-two cases, it was found that lower than prevailing wages were paid in every one of them. Powell on complaint answered that he could do nothing about this.

One of the most effective devices for hiking the profit was the manipulation of the legal status of the land on which it was built. One of two devices was used. The value of the land could be transferred to the sponsoring corporation at an exorbitant price. Franklin A. Trice of Richmond purchased the land on which the project was built for $13,987. FHA valued it at $190,000 and Trice exchanged it for $526,000 worth of corporate stock. Morris Cafritz of Washington, D. C., in his application on Parklands Manor, valued land at $20,000 an acre, which had been purchased for $690 an acre. By the use of windfall profits "in the absence of adverse economic conditions, the Cafritz children will ultimately own free and clear properties having a cost of $7.2 million and which were constructed out of a gift by Cafritz of land costing him $69,000." Mr. Cafritz' wife, Gwen Cafritz, by lavish parties outdid Mrs. Perle Mesta and became No. 1 hostess for free-drinking government officials during the Truman administration.

Often, a contribution of land was included as part of the cost when, in fact, there had been no such contribution. Thus, in the Essex House in Indianapolis, the land was, in fact, paid for by issuance of preferred stock which was redeemed out of mortgage proceeds, yet the application showed it as an equity contribution.

A much more profitable avenue of profit was to lease the land to the sponsoring corporation. In the Beach Haven apartments in Brooklyn the cost of the land was $34,500. The principals then leased the land to the sponsoring corporations at an annual rent of $60,600 for 99 years. FHA was allowed the privilege of buying this land in case the project defaulted for a price of $1,515,000.

Who paid for these watered mortgages on the building and the land? If there were a default, of course, they would be back in the lap of the government. However, in a period of inflation and housing shortages the burden was put on the tenants where it continues to remain. FHA rentals were set at 6.5 per cent net return *on the estimated cost of construction.* For every excessive $100 million in mortgages, it is estimated that tenants will be required to pay $6.5 million in excess rents each year during the thirty years of the mortgage. It was a common practice after the project was built to increase rents because of unanticipated costs. One of the devices was to switch construction costs over to operating expenses and then ask for a rent increase as was done in the case of the Shirley Duke apartments.

Rarely were normal income taxes paid on these windfall profits. The practice frequently used was for a reappraisal of the property after construction and then the lucky investors would simply pay a capital gains tax of 25 per cent. The mortgage proceeds were often used for pyramiding, that is, they were lent to another corporation, the borrower not paying income taxes on the theory that it was a loan. "A dentist turned builder, Dr. Dewey S. Gottlieb, used such tax-free funds to buy a string of race horses and a cruiser on which to entertain jockeys." By filing a consolidated tax return, the transactions were often treated as intercompany transactions and hence, in that way, income taxes were evaded.

How did they get away with it? There can be no extenuation of the swindles on the ground that they were necessary to promote housing since most of them did not occur during the acute shortage of the 1940's but in 1950 and 1951 when the housing situation had turned the corner. FHA virtually invited builders to make false statements in their applications by publicly stating it would not consider incorrect statements and applications as having any materiality. In 1951 and again in 1953, the Attorney General sought to prosecute builders for making false or incomplete disclosures and general counsel Bovard advised him that FHA was nòt deceived because it did not rely on the statements of the builders. FHA completely ignored a 1947 Act of Congress that it was to use all means to assure that estimates "will approximate as closely as possible the actual costs of efficient building operations." By 1953, the 3-year statute of limitations had run and prosecutions were barred since the 608 authority expired in March 1950.

FHA actually did missionary work on 608, advising builders how to cheat the government. A Los Angeles builder, Arthur B. Weber, told the Senate committee that he was invited to an FHA meeting at which the Section 608 program was explained and that he was told that he "should wind up the project without having any investment in it." Wilson W. Wyatt, who had been Truman's housing expediter, and Adlai Stevenson's campaign manager, had a client in a 608 operation—

SENATOR MAYBANK: Did or did not Wilson M. Wyatt suggest to his cousin that he could get a windfall?

MR. McKENNA: [deputy commissioner of the housing and

home finance agency]: Wilson Wyatt suggested to his cousin they could finance the project and make a contracting profit without putting any capital in and he suggested how he could show that they could state that the land was paid for when, in fact, it was financed, depending upon the mortgage loan to pay for the cost of the land.

SENATOR MAYBANK: Was not that the law? . . .

MR. MCKENNA: In my opinion, Wilson Wyatt's letter showed a way to evade the law but I would rather not have made that statement.

Clyde L. Powell appeared before a Senate committee in July 1949 and was asked whether he thought it possible "even for the most efficient builder to actually construct a project at 70 per cent of the estimated cost." Powell replied, "No, I do not think so. I do not see how that it is possible because we are right on top of construction costs . . . we might be off 2 or 3 per cent. I do not think that it would be physically possible to be off anything like 30 per cent." Two days previously, Powell had given permission for the payment of dividends to stockholders of $550,000 who had contributed $116,500. He was familiar with the set-up under which there was a mortgaging out of approximately $2,150,000 so that the original stockholders got $1,300,000 in dividends. Nathan Manilow, a Chicago builder, gave Powell a draft for $7500. He testified that the Illinois State FHA director telephoned him that "Powell was in a difficult situation and wanted a $7500 loan." Two weeks later, Powell granted a request to collect two months' rent in advance on his leases. Albert J. Cassel said that in December 1946, an additional FHA commitment of $709,000 was obtained for the Mayfair Mansions in Washington. When he went to Powell to pick up the commitment, Powell demanded $10,000 for his services before he would sign the authorization so Cassel gave it to him in currency. Telephone records show calls between Powell at his office and his home and many of those who received windfall profits. Powell frequently overruled local FHA officials as he did to approve a project for Dr. Gevinson in Texas.

FHA's indulgence to builders was unbounded. In the case of Patchogue Gardens, the investors took out $155,000 three months after default and FHA did nothing about it. In the project of Franklin Trice, after the project was completed and when it had half a million dollars in surplus derived from the windfall, FHA deferred the corporation's mortgage payments and waived payments to the reserve for replacements on the plea that the income to the corporation was not adequate to make the payments.

It would have been obviously impossible for these grabs to have occurred without the connivance of many FHA officials besides Clyde L. Powell. Over a period of two years, 163 cases were turned over by the FBI to FHA for investigation, of which only 9 were investigated by FHA. In early 1949, the GAO advised FHA that there was a general practice of making gifts like television sets and wristwatches to employees of the FHA office in Washington. FHA's own staff investigated and found that eight Philco TV sets were given in December 1948 and 18 wristwatches as gifts by builders. The FHA waited for 3 years after the statute of limitations had run and then turned over its report to the Department of Justice in April 1952.

Gifts were commonplace not only in Washington but in other cities like Philadelphia and Albuquerque. Builders gave parties and fishing trips for employees. Gifts were given of sums of money over $10,000, automobiles, homes purchased at a discount and other gifts.

Andrew Frost, assistant New Mexico state director, pleaded self-incrimination in questioning before the committee about fishing trips given by builders and gambling winnings with builders. He refused to answer whether in connection with a project he suggested that a party be given on the night of the ground-breaking with girls furnished by the contractor, and that there were three girls who were paid a total of between $400 and $500, the cost of which was charged to the construction job.

There were some interesting cases of "conflict of interest" in which the activities of the FHA official in his official capacity and his private capacity meshed. Ian Woodner built his apartment hotel presumably for residential purposes since FHA assistance was not recognized for construction of hotels. However, he obviously intended it as an apartment-hotel from its inception. When it was completed, he asked for permission to operate it as a hotel, which FHA refused. He discussed the matter with Franklin D. Richards, the FHA commissioner. Richards resigned on June 30, 1952. On July 22, he was retained by Woodner. Shortly afterwards, Powell reversed the local office and granted Woodner permission. Richards was paid $10,000.

Thomas Grace was New York State FHA director from August 1935 to August 1952. He remained a partner in the law firm of Grace and Grace, which was connected with 64 rental housing projects processed in the New York office while he was FHA director. These 64 projects involved mortgage commitments of $84,771,000. His brother, or the firm, received $400,000 in connection with FHA matters including $291,000 in fees. Arthur M. Chaite formerly an attorney for FHA was one of 5 former FHA people employed by Woodner. He received close to $200,000 from Woodner. Chaite said he was unable to explain $50,000 in checks which were turned into cash. Telephone records show that Powell and Chaite were in frequent communication with each other.

The full extent of the loss to the government will not be known for some time. Rents have been raised in the housing projects in order to defray the extra costs of the mortgaging out. The rental projects are new, we are in a period of inflation and comparable housing is still not available. In years to come, when tenants balk at the high rents there is certain to be a wave of defaults and the government will have to take over. At such a time, the losses may run into the hundreds of millions.

## G.I. Programs

Under the Veterans Administration loan-guarantee program for the purchase and construction of homes, 2,861,000 loans were guaranteed by 1952 with an initial principal of more than $17,641,000,000.[2] The contingent liability of the federal government under the program ultimately reached $20 billion. The frauds which were perpetrated upon the veterans were of appalling proportions. The Teague committee, a House select committee to investigate educational training and loan-guarantee programs under the G.I. bill, had a long list of whole housing projects and individual cases in which the prices of houses were raised sharply for the veterans with excess charges of all types and where construction was shoddy to the point of inhabitability. The appraisal system, which was designed to protect veterans as to the price and quality of housing, in many areas broke down. In San Diego, the operations of the loan-guaranty division completely collapsed as a result of a widespread criminal conspiracy on the part of loan-guaranty officials, V.A. fee appraisers and inspectors, officials of lending institutions and builders. Seventeen persons were indicted by a grand jury. Investigations which were made throughout the country disclosed widespread irregularities, including acceptance of gifts and gratuities by loan-guaranty personnel, acceptance of bribes, favoritism to builders and interest in outside activities such as real estate sales, construction and lending companies. VA

2. All matters discussed taken from testimony before Teague House Select Committee to Investigate Educational, Training and Loan Guaranty Programs under GI Bill (82nd Congress). Reports Nos. 2501 and 1375.

officials increased the reasonable value of property over and above established appraisals, allowed excessive cost for equipment and ignored reports that builders were failing to meet minimum construction requirements.

The most common method of rewarding cooperative loan-guaranty officials was for the contracting company to build them a house at a price far below the going market value. Sometimes the entire office was taken out en masse for a cruise at the expense of the mortgage company. Thirty-four of the thirty-six loan-guaranty officials in the Detroit office received Christmas gifts from builders doing business with the office. A loan officer in the Los Angeles office received in the 1949 Christmas season fifty-seven gifts from persons doing business with the VA.

The other aspect of the G.I. program was the educational program. The Teague committee reported that "hundreds of millions of dollars" were thrown away by the government in this program. Under the educational provisions of the G.I. bill of rights, subsistence was paid to the veteran and the educational institution was reimbursed for tuition and for books, supplies and equipment required for the course. "By the end of 1946, 2,166 privately owned schools operated for profit had come into existence and under the policies of the Veterans Administration these schools were allowed to virtually write their own charges against the Treasury of the United States without regard to the amount, type and quality of the service rendered." Private schools falsified cost data, attendance records, billed for students not enrolled, overcharged for supplies, books and tools and offered courses in fields where little or no employment opportunities existed.

The best method for obtaining graft was to overcharge for supplies. A watchmaking school charged the retail instead of the wholesale price for supplies and it is thus estimated that over a 6-year period, VA paid this one school $300,000 more than it should have obtained. In many cases, a dummy corporation was established between the real supplier and the school so that the school could get the benefit of the spread in price.

In view of the fact that the schools were competing for students and were paid for supplies, they could use the cost of supplies as a fund for enticing students into the school. One Midwestern tailoring school had a large newspaper advertisement: "Special Offer Today—a $100 suit free to veteran students. Every veteran student who enters the school during the offer will receive material to make one suit which could retail at $100." A trade school offering automotive courses advertised that it would give $100 worth of tools to each man and that students could have their cars repaired free at the school.

### Post Office

Selling of jobs in the Post Office Department seems to have been a common method of dispensing patronage. Michigan, Chicago and New York City were the spots in which charges of selling jobs for political purposes flared up. In Mississippi the practice was so brazen that it produced a Senate investigation.[3]

Mississippi voted for "states' rights" candidates in the Presidential elections of 1948. The Democratic National Committee refused to recognize the two senators from Mississippi on patronage and William Boyle, Jr., instead recognized Clarence E. Hood, Jr., as advisor on political appointments. Hood had hired Glen P. Boehm, the Washington industrial consultant, and Boehm introduced him to Donald S. Dawson. Through that channel, Hood was recognized as "acting" Democratic national committeeman from Mississippi.

Postmaster General Donaldson was told by Boyle to accept

3. See Report of Hoey investigations subcommittee (82nd Congress), "Federal Job Selling and Other Irregularities in Mississippi."

Hood's advice as to which of three top men eligible for a job should get it, whether for postmaster or rural mail carriers. Testimony before the Senate Investigations Subcommittee disclosed that these jobs were sold for fees of from $250 to $1,000. Ostensibly, the fees were contributions. One man testified "he put it [the fee] in his billfold and he says 'your thousand dollars is right here. It will be in escrow until your appointment comes through. If it doesn't, your thousand dollars is still here.' " In the testimony of another person, the question was asked, "Then it really was not a voluntary contribution, it was a voluntary purchase?" The answer was, "That's it exactly." An applicant, Grover Cleveland Smith, was testifying:

> SENATOR McCLELLAN: Would you consider yourself as making a voluntary political contribution?
> MR. SMITH: Well, Senator, so to speak, if someone had a knife in your back, telling you what to do, would you consider you were doing it voluntarily?

### Alien Property Custodian

A probe of the Alien Property Custodian has been delayed from time to time but is due to be made by the Senate. Senator Wiley has pointed out that the "gravy has been practically pouring down certain vests." At Senator Wiley's request, Harold I. Baynton, then Custodian of the Office of Alien Property, submitted the names of individuals serving as officials of each of the ten largest firms still under the jurisdiction of the office. The law firm of former Secretary of Defense Louis Johnson was paid $346,016 in legal fees through June 1951 by two corporations—General Aniline and Film Corporation and General Dyestuff Corporation. In addition, Johnson received $288,969 personally as president of General Dyestuff from July 13, 1942, until February 21, 1947. Jack Frye, another prominent Democrat and former president of TWA, succeeded Johnson as president of the two firms and drew $374,247 for himself. William Siskind, brother of Max Siskind, the law partner of former Democratic National Committee Chairman Boyle, received $70,999 in legal fees and expenses in two cases.[4]

4. See statement of Senator Alexander Wiley in *Congressional Record, Appendix,* October 20, 1951; also *New York Times,* December 8, 11, 15, 16, 1951.

# · XIX ·

# CONCLUSION

IN THE campaign of 1952, Adlai Stevenson dismissed the issue of corruption in the Truman administration by pointing to the statement of Charles Evans Hughes, "Guilt is personal and knows no party." This neatly sidesteps the question why there were so many cases of personal guilt in the Truman administration. History shows that excesses of corruption occur in particular periods for particular reasons. The unprecedented debauchery in government which flourished during the Truman administration occurred only because of a prevailing moral climate which made it possible or promoted it.

Prior to the presidency of Harry Truman there had been two administrations in which corruption had reached to the heart of the administration—that of Ulysses S. Grant and that of Warren G. Harding.

During the Grant administration, a whiskey ring was uncovered which operated from several midwestern cities. With the connivance of dishonest internal revenue officials, there was wholesale evasion of federal taxes. It was estimated that three times as much whiskey was shipped out of St. Louis untaxed as was taxed. The secretary and aide to the President, Orville E. Babcock, had been corresponding with the leaders of the ring and was tried for complicity. He was acquitted in a trial in which the President gave a deposition in his behalf. After his acquittal, Babcock returned to his desk at the White House and within a few minutes, Grant had tossed him out onto the street.

Grant's Secretary of War, William W. Belknap, was poor, and his wife was socially ambitious. She approached one Caleb B. Marsh and suggested to him that he apply for a post tradership at Fort Sill in Indian Territory. This was a valuable job and it was then held by a man named Evans. Marsh withdrew his application, and Evans, in return, agreed to pay Marsh $12,000 a year. Half went to Mrs. Belknap, who collected $20,000. Belknap was unanimously impeached by the House of Representatives but was not convicted by the Senate, mainly because he had resigned.

In the administration of Warren G. Harding, there were more serious scandals. The celebrated Teapot Dome case, which rocked the nation, can be summarized in this way. The government owned Naval Reserve No. 1 at Elks Hill, California, and No. 3 at Teapot Dome, Wyoming, a queer-shaped hill. There was fear that neighboring wells were drawing off the oil in these reserves, which alarmed officers in the Navy who felt that oil should be stored at Pearl Harbor and other places in the eventuality of war with Japan. Albert B. Fall, the Secretary of the Interior, was a resourceful man and a true patriot. He knew how to meet the emergency. He had the President sign an executive order transferring the reserves from the Secretary of the Navy to the Secretary of the Interior. The papers were signed by Navy Secretary Edwin N. Denby. It is conceded that Denby was completely innocent; although he had the appearance of a Bismarck, Denby was actually a dumbbell who signed documents without investigating the reason why or the consequences of what he was doing. Fall leased the Teapot Dome Reserve to the Mammoth Oil Company, which was an alias for Harry S. Sinclair. He then leased the Elks Hill Reserve to the Pan-American Company, which was controlled by Edward L. Doheny. These leases were made in secret and without competitive bidding. Fall proposed to use the royalties the government would collect to buy and fill fuel oil tankers for the Navy.

Fall had been in dire financial straits, and now rumors spread of his new affluence. His New Mexico ranch became stocked, and he bought neighboring land. A Senate investigation began under the relentless Senator Thomas I. Walsh, who was to prove Fall's nemesis. There were many detours. Archibald Roosevelt, a son of Theodore Roosevelt, who had worked for Sinclair, testified that he resigned after Sinclair's confidential secretary had told him that Sinclair had given Fall $68,000—Sinclair's man insisted that Roosevelt had misunderstood "6 to 8 cows" for "68 thous." Then Fall said that Edward B. McLean had lent him $100,000, but this story fell through. Finally, Doheny came forward and stated that he had lent Fall $100,000, that this money had been carried by his son in cash to Fall in a satchel. In return Doheny had received from Fall a note for $100,000 with the signature torn off.

It was then revealed that Sinclair had delivered to Fall $260,000 in Liberty Bonds. After several trials, Doheny and Sinclair escaped conviction (Sinclair served two terms for contempt), but Fall was sentenced to jail for a year, the only time in our history that a Cabinet officer has been thus disgraced.

Teapot Dome is an effective word as a symbol of corruption. It always conjures up an image of pitch-black dishonesty, the ultimate in knavery in politics. In the science of words, semantics, the trick is to latch onto the right word, the word that will ring the bell, that will bring out the desired response—Teapot Dome with its peculiar ring is certainly the right word.

The image, however, produced by the term Teapot Dome can be very readily distorted. It was not the act of an administration, but the act of a single man, a weak, greedy man who saw the chance to accumulate riches by a single stroke. The guilt of Harding lay only in his trust of Albert B. Fall. It is difficult to indict him for having had that trust, since just about everybody was deceived by Fall's bluff, hearty, wild-West exterior.

Both Grant and Harding reacted keenly to the disclosures of corruption in their administrations.

President Ulysses S. Grant was personally honest to a fault. Grant received a letter from a St. Louis banker which gave the names of many who might be called as witnesses in the whiskey ring and told of revenue officials who had been quoted as saying Grant could not give them up for fear that their disclosures might hurt the administration. Grant at once referred it to his Secretary of the Treasuy, Bristow, on July 29, 1875, with an endorsement in his own hand, which has become a historic note:

> . . . I forward this for information and to the end that if it throws any light upon new parties to summon as witnesess they may be brought out. *Let no guilty man escape if it can be avoided.* Be specially vigilant—or instruct those engaged in the prosecution of fraud to be—against all who insinuate that they have high influence to protect—or to protect them. No personal consideration should stand in the way of performing a public duty.

Teapot Dome killed President Harding. Prior to his last trip, his journey to Alaska, Harding had apparently learned the truth from his own sources. The President arranged the trip to Alaska as a means of diverting his mind. Samuel Hopkins Adams, in "The Timely Death of President Harding," gives this vivid description of the last days aboard train:

> From Tacoma on the President was in a state of chronic jitters. He could not be quiet five minutes on end. His one thought was to escape from thinking. To this end he organized a bridge game with Secretaries Wallace, Work and Howe, Speaker Gillett and Admiral Rodman. The President played to exhaustion, twelve, fourteen or fifteen hours a day, with brief time out for luncheon and dinner. The game started imme-

diately after breakfast and went on well into the next morning. Unlike other White House poker standards, the stakes were small; it was the escape from worries that the President wanted. For the other players it was an endurance test. Being two more than required, they met it by cutting in and out for a respite of two or three hours each. The President played through each session.

By the time the West Coast was reached, his nervous demoralization was painfully apparent. It reached a point at which he felt the need for real relief. He sought out Secretary Hoover. "Mr. Secretary," said he, "there's a bad scandal brewing in the administration."

The President did not disclose the nature of the scandals to Hoover, who had an inkling of what it was all about. Hoover urged the President to meet the scandals with public frankness, but the President's tension and anxiety were not assuaged. When the Presidential party reached San Francisco, the President had a stroke and died.

The new President was Calvin Coolidge. When Teapot Dome erupted publicly, he immediately appointed a Republican, Owen J. Roberts, and a Democrat, ex-Senator Atlee Pomerene to prosecute the wrong-doers. He gave them his full support. He ousted Denby from his cabinet and fired Attorney-General Daugherty without haggling when Daugherty refused to open up Justice Department files. In January, 1924, Coolidge made this announcement:

> If there has been any crime it must be prosecuted—no one will be shielded for any party, political or other reasons . . . if there is any guilt it will be punished, if there is any fraud, it will be revealed; and if there are any contracts which are illegal, they will be cancelled.

The attitude towards corruption of previous administrations should be contrasted with that of the Truman regime.

All previous cases of corruption, serious as they were, are very small compared with the corruption which took place in the administration of Harry S. Truman. Never had there been so much corruption practiced by so many public officials in so many different places.

The first count in the indictment is that the corruption was of far greater danger to the nation than in any previous cases. Corruption invaded almost every department of the government, not only in Washington but all over the country. They were graver for another reason too. The tax-collection machinery of the nation was infested with graft from top to bottom. On the machinery for collecting revenue rests the security of the nation and that of the free world. The collection of taxes of $60 billion a year cannot be carried on through coercion but depends upon the confidence of the average citizen in the good faith of the tax collectors. Groaning under the burden of the highest taxes in history, the disclosure of frauds within the Internal Revenue department could incense the mass of taxpayers to the point of wholesale evasion. This was a real, not an imaginary threat. In October 1951, the new commissioner of internal revenue, John Dunlap, suggested to the press that they "draw back" and consider whether "unfair" publicity might not destroy public confidence in the tax system. In February 1953, Chairman Robert W. Kean, opening the hearings of the House subcommittee investigating the Internal Revenue Bureau said, "If the Bureau of Internal Revenue had continued to operate as it did in the last few years, there was great danger that, through lack of confidence by the public, our whole tax-collection system might have fallen down."

The civil recovery in Teapot Dome amounted to $13 million. The amount lost through the wholesale tax frauds must have run into the billions. As an example, in March 1951, the Internal Revenue Bureau, following complaints of laxity in tax collections from racketeers, started a collection drive which in one year netted over $180 million. Comptroller General Warren estimated the loss to the Treasury by fraud or liberality in the termination of war contracts at over $500,000,000.

The Teague committee of the Democratic 82nd Congress estimated the loss in the graft-ridden G.I. educational programs in the "hundreds of millions." In the Section 608 swindles under FHA, profits of 20,000 per cent in less than two years were not uncommon, as we have seen, and one financing company netted $26,000,000.

The second count in the indictment is that the scandals of the Truman administration were epidemic. Teapot Dome and other cases of corruption were isolated transactions of individuals accomplished by stealth. The cases in the Truman era were a continuous band covering many agencies and localities. Corruption was a basic contagion.

The third count in the indictment is that the frauds were not only *epidemic,* but they were a disease *endemic* to the Truman administration. It was a necessary and natural consequence of a philosophy of government, which was in essence political. It was not idealistic or doctrinaire in its approach. The pragmatic thesis which underlay it was the purpose and expectation of winning the next election. It was built around big city machines; it not only co-operated with these machines, but nurtured and fattened them. It was no accident that the gravest frauds occurred in the Internal Revenue Bureau and the Department of Justice. The Attorney General of the United States, J. Howard McGrath, moved over from the job of chairman of the Democratic National Committee in the 1948 campaign. The chairman of the Democratic National Committee in the 1944 campaign, Robert E. Hannegan, had moved over from the job of commissioner of internal revene. When he left in 1944 to be national chairman, he turned the office over to his close New York political friend, Joseph D. Nunan.

This aspect of the administration accounts for the fact that the frauds did not stem out of individual venality and cupidity alone. There was a concurrent motive to benefit and aggrandize the Democratic party, on the welfare of which the careers of many politically-minded men depended.

The fourth count in the indictment is that the administration of Harry Truman, far from taking effective action to wipe out corruption, was in some cases protecting the wrongdoers, in other cases was indifferent and in other cases the machinery of the administration was used to block and thwart the investigators of corruption. The frauds were revealed not because of the administration, but in spite of it.

Various counts of this indictment are summarized in a statement which was made by Representative Cecil R. King (Democrat of California), chairman of the Ways and Means Subcommittee investigating the tax scandals, on the last day of the hearings in San Francisco:

> Control of the office over a long period had fallen into the hands of a top echelon of political appointees whose chief failing was their gross incompetence. Their second, and also serious, failing, was a devotion to political interests which transcended their loyalty to the Revenue Service and caused them to engage in petty and sometimes criminal manipulations. In these they were encouraged and protected by the complacency and indifference of an inept top administration in Washington. Political and personal favoritism in the treatment of taxpayers and in the handling of personnel problems has been the result.
>
> There is nothing unique about what happened here. We have found fundamentally the same thing from Boston to New York to Brooklyn to St. Louis to San Francisco. Everywhere the pattern has been the same.

A graver indictment may yet emerge against the Truman administration. As a result of the public clamor, runaway grand juries and Congressional investigations, the Truman administration was forced to take action against wrongdoers. Significantly, however, the administration did its best to save its reputation—former Commissioner Nunan was charged with income tax evasion rather than tax fixing and collector James P. Finnegan of St. Louis was convicted of misconduct charges rather than more serious charges that might have been brought against him. Corruption was so rampant and so widespread, and officials within the Administration acted so often in concert that the shape of a general conspiracy to obstruct justice is indicated. It was in St. Louis, the home area of the President and his top lieutenants, that intense efforts to prevent a grand jury investigation occurred in 1951. It is in St. Louis today that a grand jury probe which has already resulted in indictments of Assistant Attorney General Caudle and Presidential Secretary Connelly may reveal a story even more shocking than the one we know today.

# INDEX

# INDEX

319